Across the world, the work of caring for and maintaining life is devalued and outsourced largely to women of colour, who are poor and working class. *Emancipatory Feminism in the Time of Covid-19* is a timely conversation with Marxist, ecosocialist and indigenous perspectives, analysis and practice. In the intersecting crises capitalism has catapulted us into, it shares powerful forms of solidarity, resistance and ways of being.

—Pregs Govender, writer and author; former union educator;
MP and human rights commissioner

This volume illuminates the power of emancipatory feminist alternatives in a world of polycrisis. It reminds society that women-led agentic practices create transformative strategies for rethinking work, development and activism. The ideological resources it provides for intersectional movement building are invaluable.

—Khwezi Mabasa, lecturer, University of Pretoria;
research associate at the Society, Work and Politics Institute,
University of the Witwatersrand and at the Friedrich Ebert
Stiftung Institute South Africa Office, Johannesburg

Emancipatory feminist solutions are key to dismantle exploitative structures and systems by bringing in the voices, knowledge and innovations of those most impacted by crisis and pandemics like Covid-19. This volume provides inspiring examples of frontline transformative resistance by grassroots women.

—Dorah Marema, Senior Atlantic Fellow, Atlantic Fellowship for
Racial Equity; President, GenderCC-Women for Climate Justice

Satgar and Ntlokotse bring us a stunning collection of essays on grassroots women-led political resistance. Liberal feminism has clearly failed – and with the patriarchal capitalist crises of social reproduction ever more intense under pandemic conditions, women continue to serve as shock absorbers for the status quo. Here is an emancipatory feminism, grounded in practical initiatives for women's food sovereignty, a climate justice charter and socio-ecological alternatives inspired by ubuntu, eco-feminism and jineology. Time for all to take note!

—Ariel Salleh, author of *Ecofeminism as Politics* (1997/2017);
Distinguished Visiting Scholar, Queen Mary University of London, 2023

T0366517

DEMOCRATIC MARXISM

DEMOCRATIC MARXISM SERIES

Series Editor: Vishwas Satgar

The crisis of Marxism in the late twentieth century was the crisis of orthodox and vanguardist Marxism associated mainly with hierarchical communist parties, and imposed, even as state ideology, as the 'correct' Marxism. The Stalinisation of the Soviet Union and its eventual collapse exposed the inherent weaknesses and authoritarian mould of vanguardist Marxism. More fundamentally vanguardist Marxism was rendered obsolete but for its residual existence in a few parts of the world, including within authoritarian national liberation movements in Africa and in China.

With the deepening crises of capitalism, a new democratic Marxism (or democratic historical materialism) is coming to the fore. Such a democratic Marxism is characterised by the following:

- Its sources span non-vanguardist grassroots movements, unions, political fronts, mass parties, radical intellectuals, transnational activist networks and parts of the progressive academy;
- It seeks to ensure that the inherent categories of Marxism are theorised within constantly changing historical conditions to find meaning;
- Marxism is understood as a body of social thought that is unfinished and hence challenged by the need to explain the dynamics of a globalising capitalism and the futures of social change;
- It is open to other forms of anti-capitalist thought and practice, including currents within radical ecology, feminism, emancipatory utopianism and indigenous thought;
- It does not seek to be a monolithic and singular school of thought but engenders contending perspectives;
- Democracy, as part of the history of people's struggles, is understood as the basis for articulating alternatives to capitalism and as the primary means for constituting a transformative subject of historical change.

This series seeks to elaborate the social theorising and politics of democratic Marxism.

Published in the series and available:

Michelle Williams and Vishwas Satgar (eds). 2013. *Marxisms in the 21st Century: Crisis, Critique and Struggle*. Johannesburg: Wits University Press.

Vishwas Satgar (ed.). 2015. *Capitalism's Crises: Class Struggles in South Africa and the World*. Johannesburg: Wits University Press.

Vishwas Satgar (ed.). 2018. *The Climate Crisis: South African and Global Democratic Eco-Socialist Alternatives*. Johannesburg: Wits University Press.

Vishwas Satgar (ed.). 2019. *Racism after Apartheid: Challenges for Marxism and Anti-Racism*. Johannesburg: Wits University Press.

Vishwas Satgar (ed.). 2020. *BRICS and the New American Imperialism: Global Rivalry and Resistance*. Johannesburg: Wits University Press.

Michelle Williams and Vishwas Satgar (eds). 2021. *Destroying Democracy: Neoliberal Capitalism and the Rise of Authoritarian Politics*. Johannesburg: Wits University Press.

EMANCIPATORY FEMINISM IN THE TIME OF COVID-19

TRANSFORMATIVE RESISTANCE AND SOCIAL REPRODUCTION

Edited by Vishwas Satgar and Ruth Ntlokotse

WITS UNIVERSITY PRESS

Published in South Africa by:

Wits University Press
1 Jan Smuts Avenue
Johannesburg 2001

www.witspress.co.za

First published 2023

http://dx.doi.org. 10.18772/22023078264

978-1-77614-826-4 (Paperback)
978-1-77614-827-1 (Hardback)
978-1-77614-828-8 (PDF)
978-1-77614-829-5 (EPUB)
978-1-77614-830-1 (Open Access PDF)

The publication of this volume was made possible by funding from the Rosa Luxemburg Stiftung.

ROSA
LUXEMBURG
STIFTUNG

EMANCIPATORY
FUTURES STUDIES

Project manager: Inga Norenius
Copyeditor: Inga Norenius
Proofreader: Lee Smith
Indexer: Margaret Ramsay
Cover design: Hothouse, South Africa
Typeset in 10 point Minion Pro

*This seventh volume in the Democratic Marxism series is dedicated to
Fikile Ntshangase who paid the ultimate price in the struggle for climate and,
more generally, environmental justice. She was gunned down in her kitchen in front
of her 11-year-old grandson on 22 October 2020.*

CONTENTS

TABLES

ACKNOWLEDGEMENTS

This volume owes a special debt to the Rosa Luxemburg Foundation (RLF). Without the support given by the RLF it would have been impossible to hold an online contributors' workshop during the Covid-19 pandemic, and ensure the manuscript was prepared for publication. We are also grateful for the support given by the Co-operative and Policy Alternative Centre (COPAC), which played a central role in organising the online workshop convened with contributors and activists from various social movements. The support given by the RLF has enabled this volume in the series to be published open access. The Emancipatory Futures Studies in the Anthropocene project at the University of the Witwatersrand also provided support for the research and writing contributions by Vishwas Satgar. Moreover, it is important to acknowledge the editorial assistance provided by Jane Cherry from COPAC. Her efforts were crucial for keeping things on track. The efforts and inputs from Michelle Williams, Courtney Morgan, Awande Buthelezi and Charles Simane are also appreciated. Finally, our sincerest appreciation to the team at Wits University Press, particularly Veronica Klipp, Roshan Cader and Corina van der Spoel, for supporting this volume and the Democratic Marxism series.

ACRONYMS AND ABBREVIATIONS

Cosatu	Congress of South African Trade Unions
CRAM	Coronavirus Rapid Mobile Survey
CSG	Child Support Grant
Denosa	Democratic Nursing Union of South Africa
DRC	Democratic Republic of Congo
EN	enrolled nurse
ENA	enrolled nursing auxiliary
GDP	gross domestic product
GRB	gender responsive budgeting
HRH	human resources for health
IFFs	illicit financial flows
IFIs	international finance institutions
IMF	International Monetary Fund
IPV	intimate partner violence
ISIS	Islamic State of Iraq and Syria
MACUA	Mining Affected Communities United in Action
MPRDA	Mineral and Petroleum and Resources Development Act
MTBPS	Medium Term Budget Policy Statement
NHI	National Health Insurance
NIDS	National Income Dynamics Study
OSD	Occupation Specific Dispensation
PMBEJD	Pietermaritzburg Economic Justice and Dignity Group
PN	professional nurse
PPE	personal protective equipment
RN	registered nurse
RWA	Rural Women's Assembly
SAFSC	South African Food Sovereignty Campaign
Saftu	South African Federation of Trade Unions
Sanc	South African Nursing Council
SARS	severe acute respiratory syndrome
SASSA	South African Social Security Agency
SERT	socio-ecological reproduction theory
SRD	Social Relief of Distress Grant
SRT	social reproduction theory
StatsSA	Statistics South Africa
UASA	United Association of South Africa
UNDP	United Nations Development Programme
UNFCCC	United Nations Framework Convention on Climate Change
WHO	World Health Organization
WMO	World Meteorological Organization

INTRODUCTION

Vishwas Satgar and Ruth Ntlokotse

Our lives, on a planetary scale, changed when Covid-19 was declared a pandemic by the World Health Organization in early 2020. For many this was a crisis like no other. All living generations were marked by this moment. Our certainties about life, society and nature were all upended. Pandemic waves, lockdowns, social distancing, public health protocols and vaccines dominated our social relations. While the pandemic affected everyone, it impacted on women in a differentiated and disproportionate way. For women in precarious labour market jobs, earning below the minimum wage in the informal economy and in the domestic sphere, life shifted from hard to catastrophic. Drawing on the category of 'subaltern' utilised by the Marxist Antonio Gramsci to foreground the history and lived experience of those in the lower rungs of societal hierarchies, this volume does the same for understanding women's oppression during Covid-19.[1] Put differently, this volume centres subaltern women's oppression and resistance, as opposed to the reproduction relations of upper-middle-class, elite and wealthy women. Subaltern women's oppression – among poor, working-class and peasant women – took on a grotesque aspect, and thus placed these women at the centre of the societal crisis of social reproduction. Social reproduction refers to the production of workers and peoples and, more generally, society. It is an invisible process that sits behind and is determined by profit making in production, finance and consumption relations and involves unpaid female labour, public institutions, communities and non-human nature. In the twentieth century different forms of social reproduction regimes with different degrees of state support emerged in the global South and North. However, over the past four decades of financial discipline, precarity and the commodification of everything through neoliberal marketisation, subaltern women have been squeezed in the vice grip of inequality.

In this context, ruling classes scrambled to construct a 'Covid-19 regime of social reproduction' to address the suffering of societies. A moment arrived to place human needs before profit making. New economic policy scripts, regulation, support measures for businesses and households, together with public health protocols attempted to hold societies together and ameliorate the wrenching impacts of economic fallout. Yet major shortcomings and challenges were revealed in a highly unequal world in which women carry the burden. These issues are explored in this volume.

Moreover, the realities of crisis far exceed Covid-19. In fact, the pandemic as a biological disaster merely intersected with a host of cascading crises which have made the already oppressive and tenuous lived realities of women at the grassroots unliveable. Economic precarity, climate shocks, extractivist resource practices, hunger and many other systemic crises are converging. Subaltern women are not merely in a battle to eke out an existence on the margins of society but are trying to preserve life; they face shocks and burdens that threaten to wipe them out. To understand this, the volume challenges social reproduction theory and analysis to revisit its analytical remit. Is it just about understanding the contraction of the welfare state in the global North and its implications for social reproduction, or about precarious working conditions for women, or about highlighting unpaid labour in the household? Does social reproduction theory assist in understanding the total crisis of contemporary capitalism? Can social reproduction theory and analysis enable and further strengthen the necessary world-making role of emancipatory feminism? How does transformative resistance extend and enrich social reproduction theorising? This volume wrestles with these challenges from the standpoint of grassroots women's struggles in South Africa, the larger African context and in the Kurdish world. The scope of this volume was grounded in an appreciation that social reproduction feminism works with universals, recognising that women are not only exploited all over the world but are also oppressed within the realm of social reproduction. What this volume offers is an enquiry about how social reproduction crises and resistance in three spatial contexts can be analysed, theorised and rethought. This is certainly not exhaustive, but South Africa is an interesting case of how feminist organising and politics faltered in the context of institutionalising a shallow market democracy, defined by sharp race, class and gender inequalities. New forms of grassroots feminism are attempting to understand and transform a South Africa in crisis. The larger African context is the terrain of organising for WoMin African Alliance, involved in 13 countries, and actively building women's power around energy and climate justice, against militarisation and for development alternatives. Informed by this positioning, understanding the depth of crisis confronting women on the continent and their responses is crucial. Rojava, in the Kurdish world, is a striking example of how a women-centred paradigm of politics is central to the emancipation project of the Kurdish people; it is about abolishing 5 000 years of patriarchy (a system of male-centred power) and is a 'women's revolution'. This women-centred politics also works with its own conception of crisis and transformative resistance, which warrants learning from.

At the same time, feminist struggles that existed before Covid-19 intensified during the pandemic. Implicated in the marketisation of societies, for over four decades, has been the hegemony of liberal feminism, in support of techno-financialised capitalism. Yet, its vaunting of upper-middle-class and wealthy women's success stories in a world of economic competition, formal women's rights, gender equality in the marketplace, excessive glamorous and conspicuous consumption and private property has reached its limits. Finding equality within patriarchal capitalism has been a dead end for most women. Liberal feminism has not been transformative and in its shadow new forms of women's counter-hegemonic power and feminist practice have been developing. This has been incubating in ecological, economic and state relations led by grassroots women. In this volume these new practices of emancipatory feminism are explored, including women resisting mining and women in mining; women ensuring national sovereignty is about women's emancipation in the context of ecological and climate justice struggles; food sovereignty pathway building; women in struggles to achieve class mobility through education and skills; women contesting economic relief and 'build back better' policy; and women challenging onerous working conditions in the public health-care system. The volume thus highlights an emergent grassroots and subaltern emancipatory feminism, anchored in transformative resistance that seeks to institutionalise new forms of women's power.

In short, this seventh volume in the Democratic Marxism series builds on the concerns and focus of Jacklyn Cock and Meg Luxton, both veteran activists and feminists, who raised the need in volume 1 of the series, *Marxisms in the 21st Century: Crisis, Critique and Struggle*, to find a way forward for the rocky relationship between Marxism and feminism. They argued then that socialist feminism, an independent current within feminism, is crucial for the renewal of feminism. In their view, such a feminism is committed to ensuring that Marxism takes seriously sexism, heterosexism, racism and, more generally, the systemic subordination of women while at the same time challenging feminist thought to integrate an anti-racist class analysis to ensure that the liberation of women is conjoined to the liberation of all people.

THE COVID-19 CONJUNCTURE

A pathogen possibly originating from a wild animal changed everything. About 7.7 billion people could not work, attend school, move around and generally could not be social beings. The structural consequences of this pathogen were unprecedented. It brought the national and global economy to a halt; airlines and shipping were gridlocked; extracted resources could not move and border posts between states were closed. Ruling classes and power structures in this context had to find new modes of ruling. The existential risk to society induced an urgency to protect society. This was the conjunctural significance of Covid-19. Decades of restructuring economies and societies to meet the requirements and needs of capital were suspended (or so it seemed). The competitive and acquisitive individual was no longer more important than our common wellbeing. The rhetoric of care from politicians and rulers seemed to suggest that preserving human life trumped everything else.

In specific countries, patriarchal nationalists, staunch neoliberals and even twenty-first century fascists had to place the exigencies of the public health crisis before their narrow political agendas. This tested the capacity (or lack thereof) of states, economies and society more generally. Decades of undermining public health through austerity, privatisation and mismanagement revealed health inequalities. Economies that have been deeply globalised exposed their limits. Criminalised politicians even had to feign responsiveness to societal need and rapacious looting appetites had to be pushed into the background. However, subaltern women entered the pandemic extremely challenged. Such women have been the main losers under deep globalisation and economic adjustment over the past four decades of neoliberalisation. In the early 1980s the United Nations made the following observations about the plight of women in the world (Peet and Hartwick 1999: 164): women make up half the world's population, perform two-thirds of the world's working hours, receive one-tenth of the world's income and own only one-hundredth of the world's property.

After more than four decades of neoliberal restructuring of the global economy and the remaking of states as enablers of the sovereignty of capital, subaltern women continue to face a desperate situation of gender inequality. According to Oxfam, this desperate situation is manifest in:[2]

- Low wages: across the world, women are in the lowest-paid work. Globally, they earn 24 per cent less than men and at the current rate of progress, it will take 170 years to close the gap. There are 700 million fewer women than men in paid work.
- Lack of decent work: 75 per cent of women in developing regions are in the informal economy, where they are less likely to have employment contracts, legal rights or social protection, and are often not paid enough to escape

poverty. Six hundred million women are in the most insecure and precarious forms of work.

- Unpaid care work: women do at least twice as much unpaid care work, such as childcare and housework, as men – sometimes ten times as much, often in addition to their paid work. The value of this work each year is estimated to be at least US$10.8 trillion – more than three times the size of the global tech industry.
- Longer workdays: women work longer days than men when paid and unpaid work is counted together. That means globally, a young woman today will work on average the equivalent of four years more than a man over her lifetime.

South Africa mirrors many of these dynamics of gender-based exploitation, exclusion and oppression. Pioneering and important social reproduction analyses, done over the past two decades, bring this into focus in relation to households and communities, highlighting African working-class women as the 'shock absorbers' of the crisis of social reproduction.[3] During the initial pandemic lockdown in 2020, about four million women (including domestic workers) in the informal economy lost income-earning opportunities overnight. Moreover, African working-class women continued to be the most vulnerable, with a 41 per cent unemployment rate in 2021 – higher than any other population group. Such subaltern women, oppressed by patriarchal relations, were forced to cook, clean and provide care labour for more family members during lockdown, and where meagre incomes existed these were spread more thinly (including from state support programmes) as increases in food prices registered. According to a Pietermaritzburg Economic Justice and Dignity Group report, in late 2021 an essential food basket for a low-income household of seven members cost on average R4 275.94 per month. The minimum wage of a full-time domestic worker is approximately R3 207.12, assuming a wage of R19.09 per hour (and many domestic workers do not earn nearly as much as this) (PMBEJD 2021: 1). The hunger squeeze on poor and working-class households intensified during Covid-19. Violence against women in South Africa escalated. In 2016, South Africa had the fourth highest female interpersonal violence death rate out of 183 countries. Contrast this with the global female homicide rate in 2019, which was 2.3 per 100 000 of the global population; in South Africa the rate was a staggering 10.1 per 100 000. During the first three weeks of lockdown in 2020, the government's Gender-Based Violence and Femicide Command Centre received over 120 000 cases and the Foundation for Human Rights suggested a 54 per cent increase in gender-based violence.

Table 0.1: Unpaid care and domestic work in households during 2020

Chore	Women (%)	Men (%)
Increase in cooking and serving meals	38	18
Don't usually cook or serve a meal	17	48
Increase in cleaning	45	35
Increase in repairs and household management	29	24
Increased time for pet care	13	14
Increase in caring for children	36	30
Increase in teaching children	32	29
Increase in playing with children	34	28

At a global level, a United Nations Women study on care and domestic work conducted between April 2020 and November 2020, involving 47 countries, found the realities shown in Table 0.1.

Essentially, 60 per cent of women reported an increase in care work compared to 40 per cent of men. The Philippines was the outlier, where 80 per cent of men reported an increase in unpaid domestic work while only 62 per cent of women said the same. Moreover, 28 per cent of women said the intensity of care work increased, while only 16 per cent of men said the same. Finally, 64 per cent of parents observed a high involvement of girl children in household chores (UN Women n.d.).

Similarly, the International Labour Organization (2021: 4) observed that women in the world faced the following situation during the pandemic:

> The disruption to labour markets has had devastating consequences for both men and women, yet women's employment declined by 5 per cent in 2020 compared with 3.9 per cent for men … A cross-cutting issue affecting women in all countries, sectors, occupations and types of employment is that the burden of intensified childcare and home-schooling activities has disproportionately fallen on them, leading to a rise in unpaid working time for women that reinforces traditional gender roles. Moreover, women often work in front-line occupations, such as care workers or grocery clerks, that face elevated health risks and difficult working conditions.

Breaking the glass ceiling in job-shedding economies and precarious labour markets has certainly not been a concern in this conjuncture of deep systemic crisis for subaltern women. Public policy debates about bringing the state back in to address the crisis of social reproduction by ensuring adequate socio-economic mitigation has loomed large across the world. How states should use their resources to protect their societies from harm during the pandemic has become a crucial debate. How should recovery happen to benefit the most vulnerable? By January 2021, in aggregate, governments in different parts of the world had injected US$14 trillion into economic support, with the US having the largest injection of $2.2 trillion (Tooze 2021: 473). Several policy positions have emerged to construct a state-supported Covid-19 social reproduction regime, including arguments for gender mainstreaming in pandemic budgets, a universal basic income/grant/guarantee, income transfers for unpaid labour, increased spending on health care, increased wages for essential services workers, opening the food commons through solidarity and food sovereignty and democratising power. However, while governments have deployed various socio-economic mitigation measures, these have been uneven, inadequate and generally the situation on a world scale has continued to be disastrous. For global monopoly capital, particularly digital, financial and agricultural, profit rates continued to increase and wealth further concentrated at the top. Mainstream pandemic economics has really been about widening inequality, including gender-based inequality.

HEGEMONIC LIBERAL FEMINISM IN THE WORLD AND SOUTH AFRICA

With the global shift to neoliberalism in the 1980s, corporate boardroom feminism and, more broadly, feminism of upper-middle-class and wealthy liberal women, became dominant. The neoliberal class project of entrenching financial discipline in states and societies articulated with several social issues in a manner that did not question the systemic roots of oppression but reinforced its hegemony. Breaking the glass ceiling, having more skirts in boardrooms and on chairs, more women CEOs and political leaders, private property rights for peasant women in the global South, deregulating labour markets to create precarious jobs for women, equal rights before the law and generally more women in patriarchal command centres of techno-financialised capitalism became the rallying cry. Feminist issues became wealthy women's issues and vice versa.

By the fourth decade of neoliberalisation, the world was restructured and remade in the image of US-led transnational capital. We were all living in a global capitalist civilisation with the white male, homo-economicus, as our civilisational standard; everybody needed to become a businessperson, an entrepreneur and ultimately a capitalist. Liberal feminism was centrally implicated in this process of civilisation making and contributing to a highly individuated and market-centred political subject; it has been the handmaiden to a form of deleterious financialised techno capitalism. At the same time, Donald Trump and a slew of authoritarian neoliberals ascended into power. This posed a dilemma for feminism internationally: break with liberal feminism and a rising authoritarian neoliberal feminism or remain trapped. This came to the fore sharply in several women's strikes in 2016, 2017 and 2018 which, in different parts of the world, sought to resist exclusionary nationalism and the neoliberal attack on decent work, health care, pensions, housing, education and public transport (Arruzza et al. 2019). In the heat of these struggles, hegemonic liberal feminism was critically scrutinised, critiqued and rejected. In essence, the critique asserted was this:

> Fully compatible with ballooning inequality, liberal feminism outsources oppression. It permits professional-managerial women to lean in precisely by enabling them to lean on the poorly paid migrant women to whom they subcontract their caregiving and housework. Insensitive to class and race, it links our cause with elitism and individualism. Projecting feminism as a 'stand-alone' movement, it associates us with policies that harm the majority and cuts us off from struggles that oppose those policies. In short, liberal feminism gives feminism a bad name. (Arruza et al. 2019: 37–38)

South African feminists face the same dilemma regarding a hegemonic liberal feminism that has not worked for the many. According to the Wikipedia entry on feminism in South Africa, this concerns 'the organised efforts to improve the rights of girls and women in South Africa'.[4] It goes on in this vein, even providing a sanitised version of women's struggles and reducing them to racial and gender equality, suffrage and equal pay for men and women. This is quintessential liberal feminism appropriating feminism in South Africa. Moreover, liberal feminists trumpet how many legal rights have been won. For Jen Thorpe (2018), women have a barrage of laws and rights in the new South Africa and all that is needed is to improve state implementation capacity. While this holds some truth, it falls short in explaining how the post-apartheid neoliberal political economy has undermined these rights and made them inaccessible to most subaltern women. Moreover, liberal feminism has also been explicit in vaunting the leap through the glass ceiling as a model – a standard-bearer – for women more generally in South African society. A collection of essays, *Feminism Is: South Africans Speak Their Truth*, attempts to universalise the experience and politics of privileged, professional middle-class women as feminism. While it celebrates diverse racial experiences, it is unsatisfying in how it occludes the lived realities that the majority of subaltern women face within the exclusionary practices of patriarchal and globalised South African capitalism.[5] However, in reality this feminism, as part of the neoliberal class project, has become the dominant type of feminism we see promulgated in the mainstream. It is in crisis together with the capitalist status quo it wants to be part of and which it defends.

So how did liberal feminism, even its black variants, with its emphasis on class mobility, conspicuous acquisition, institutional representation and legal rights become the dominant feminism in South Africa? It certainly was not inevitable or predetermined, given the radical histories of resistance by subaltern women in South Africa – from resisting high rents, opposing pass laws (such as the powerful women's march to government buildings in Pretoria on 9 August 1956), engaging in student protests, strengthening and leading mass organisations to building trade unions and establishing women's grassroots organisations. Several historical conditions explain this. First, the hegemonic place of Marxist and socialist feminism in the 1970s and 1980s, which provided crucial intellectual resources through conceptual approaches that linked gender oppression to race, class and capitalism, was simultaneously buoyed by the strength of mass politics and a radical intelligentsia, including feminist theorists.[6] In South Africa's transition to democracy the de-radicalisation of mass politics, including through demobilising the United Democratic Front, and co-opting trade unionists, civic leaders and communists into state institutions (including parliament, administration and local government), contributed to eviscerating a radical impulse for change from below. Academics also slid into a post-modern register and mode of thinking about the world, and identity politics became fashionable. In this context, Marxist and socialist feminism lost ground in the everyday lives of subaltern women. Second, the normalcy of a market democracy as the terrain for feminist struggle locked in how women's rights were constitutionalised. For instance, the National Women's Coalition championing the Women's Charter, the creation of the Commission of Gender Equality (a constitutional statutory body), the creation of the Office of the Status of Women and the joint Parliamentary Committee on the Quality of Life and Status of Women failed to transition into a mass movement of ongoing resistance championed by subaltern women. As many feminists have observed, this was the high point of collective and national-level mass women's organising in the post-apartheid period and the state–women's movement relation that developed undermined the capacity for mass-based women's organising from below.[7] Third, the shift to deep globalisation and neoliberalisation after 1996 signalled a shift to deracialising capitalism as the dominant national liberation project. Black economic empowerment transactions and 'two economies' discourse merely reinforced the importance of capitalist accumulation as the means to liberation, even for women. In this context, Thabo Mbeki affirmed a liberal gender representation politics as central to both the state and the economy.[8]

However, hegemonic liberal feminism with all its claims, gestures and performative assertions has not contributed to changing the lives of the vast majority of subaltern women.[9] Its own functionalism and legitimating role for deep globalisation and the neoliberal class project have contributed to creating an unequal, desperate and unviable society, giving rise to social conservatism, revanchist and nativist nationalism and explicit expressions of misogyny and patriarchy in the mainstream of South African society.[10] The rise of Jacob Zuma, and his brand of African masculinity and patriarchy, the sexist practices of political parties, trade unions and community organisations and, more generally, the war on women in South African society cannot be separated from the role hegemonic liberal feminism played in the making of a crisis-ridden market democracy. This pattern is not unique to South Africa, with inequality breeding reaction.[11] The rise of extreme right-wing politics, married to religious fundamentalism, patriarchy and exclusionary nationalism, is expressing itself in the USA, Europe, Brazil, India and in many other parts of the world. Liberal feminism helped engender this. It is now in crisis together with the societies it has tried to make in its own image as part of a globalised, marketised and mass consumption capitalism.

THE RETURN OF SOCIAL REPRODUCTION THEORY

It is commonplace to periodise feminism and from most accounts it has gone through three waves: the late nineteenth century, shaped by the rise of mass labour movements and workers' parties wrestling with classical Marxism and the women's question, the suffragettes struggling for the right to vote and the Russian Revolution. The second wave, from the 1960s till the early 1980s, involved the rise of socialist feminism with its critique of classical Marxism – particularly its failure to fully appreciate the salience of women's work and the sexual division of labour;[12] radical feminism, with its emphasis on lived experience and patriarchy as the basis of women's oppression; liberal feminism, with its emphasis on gender equality within capitalism; and Third World liberation struggle approaches to the women's question. A third wave in the late 1980s has been marked by hegemonic liberal feminism, post-modernism and eco-feminism. As mentioned, hegemonic liberal feminism championed the class mobility of elite and wealthy women into the centres of globalising capitalism and validated a shallow form of gender and race equality: equality in the market, in the boardroom and in the wealthy family. Post-modern feminism rejected universals like class exploitation and meta-narratives and merely validated the identities and role of particularist feminisms, issue-centred intersectional politics and performative populism. Eco-feminism, emerging during second-wave feminism, found its moorings through providing a decolonial and subaltern feminist critique of the ecologies of capital, eschewing catch-up modernisation and affirming an eco-feminist politics of subsistence and indigenous knowledge.

In the ferment of this ideological landscape, social reproduction theory (SRT), rooted in Marxist and socialist feminism, has made a comeback as part of a fourth wave of feminism. It emerges out of the crises of global capitalist restructuring (using debt in the global South, austerity and precarity in the labour market in the global North), in resistance to the emergence of extreme right-wing politics, and through living during a time of a global pandemic. In general terms, social reproduction relates to life making in relation to the biological reproduction of our species (sex), the material existence of the working class (household income) and care labour (for instance, child rearing, cooking, cleaning, taking care of the elderly) within a gendered division of labour. The lack of a coherent and fully articulated conceptualisation of production and social reproduction in Marx's and Engels' work led to the development of SRT. It first made its appearance in first-wave feminism amongst Marxist feminists seeking to understand the 'double burden' facing women as workers and wives. During the Russian Revolution, Alexandra Kollontai went the furthest to argue that addressing childcare and the transformation of the family was a necessary precondition to achieving equality of the sexes and socialism (Bryson 2005: 131). In second-wave feminism, SRT found its place in socialist feminist theorising (Cakardic 2020). On the one hand, socialist feminists theorised home-based work as creating value and as actually unpaid labour.[13] On the other, a more unitary theory emerged, recognising domestic labour as creating use values to meet needs, but at the same time appreciating production and reproduction as connected. Thus in second-wave feminism, domestic labour contributed crucially to reproducing the entire capitalist system and the working class. Women's oppression was wired into structural relations and was not a simple add-on to capitalism. Today SRT is making a comeback. Several important interventions are bringing it to the fore through repositioning a Marxist/socialist-inspired feminism in relation to feminism in general. Such attempts include revisiting the 'unhappy marriage' of Marxism and feminism (Mojab 2015), Marxist feminists rejecting liberal feminist hegemony and shallow intersectionality feminism to 'go it alone' politically (Bhattacharya 2017), and finding the place of SRT in 'dangerous liaisons' in actual struggles (Fakier et al. 2020).

RETHINKING SOCIAL REPRODUCTION AND EMANCIPATORY FEMINISM

Feminism has never been static and has changed under variegated historical and socio-ecological conditions. It is important to recognise the context in which social reproduction theory is making a return as part of the fourth wave of feminism. At the same time, organic emancipatory feminism is informed by the shortcomings of hegemonic liberal feminism, as well as lived experience, resistance and struggles for systemic alternatives to capitalism's total crisis. What it expresses is the following:

- Critical lessons have been learned from previous waves of feminism for theory and struggle to overcome all oppressions faced by women.
- In confronting patriarchal capitalism and its crises of socio-ecological reproduction, it is converging around Marxist, socialist, ecological and indigenous feminisms with an anti-capitalist and, more specifically, a democratic eco-socialist imaginary. It is seeking to build genuine universal subaltern solidarity, in opposition to capitalist oppression, while recognising the particularities of culture and identity.
- It is decolonising in its resistance to white supremacy and Euro-American modernity while recognising that democracy – procedural, institutional and rights – does not belong to capitalism but is the product of a people's history of struggle going back to ancient times of sharing the commons, resisting slavery, revolutions, anti-colonial struggles, cooperative movement building, traditions of worker control and digital commoning. It seeks to expand and deepen democracy.
- In its desires and visions for subaltern women-led transformation it is constitutive of power from below and works at different scales to build mass movements that will drive democratic systemic reforms to advance political projects capable of overcoming patriarchal capitalism while building the next society in the present. In this sense it expresses a new form of transformative resistance, different from lobbying, symbolic protest and seeking identity recognition.

The chapters that follow capture different aspects of this emergent emancipatory feminism and its relationship to social reproduction theoretical analyses.

INDIGENOUS EMANCIPATORY FEMINISM AND TRANSFORMATIVE RESISTANCE

Samantha Hargreaves, in chapter 1, places the concept of extractivist patriarchal capitalism at the centre of her analysis. She brings to the fore multiple and interconnected systemic crisis dynamics shaping the lives of peasant and African working-class women on the African continent. She demonstrates how the crisis of climate and ecology, debt and financial flows from Africa, the rise of pandemics (including Ebola), war displacement and violence against women are all imbricated in the making of extractivist patriarchal capitalism. The flip side of this reality is a general crisis of social reproduction facing unpaid women labour in peasant and working-class households on the continent; they carry the burden of all these crises. Far from surrendering to the dystopian and unliveable realities facing women on the continent, Hargreaves highlights the axes of eco-feminist ideological renewal crucial to advance decolonisation and dreams of African alternatives to 'build back better' coming out of Covid-19. With grounded insights from the work of WoMin African Alliance, she underlines the importance of customary relationships with land and nature, the philosophical importance of ubuntu for remaking the human–nature relationship and the importance of reclaiming pan-Africanism by drawing on its radical intellectual roots. This is an emancipatory feminism in the making.

Hawzhin Azeez, in chapter 2, amplifies the critique of liberal feminism by situating it in relation to Eurocentricism, the making of capitalist patriarchy and imperialism. She demonstrates how liberal feminist political leaders in various parts of the world also failed in their responses to Covid-19, particularly in relation to the subaltern other. As an alternative emancipatory feminism she highlights jineology, a feminism central to the Kurdish struggle in the Middle East, particularly Rojava in Northern Syria. As a grassroots approach to feminism, jineology derives from the thought of Abdulla Ocalan and is central to the practice of 'democratic confederalism' in Kurdish territory. The collective and social ecology emphasis of jineology is a living, counter-hegemonic example to the elitism and exclusionary practices of liberal feminism. Azeez demonstrates how this works in Rojava and how it has made a practical difference in how women have played a central role in the response to Covid-19 and the challenges of social production it brought to the fore. Food-producing cooperatives, mask making, tree planting, defence, education and awareness-raising have all been led by women. The flourishing of this feminism has been a deliberate process of raising consciousness through intensive political education and ensuring women's power prevails in all spheres of Kurdish struggles for emancipation. Put more sharply, jineology means Kurdish emancipation is either feminist or it is nothing.

ECOLOGY AND TRANSFORMATIVE WOMEN'S POWER IN SOUTH AFRICA

Inge Konik, in chapter 3, provides an overview of some central differences between materialist ecological feminism and liberal feminism. This overview and juxtaposition critically highlights the main preoccupations of liberal feminism as it relates to a hyper individualism and single-issue politics and a consumption feminist image. On the other hand, eco-feminism emerges from the 1970s grassroots struggle to defend non-human nature and has a more holistic understanding of humans-in-nature; provides a critique of capitalist patriarchy as it oppresses both natural relations and women; and furnishes a non-economistic and ecological approach to caregiving in the process of social reproduction. In short, Konik sheds light on why materialist ecological feminism is better equipped than liberal feminism both to analyse and to resist the exploitative practices of neoliberal capitalism. The capacity of each movement to address contemporary social and ecological challenges such as Covid-19 is shaped by important epistemological differences between them. Konik explores these issues through highlighting crucial lessons for eco-feminism and more generally emancipatory feminism.

Dineo Skosana and Jacklyn Cock, in chapter 4, explore the lived realities and struggles of African working-class women in two mining-affected communities. Rich in empirical insights, they explore an African eco-feminist practice with due sensitivity to how women in these communities understand socially constructed gender relations. In theorising from this they provide a rigorous analysis about women as shock absorbers of the multidimensional crisis created by Covid-19, pollution and climate shocks. They also explore the complexities, ambiguities and challenges of building grassroots resistance. Finally, they assess the role of WoMin and the Rural Women's Assembly in advancing and developing an African eco-feminism based on the lived experience, struggles and solidarity-based movement-building practices they champion at the grassroots. This chapter gives meaning to the idea of 'our existence is resistance'.

Courtney Morgan and Jane Cherry, in chapter 5, utilise an eco-socialist feminist lens to explore the intersection of the Covid-19 lockdown, hunger and the role that women play in the transition to food sovereignty through their transformative practices. The chapter situates the international itinerary of food sovereignty, its history and its emergence as an alternative system to address hunger through La Via Campesina, an international grassroots feminist farmers' organisation. This perspective is extended into the South African context to highlight the campaigning work of the South African Food Sovereignty Campaign before and during Covid-19. Given that hunger is central to the crisis of social reproduction, this chapter highlights food sovereignty as power, as a response to the gendered powerlessness of hunger. The chapter provides crucial insights into how food sovereignty can be used to address this crisis in a way that empowers women. Through the interviews they conducted, the authors place in the spotlight South African women who are not only talking about food sovereignty but also employing its practices in their everyday lives to alleviate hunger and build new food sovereignty systems in their communities. The women profiled in this chapter wield power in four meaningful ways: movement power, structural power, direct power and symbolic power.

ECONOMIC TRANSFORMATION, PUBLIC SERVICES AND TRANSFORMATIVE WOMEN'S POWER IN SOUTH AFRICA

Asanda Benya, in chapter 6, explores the role of women in mining. She explores this question historically and in relation to contemporary platinum mining. The discursive delegitimising of women in mining and their controversial inclusion is the starting point for this chapter. The androcentric arguments against the inclusion of women in mining are interrogated while the reasoning for the inclusion of black male bodies is juxtaposed as part of the making of a patriarchal and racist mining capitalism. However, given the androcentric hegemony within the division of labour within the mining process, Benya explores how the marginality of women in mining has become a source of autonomous agency to resist incorporation into a male and racist conception of mining labour practice. She highlights numerous 'strategic refusals' including leaving stopes and negotiating work, rejecting fanakalo (a language spoken by male mineworkers) and 'honorary citizenship', and contesting naming and union membership. This is pathbreaking ethnographic work which shows that African working-class women in mining are reaching for more than liberal equality in the workplace.

Jane Mbithi-Dikgole, in chapter 7, provides a perspective of class and social mobility amongst African women in South Africa. Through qualitative research, she explores middle-class and working-class African women entrepreneurs' career aspirations and labour market choices to assess how this impacts on social mobility. Drawing on in-depth interviews with 103 African women entrepreneurs located in three provinces in South Africa (Gauteng, Mpumalanga and Limpopo), she provides rich research material that shows women's class location has enduring effects on their future work expectations and social mobility. Social class, like gender, generates meanings and expectations that influence women's perceptions of the opportunities available to them. The central aim of this chapter is to explore how race, class and gender affect the labour market decisions of African women, and how this triple oppression has been used to understand the conditions of African women. Class location affects an individual's life choices as life contexts shape women's expectations about work prospects and ultimately shape their lives and social mobility probabilities. Mbithi-Dikgole shows how class location influences labour market choices and employment beliefs and further situates these lived realities against liberal feminism. Ultimately this chapter argues that the crisis of social reproduction disadvantages African women as the gendered division of labour is constructed and maintained in various ways. This crisis means more oppression for African working-class women.

Sonia Phalatse and Busi Sibeko, in chapter 8, unpack the relationship between social reproduction and fiscal policy in the context of crisis and post-crisis recovery. The authors discuss the role of fiscal policy in addressing the crisis of social reproduction which has been shaped by the trajectory of capital accumulation in South Africa. They argue that the government's Covid-19 fiscal response was inadequate, punitive to women, and is exacerbating existing structural inequalities. The Supplementary Budget austerity measures disproportionately affected women as they bear the major part of the burden of social reproduction. They therefore require greater and easier access to public services, but austerity takes that away. These austerity measures were further reinforced in the 2020 Medium Term Budget Policy Statement. Constrictive fiscal policies that have prioritised debt stabilisation at the expense of developing a comprehensive social provisioning policy – which has only deepened since the onset of the global pandemic – have locked in the economy to austerity policies that have worsened conditions for working-class women. A post-Covid-19 economic recovery will require undertaking a state-led expansionary fiscal policy that restores greater investments in social infrastructure, particularly care infrastructure. In this context, it is important to develop tactics to address the crisis of social reproduction in a manner that reprioritises care and decentres profit. This means the South African economy will need to structurally transform to ensure that a number of intersecting inequalities are reversed.

In chapter 9, Christine Bischoff focuses on nurses as part of the health-care workforce, and explicates the idea that paid health-care work is a form of social reproductive labour. Care work describes spheres of work that are usually feminised and comprise the nurturing of others. Many nurses are from poor working-class backgrounds. In South Africa, the dual health-care system persists and there is inequality in the distribution of resources between the private and public health-care sectors. Typically black and female, health-care workers are poorly treated and this impacts on the quality of health-care services offered. Their working conditions are poor: nurses work for long hours, receive low pay and have many financial dependents. There is an increasing casualisation amongst the health-care workforce and nurses are also at risk of being victims of violence in the workplace, as there are chronic nursing staff shortages. Their working conditions became even more dire during Covid-19, since nurses are part of the frontline service personnel who were most at risk of infection and passing that risk on to their families and dependents. Ineffectual trade union responses and austerity measures in the public sector only exacerbate the crisis of social reproduction.

WHERE TO FOR EMANCIPATORY FEMINISM?

While this volume highlights an emergent emancipatory feminism and its transformative forms of resistance and potentials, it also opens up ways of rethinking SRT and modes of doing transformative politics to realise emancipatory feminism, as part of a fourth wave of feminism confronting the total crisis of contemporary capitalism. However, this journey is fraught with challenges. Central to the realisation of emancipatory feminism is the convergence between Marxist, socialist, ecological and indigenous feminisms. This volume demonstrates that it is possible. At the same time, there is a need for dialogue with intersectional feminism. Vishwas Satgar, in chapter 10, engages with these issues. He highlights the dominant modes of Marxist-feminist social reproduction theoretical analysis that have emerged as part of the fourth wave of feminism. While embracing this conceptual approach, he also highlights three crucial problems with Marxist social reproduction analysis that need to be addressed in order to take on board the total or civilisational crisis of contemporary capitalism. This includes a need to appreciate that the systemic crisis tendencies and contradictions of contemporary capitalism are registering as crisis in everything. The dividing lines between background and foreground conditions are blurring as the system reveals its failings, vulnerabilities and limits. Moreover, ecology has to be central to how social reproduction theory and analysis is put to work. This requires a revisit of Marx's ecology, his conception of the human and the important contributions of ecological feminism. From this perspective it might be more appropriate to think of 'green' social reproduction theory as socio-ecological reproduction theory. Another crucial challenge is to clarify the role of intersectionality and Marxist oppression analysis within such a framework. The chapter concludes with a focus on how conceptualising the social reproduction crisis as socio-ecological crises complements emancipatory feminism while highlighting challenges that have to be overcome for such a feminism to flourish.

NOTES

1 During 1934, in Mussolini's prison, Antonio Gramsci in his *Prison Notebook 25* specifies the concept of the subaltern as referring to slaves, peasants, women, different races and the proletariat as subordinate social groups. As Green (2011: 66) highlights, the usage in the *Prison Notebooks* is cryptic but relates to Gramsci's interest in producing a methodology of subaltern history, a history of subaltern classes and a political strategy based on the subaltern. These concerns are also central to a subaltern emancipatory feminism.

2 See https://www.oxfam.org/en/why-majority-worlds-poor-are-women.

3 Fakier and Cock (2009) explore dynamics of physical and emotional care labour as unpaid care labour in a poor working-class community, Mosoetsa (2011) explicates the dynamics of survival in working-class female-headed households and Williams (2018) foregrounds the struggles of women in rural South Africa in the context of a post-wage existence.

4 See https://en.wikipedia.org/wiki/FeminisminSouthAfrica.

5 A similar volume with a misleading title, given the high-profiled women it celebrates, is Engelbrecht and Tywakadi's (2020) *Forgotten Women: The South African Story*.

6 In this regard see Bozzoli (1983), who explores the conceptual challenges and problems with some of the Marxist approaches to feminism in South Africa that developed during the 1960s and 1970s.

7 Amongst others, see Horn (1995), Hassim (2005) and Meintjies (2011).

8 Hassim (2014) provides an important critical analysis of the limits of quotas and gender-based representational politics in local government.

9 See Fakier and Cock (2009), Mosoetsa (2011) and Williams (2018).

10 This critique is developed further by other contributors to this volume.

11 See Williams and Satgar (2021), Volume 6 in the Democratic Marxism series, entitled *Destroying Democracy: Neoliberal Capitalism and the Rise of Authoritarian Politics*, which explores these issues. Also see Panitch et al.'s (2021) *Socialist Register 2022*, in which analyses focus on these issues as well.

12 The work of Silvia Federici (2021), within second-wave feminism and now, has been crucial in drawing attention to women's unpaid reproductive labour within the gender division of labour underpinning the realm of social reproduction, including the notion of the 'patriarchy of the wage'.

13   An International Wages for Housework Campaign developed out of this analysis in the early 1970s. Silvia Federici was one of the socialist feminists involved with this campaign.

REFERENCES

Arruzza, C., Bhattacharya, T. and Fraser, N. 2019. *Feminism for the 99% – A Manifesto*. London and New York: Verso, e-book.

Bhattacharya, T. 2017. *Social Reproduction Theory: Remapping Class, Recentering Oppression*. London: Pluto Press.

Bozzoli, B. 1983. 'Marxism, feminism and South African studies', *Journal of Southern African Studies* 9 (2): 139–171.

Bryson, V. 2005. 'Production and reproduction'. In G. Blakeley and V. Bryson (eds), *Marx and Other Four-Letter Words*. London and Ann Arbor, MI: Pluto Press, pp. 127–142.

Cakardic, A. 2020. 'Marx and social reproduction theory: Three different historical strands'. In N. Engelbrecht and Y.K. Tywakadi (eds), *Forgotten Women: The South African Story*. Johannesburg and Pretoria: Women of Stature Foundation and Blank Page Books.

Engelbrecht, N. and Tywakadi, Y.K. 2020. *Forgotten Women: The South African Story*. Johannesburg and Pretoria: Women of Stature Foundation and Blank Page Books.

Fakier, K. and Cock, J. 2009. 'A gendered analysis of the crisis of social reproduction in contemporary South Africa', *International Feminist Journal of Politics* 11 (3): 353–371.

Fakier, K., Mulinari, D. and Rathzel, N. (eds). 2020. *Marxist-Feminist Theories and Struggles Today: Essential Writings on Intersectionality, Labour and Eco-feminism*. London: Zed Books.

Federici, S. 2021. *Patriarchy of the Wage: Notes on Marx, Gender and Feminism*. Oakland, New York and Toronto: PM Press, e-book.

Green, M.E. 2011. 'Gramsci cannot speak: Presentations and interpretations of Gramsci's concept of the subaltern'. In M.E. Green (ed.), *Rethinking Gramsci*. Oxon and New York: Routledge, pp. 65–86.

Hassim, S. 2005. 'Voices, hierarchies and spaces: Reconfiguring the women's movement in democratic South Africa', *Politikon* 32 (2): 175–193.

Hassim, S. 2014. 'Persistent inequalities: A comparative view of Indian and South African experiences of local government quotas for women', *Politikon* 41 (1): 85–102.

Horn, P. 1995. 'Where is feminism now?', *Agenda: Empowering Women for Gender Equity* 26: 71–74.

International Labour Organization. 2021. *World Employment and Social Outlook Trends 2021: Executive Summary*. Accessed 25 January 2022, https://www.ilo.org/wcmsp5/groups/public/---dgreports/---dcomm/documents/publication/wcms794452.pdf.

Meintjies, S. 2011. 'The women's struggle for equality during South Africa's transition to democracy', *Transformation* 75: 107–115.

Mojab, S. 2015. *Marxism and Feminism*. London: Zed Books.

Mosoetsa, S. 2011. *Eating from One Pot*. Johannesburg: Wits University Press.

Panitch, L., Albo, G. and Leys, C. 2021. *Socialist Register 2022: New Polarizations, Old Contradictions*. London: Merlin Press.

Peet, R. and Hartwick, E. 1999. *Theories of Development*. New York: Guilford Press.

PMBEJD (Pietermaritzburg Economic Justice and Dignity Group). 2021. 'Household Affordability Index: December 2021'. Accessed 25 January 2022, https://pmbejd.org.

za/wp-content/uploads/2021/12/December-2021-Household-Affordability-Index-PMBEJD_29122021.pdf.

Thorpe, J. 2018. 'Feminism and the law'. In J. Thorpe (ed.), *Feminism Is: South Africans Speak Their Truth*. Cape Town: Kwela Books, pp. 259–268.

Tooze, A. 2021. *Shutdown: How Covid Shook the World Economy*. New York City: Viking.

UN Women. n.d. 'Whose time to care?: Unpaid care and domestic work during Covid-19'. Accessed 25 January 2022, https://data.unwomen.org/sites/default/files/inline-files/Whose-time-to-care-brief_0.pdf.

Williams, M. 2018. 'Women in rural South Africa: A post-wage existence and the role of the state', *Equality, Diversity and Inclusion: An International Journal* 37 (4): 392–410.

Williams, M. and Satgar, V. (eds). 2021. *Destroying Democracy: Neoliberal Capitalism and the Rise of Authoritarian Politics*. Johannesburg: Wits University Press.

INDIGENOUS EMANCIPATORY FEMINISM AND TRANSFORMATIVE RESISTANCE

CHAPTER

1

EXTRACTIVISM AND CRISES: ROOTING DEVELOPMENT ALTERNATIVES IN EMANCIPATORY AFRICAN SOCIALIST ECO-FEMINISM

Samantha Hargreaves

INTRODUCTION

In Africa, Covid-19 meets a multiplicity of other crises all interlinked, mutually reinforcing and connected to the same systemic source: extractivist patriarchal capitalism.[1] The crises include climate and ecology and accompanying humanitarian distress; debt (sovereign and individual); hunger; water deprivation; war, civil conflict and associated displacement. These crises layer one upon the other, deepening existing crises and introducing new crises. Read together, for the majority of the world's poor these manifold crises strip away their ability to live, resulting in a profound crisis of social reproduction.[2]

The impacts of these crises are unequally distributed and felt within Africa and, more generally, the global South in its most expansive definition.[3] Bearing the brunt of the impacts are working-class and peasant women within the most impacted regions, who carry these many crises in their bodies, minds and hearts – for the work of social reproduction and care embraces this all.

As we look beyond Covid-19 and the many crises confronting Africa, the new guiding discourse amongst allies and friends (workers, civil society movements, progressive NGOs and so on) and enemies (the World Bank and other

23

international finance institutions [IFIs], the United Nations [UN], the G20 and more) is that of *recovery*, variously just, resilient, sustainable, inclusive and 'green'. The political analysis, principles and strategies, and the goal of transformation guiding the content of the discourse and the pathways chosen, are wildly divergent, with capital and interests allied to corporations and the elite seeking to advance their genocidal and ecocidal ambitions under the veil of 'reconstruction and development'. Trade unions, peasant and other social movements and progressive feminist organisations are keeping a vigilant and critical eye on these dangerous actors, working collectively and individually to counter their narrative with a vision and discourse of an alternative pathway to a different world that centres people, care, ecosystems and the earth.

This chapter builds on the analyses written by the WoMin African Alliance (where I am based) during the Covid-19 crisis, and our early explorations of pan-Africanism built from below in and through African women and their communities' resistance to extractivism, and their struggles for justice and reparations. WoMin works on the frontiers of extractivism in the African context and the costs this model of capitalist accumulation externalises to women, their bodies and their labour.[4] In our efforts, and increasingly so since the onset of the Covid-19 crisis, we have centred the reparations due to African people for the climate debt, the sovereign debt, the colonial and neocolonial debt, and the reproductive debt to African working-class and peasant women. The reparations angling is radical and restorative, acknowledging the centuries of exploitation, theft and violence perpetrated against African peoples, which enabled the development of economies and societies in imperial Europe and North America. A just transition to a just future for Africans now and the generations of Africans to follow must be secured by the settlement of these debts as the basis for reconstruction and development that is guided by justice, determined by the majority, and guarantees a life for all on this earth.

Whilst WoMin has always identified as an African alliance, we have never expressly adopted a politics informed by pan-Africanism. To conceptualise alternatives to development, we have drawn upon political ideas that have emerged in contexts other than our continent: *buen vivir*; extractivism, post-extractivism and neo-extractivism; the commons; degrowth (for parts of the overdeveloped global North); circular economies and so forth. The growing crises and threats to life on our continent have prompted WoMin to search for living African alternatives as well as alternatives eclipsed by successive waves of colonisation and neocolonial extractivist capitalism. The frame guiding our work with women is thus ecological, feminist, socialist and expressly pan-African.

Since 2021, we have been supporting dialogues with working-class and peasant women in communities of resistance across the continent. This process will culminate in subregional convergences and a 2024 pan-African assembly which will adopt a statement crafted by women and share a collection of women's stories and visual representations in beadwork and/or tapestry of the alternatives that women dream of.

The lexicon of alternatives which WoMin is now exploring encompasses pan-African solidarity which deliberately embraces the diaspora and contests colonial boundaries and accompanying xenophobias; endogenous practices and philosophies such as ubuntu and ways of addressing bodily and emotional trauma that draw upon African spiritualities; and a deepening understanding and defence of the living land commons: the customary communal land tenure systems which are widespread across our continent. This chapter explores some of the key political ideas that will shape WoMin's journey with women in the next decade to decolonise 'development' and liberate the continent and its diverse peoples.

UNDERSTANDING THE INTERSECTING CRISES IN THE AFRICAN CONTEXT

The crisis of climate and ecology

Global average temperatures have increased a frightening 0.8°C since 1880. The year 2019 broke all previous average temperature records and despite the economic slowdown triggered by the Covid-19 crisis, the Carbon Brief has forecast that 2020 is still set to hit record highs (Hausfather 2020; see also Barkham 2020). At the current trajectory, in terms of unconditional government pledges through the United Nations Framework Convention on Climate Change (UNFCCC), average temperatures will, estimated very conservatively, increase by just over 3°C by 2100.

At the time of writing, scientists studying the frozen methane deposits in the Arctic Ocean – the 'sleeping giants of the carbon cycle' – reported that the methane is 'seeping' from the melting peat bogs over millions of hectares in Siberia (Tomala 2019). Methane has more than 80 times the warming power of carbon dioxide in the first 20 years after it reaches the atmosphere and therefore sets the pace for warming in the short to medium term. Researchers are concerned, given the volume of deposits, that a new climate feedback loop[5] that could heighten the pace of global heating has been triggered. This process was accelerated by the Siberian wildfires in July 2020, as well as other wildfires that have raged across parts of the United States, Australia and Europe over the past few years.

Climate change is affecting different regions of the world differently, with Africa heating disproportionately quickly, and with little infrastructure and few resources to mitigate heating and adapt to a warmer world. This is a grave injustice, given that Africa accounts for only two to three per cent of the world's carbon dioxide emissions from energy and industrial sources since the start of the Industrial Revolution in Britain and Europe. This percentage includes South Africa, which was ranked fourteenth in the list of the world's top carbon emitters in 2018, which means that the relative contributions of all other African countries are microscopic in comparison.

The World Meteorological Organization (WMO) released its *State of the Climate in Africa 2019* report in October 2020 and draws the conclusion that average temperatures in Africa have increased over 1°C (greater than the global average indicated above) since 1901. Warming in large areas of the continent will well exceed 2°C by 2080 to 2100 if emissions continue at their current levels. With this climate warming, the deterioration of food security has resulted in a 45.6 per cent increase in the number of undernourished people since 2012 (WMO 2020). In the Sahel region, Robert Muggah and José Cabrera (2019) report that roughly 80 per cent of the farmland is degraded by rising temperatures and that conflicts rage as desperate people fight to control farmlands and scarce water bodies. Women constitute a sizeable percentage of the world's poor, and about half of the women in the world are active in agriculture. The WMO estimates that in developing countries, women constitute 60 per cent of food producers, and in low-income, food-deficit countries, 70 per cent of the same; the projected impacts of climate warming on agriculture will affect them severely.

Droughts, floods, hurricanes, persistent malaria and generalised water scarcity are likely to increase in the next few decades. In low-lying coastal areas, rising sea levels have taken metres of coastline, along with people's land, housing and communal social services (WMO 2020).

Finally, it is important to recognise the direct links between climate change and biodiversity loss. We need to address both in order to maintain nature and our well being. Biodiversity (the diversity within species, between species and within ecosystems) is declining faster than it has at any other time in human history. Thales Dantas (2018) asserts that the current rate of extinction is ten to hundreds of times higher than the average over the past ten million years and is accelerating. Humanity has already caused the loss of 83 per cent of all wild mammals and half of all wild plants. If low estimates of the number of affected species are accurate, between 200 and 2 000 extinctions are occurring every year.

Debt and financial flows out of Africa

The looting of Africa's wealth and deepening debt have rendered the continent's governments incapable of meeting basic social needs, mitigating climate crisis and supporting adaptation needs of citizens. Seamus Cleary (1989), Thandika Mkandawire and Chukwuma Soludo (2003), and Ndongo Sylla (2018) have evidenced that successive neoliberal structural adjustment policies and the accompanying privatisation of key public services (education, health care, water and sanitation) under the direction of IFIs such as the International Monetary Fund (IMF) and the World Bank have hollowed out state capacity, thus gravely undermining the readiness of African countries to deal with Covid-19, as well as other pandemics such as Ebola and HIV/AIDS.

The rise of the extractive sectors in Africa in the past decade or more has led to the vast looting of Africa's wealth, well captured in the results of the High-Level Panel on Illicit Financial Flows from Africa (High-Level Panel 2015), and severely compromises the ability of states to fulfil their developmental responsibilities. In February 2015, after three years of research and analysis, this panel reported that Africa was losing more than US$50 billion every year to illicit financial flows (IFFs). This is defined as money which is earned, transferred or utilised through illegal means and originates from (i) corporate tax evasion, trade mis-invoicing and unlawful transfer pricing; (ii) criminal activities; and (iii) corruption of government officials, with the latter accounting for only three per cent of total outflows, according to Open Society Initiative of West Africa (OSIWA) estimates.[6] The case of Nigeria is powerful: the oil and gas sector of the Nigerian economy is responsible for 92.9 per cent of IFFs, with over US$217.7 billion said to have flowed out of the country between 1970 and 2008, according to research conducted by the Partnership for African Social and Governance Research (PASGR). They argue that the extractives sector leads in wealth outflows from the world's periphery to the wealthy centres, which in the Nigerian case are the US, Spain, France and Germany.[7]

The High-Level Panel only addressed illicit flows, thus neglecting significant corruption and revenue loss due to licit (or legal) financial outflows. To attract investment in the mining and other extractives sectors, governments 'bend' (with the pressure of corporations and often supported by corruption) the tax and revenue collection rules and systems, and waive duties required by law. Mining companies are thus able to negotiate tax rates favourable to themselves but inconsistent with the laid down laws of the country in question. By way of example, in Sierra Leone, the corporate income tax for mining companies is 37.5 per cent as set out in the Income Tax Act of 2002. However, in 2010/11 two iron ore mining companies,

African Minerals and London Mining, had individual agreements with the government to pay only 25 per cent. In London Mining's initial agreement, the company retained a six per cent income tax rate for three years (WoMin 2020).

Debt is weighing heavily on the national budgets of African countries and has been exacerbated, in recent years, by 'Eurobonds', a debt instrument that is denominated in a currency other than the home currency of the country. This leaves African countries extremely vulnerable to commonplace volatility in foreign exchange currency rates.

In the joint 2020 Committee for the Abolition of Illegitimate Debt/WoMin statement on the African debt crisis, sub-Saharan Africa's outstanding public external debt doubled between 2010 and the end of December 2018, from US$160 billion to US$365.5 billion. At the time of writing, Africa's public debt stands at more than US$500 billion (CADTM and WoMin 2020). In some countries, debt servicing represents more than 25 per cent of their revenues, and most countries spend more on debt than on health. For example, Cameroon spends 23.8 per cent of its revenue on debt servicing, compared to 6.9 per cent on health. This year, the continent will pay a total of US$44 billion in interest alone to its external creditors.

The CADTM/WoMin statement indicates that African governments are struggling to find the money to fight the Covid-19 pandemic and save lives, and to support the very necessary recovery plans – imperatives undermined by the demands of debt servicing. In contrast, rich countries are investing about eight per cent of their gross domestic product (GDP), on average, on economic interventions and stimulus measures, while African countries are spending an average of 0.8 per cent of their GDP, which measure hides significant differences across African countries (CADTM and WoMin 2020).

The extractives sector, and extractivism as a model of development, is inextricably linked to the debt crisis. WoMin and other allies project a greater demand for the extraction of Africa's wealth in natural resources in the coming years, to settle existing debts and procure new loans for 'reconstruction'. This will only fuel the unsustainable cycle of mega resource extraction, greater illicit and licit financial flows out of Africa, deepening climate and ecological crisis, expanding indebtedness and yet more extraction in a desperate quest to head off the growing interconnected crises.

The rise of pandemics

HIV/AIDS, avian flu, the swine flu pandemic, severe acute respiratory syndrome (SARS), the Ebola fever and now Covid-19[8] are the main infectious diseases, stemming from the spread of pathogens ordinarily found in animals, usually wildlife, to humans, which have afflicted Africa in the past 50 years.[9] Vandana Shiva, the esteemed scholar and activist, argues that 'more than 300 new pathogens have emerged over the past 50 years as the habitat of species is destroyed and manipulated for profits' (Shiva 2020).

The root of most new infectious diseases lies in the rapid expansion of the extractives sector, which includes logging and industrial plantation style mono-cropping (such as palm oil and cocoa), livestock production and, more recently, the mining sector's violent encroachments on land and forests in contexts of deep structural poverty.

The Ebola crisis, which raged through West Africa during 2013–2016, killing more than 11 000 people, and mainly affecting Sierra Leone, Liberia and Guinea, powerfully illustrates this relationship. Significant capital investment in the extractives sector (rubber tapping, cocoa and palm oil production specifically) had contributed to West Africa suffering the highest deforestation rate in the world at this time. Scientists studied 27 Ebola outbreak sites in sub-Saharan Africa and discovered that an outbreak is most likely to strike in or near areas that have experienced deforestation in the previous two years (McQue 2018).

In 2019, the Ebola virus reared its head again, this time in the war-torn eastern Democratic Republic of the Congo (DRC), where gold mining by large multinational companies is widespread. It is estimated that more than 2 000 people died in this year-long epidemic (Keneally 2014). In this instance, Ebola was directly linked to the mining industry, confirming the analysis of scientists that mining, the felling of trees to build roads, and the construction of settlements in previously pristine jungles bring humans into contact with animal species they may never have been near before (Keneally 2014).

Ebola has taken root in contexts characterised by deep structural poverty. At the time of the 2013–2016 crisis, Sierra Leone, Guinea and Liberia were ranked 183, 175 and 179 in the UN Human Development Index, with the DRC (in 2019) sitting at 179 on the same index. This poverty in contexts that have withstood the ravages of resource grabs during the colonial, post-colonial and neocolonial periods, undermines the readiness of African states and African peoples to respond to pandemics and other crises of climate, ecology and war. By way of illustration, in 2018 the World Health Organization (WHO) outlined the direct and indirect impacts of climate change on human health as malnutrition, tropical and diarrhoeal diseases, malaria, dengue fever, as well as meningitis and cardio-respiratory diseases.[10]

Early projections concerning the impact of Covid-19 on African countries, which are characterised by weak health systems, and existent diseases of poverty (HIV/AIDS, tuberculosis and malaria) were dire. However, the reported infection and death rate was low compared to most regions of the world, with 51 000 African deaths confirmed at the time of writing. The head of the Africa Centres for Disease Control and Prevention indicated that the miscounting of deaths was minimal. In contrast, South African epidemiologists argued that the actual death rate there was 2.5 times greater than officially reported.[11]

War, displacement and violence against women

Scientists have generally avoided making a direct link between climate change and conflict, but are more recently converging around the idea that climate change adds to already existing stresses in societies and can therefore be characterised as having a 'threat multiplier' effect. 'Think of climate change as "loading the dice", making conflict more likely to occur in subtle ways across a host of different country contexts' (United Nations 2019; O'Loughlin and Hendrix 2019).

The Sahel is an important illustration. Dependent on rain-fed agriculture, the Sahel is frequently impacted by droughts and floods, with significant impacts on people's food security.[12] The combined contribution of violence, armed conflict and military operations has displaced more than 4.9 million people and left approximately 24 million people in need of humanitarian assistance. The UN concludes that climate change is partly to blame. Roughly 80 per cent of the Sahel's farmland is degraded, and temperatures there are increasing at one and a half times the global average. The effect of this is that droughts and floods are growing longer and more frequent, which undermines food production. The land available to the more than 50 million pastoralists and their dependents is shrinking (Muggah and Cabrera 2019), a reality aggravated by rising population numbers pushing farmers northward in search of cultivable land. Add the shrinking of Lake Chad to the picture and these combined factors provide a verdant breeding ground for terrorist groups as social values and moral authority evaporate.

Large-scale extraction of natural resources often lies at the heart of wars and civil strife. Gargantuan mining and resource companies like ExxonMobil and BHP Billiton manoeuvre for control of enormously valuable oilfields and mineral lodes. Add to the mix other players, such as shadowy resource traders, smugglers, corrupt local officials, arms dealers, transport operators and mercenary companies, and the potential for conflict at scales ranging from local to national and well beyond, multiplies. Increasing scarcity of resources further sharpens such conflicts, in which powerful governments and their military/intelligence arms are usually implicated.

In Liberia and Sierra Leone, decades of civil strife are linked to control over the diamond fields and involve corporations, illicit trading, elite grabs and the corruption of traditional leaders. The International Rescue Committee's mortality studies on the humanitarian impact of civil conflict and inter state wars linked to control over natural resource wealth, mainly on the eastern side of the DRC, estimate that 5.4 million people have died since 1998, making this the deadliest conflict since the Second World War, yet barely acknowledged internationally (Moszynski 2008). The same is true of Angola's oil and diamond fields, and Nigeria's Niger Delta, which has been characterised by decades of insurgencies and local resistances, military occupation, and extreme violence perpetrated against women – all linked to oil company controls over the extremely profitable exploitation of reserves.

War and conflict, and the other crises cited here, elevate domestic and sexualised violence as families confront extreme social and economic stress (Gevers et al. 2020; Harvey 2020; UN Women n.d.). In Uganda, research undertaken by the United Nations Development Programme (UNDP) revealed that women and girls are that much more vulnerable to rape and harassment as they walk longer distances to access food and water in situations of climate-related drought. WoMin drew the same conclusions through feminist participatory research undertaken with women in northern KwaZulu-Natal in South Africa, where the combined impacts of water grabbing by the Tendele coal mine and drought left women and girls walking round trips of two hours for 25 litres of water. Women reported experiences of sexual harassment and rape during these walks (WoMin 2017).

Ecological and climate crisis, arising from an extractivist logic, are concrete expressions of the eroded relationship between humanity and nature under Western industrialised capitalism. When nature's territory is violently damaged and destroyed by the externalised impacts of industrialised extractivist processes (water, air and soil pollution, and biodiversity losses), the body territory is also polluted. People fall ill with cancers, respiratory diseases, reproductive health problems, eye diseases and substance addictions, which not only contribute to the increased labour of care carried by women in impacted communities but also contribute to a crisis in the ability of people to reproduce themselves daily (the crisis of social reproduction). The destruction of nature territory and body territory through pollution, ecological destruction and climate change, and the violence perpetrated against workers, communities and especially women are intertwined. Violence against women must, therefore, be addressed as intrinsically linked to the ecological and climate crisis (World Rainforest Movement 2016).

Conservative and liberal commentators from the territorial global North have projected Africa's conflicts and wars as 'domestic' issues related to its underdeveloped status and corrupt leaders. However, the continent's battles arise, in large part, from corrupt transnational corporations and their quest for control over and maximum profit from Africa's wealth and the unsustainable energy systems, lifestyles

31

and consumption patterns of the middle classes and elites in the same dominant territories, which fuel climate and ecological crises.

Concluding thoughts on the interconnected crises

The mounting ecological and climate crises and rising consciousness of their roots meet the Covid-19 pandemic to lay bare the same systemic roots. The historical and structural realities described above, which afflict Africa and its poor and working populations in very particular ways, stem from the same root: extractivist neocolonial patriarchal capitalism. This system exploits the cheap labour of black working-class men in mines and plantations and rests on the unpaid labour of women as they work to house, provide water and food, care for and satisfy the needs of labour. The peasantry and the working classes are dispossessed of land, water, forests, fisheries and minerals to profit the system, which relies on nature as a free or cheap input to production and a 'sink' for the externalised environmental costs of production. Capital also depends on women's unpaid labour to absorb the externalised social and economic costs of production and the rehabilitation of damaged nature (Hargreaves 2019).

Reputable scientists, academics, analysts and organisations[13] are linking Covid-19 to the encroachments of extractivist capital upon forests and ecosystems as corporates pursue profit through ranching, logging and mining. The logic of reducing nature and its beings to assets to be exploited for profit therefore lies at the very heart of the Covid-19 pandemic, the very same logic that is causing the global climate crisis.

Working-class and peasant women in Africa carry the burden of all the crises listed above because of their designation as the primary household food producers, caregivers and harvesters of water, energy and other basic goods needed for the reproduction of life and the wellbeing of people. But these roles also place them at the frontlines of the battle to defend nature and its right to exist, without which the survival of all beings would not be possible.

Political analysis and perspectives which link ecology, feminism and socialism with critical analysis about who carries the cost of a violent extractivist development model – LGBTIQ, black and brown, working-class, peasant and female bodies – have been more evident during the height of the Covid-19 pandemic on the African continent. What has, however, been largely lacking in the Anglophone African literature on crises and frames for economic, political and societal responses has been a reclaiming and reconceptualisation of a radical pan-Africanism which can inspire movement, frame resistance and drive African development alternatives.

The following section addresses just three dimensions of a decolonising process of dreaming and imagining African alternatives – a process that WoMin has started exploring in its work with women. These include African commoning and the protection of land and nature through customary laws and practices; the philosophy and practice of ubuntu (I am because we are); and, embracing these two dimensions, the recovery of pan-Africanism in and through women's resistances to extractivist capital.

'BUILDING BACK' WITH AFRICAN HISTORY, POLITICS AND PHILOSOPHY AT THE CENTRE

There are powerful political ideas, theories and practices that have informed and continue to guide progressive social movements and formations as we make sense of the contexts we live in, dream of a different world and build strategies for reaching our destination within wider political movements. The WoMin African Alliance subscribes to the political ideas of extractivism (and its variants), eco-feminism, the commoning of resources, decolonisation, ecological socialism and post-development thinking.

Most importantly, WoMin has also been deeply shaped by the experiences of women in extractives-impacted communities; by the droughts, flooding, cyclones and hurricanes which characterise the climate crisis; by the violence and injustices the women we work with confront daily;[14] and by the close political allies with whom we analyse, organise and campaign.

As we build an imagination of and pathway towards a post-Covid world that acknowledges the multiple crises which the peoples of Africa live with daily, progressive African feminists and anti-capitalist movements are charged with acknowledging the living African alternatives that exist in the everyday systems and practices of holding land, making decisions, keeping and sharing seed, producing food, sharing labour demands collectively, dealing with traumas, relating to ecologies and offering social support. At the same time, we must collaborate with communities – and women specifically – to recover historical practices which have been eroded by successive waves of colonisation and neocolonisation. While the recovery and deepening of these more micro-level alternatives will be critical to building resilience and adapting to a rapidly warming climate, these must be located within a wider political struggle against the deep roots of Africa's historical oppression. This requires a recovery and embracing of radical pan-Africanism which is socialist, ecological and feminist and which can grapple with new configurations of imperialism.

The living, breathing African commons: Customary land tenure systems

Land on large swathes of the continent is held under common or communal property systems. Liz Wiley (2018), writing for the Forest Peoples Programme, estimates that 90 per cent of rural dwellers acquire, hold and transfer lands as members of communities, in accordance with agreed community norms. She estimates that between 800 and 880 million people on the continent were living under common property regimes at the time of writing, and that this number will increase to around one billion people in 2050. Only four (Mauritania, Eritrea, Senegal and Egypt) out of 54 countries had fully extinguished customary tenure, although communities continue to use land and resources in common. Despite the scale and extent of customary landholding, many African governments do not recognise or support it, with the result that these systems are under threat. Customary tenure systems are generally characterised by some of the following features:

- Those who dwell on the land are the keepers/carers/custodians for generations to come.
- Land may not be owned as private property and cannot be sold on the open market. Having said that, rights to communal land are strong; rights can be bequeathed within the family (variously to the oldest or youngest male child as a commonplace practice) and can only be alienated by collective decision upon serious violation of communal rules.
- Decisions about the use of land must be made collectively by the group/tribe/community.
- Representatives/leaders of the group are required to facilitate collective decisions of the group and represent these to 'outsiders'.
- Land rights and the strength of tenure security determine membership of the group and rights to participate in and influence decision making at a collective level.
- There are strict rules for the entry of outsiders to the group in order to preserve the integrity and common rules of the collective.

This is a description of 'ideal' and generalised rules for common property systems at the local or micro scale, benefiting a clearly defined group, community, tribe or entity. There is, of course, variation from one context to the next. The practices and beliefs of these systems have been eroded and manipulated by states and the powerful during colonisation, apartheid (in South Africa), neoliberal capitalism and neocolonisation. Community and traditional leaders often exercise too much power, fail to respect community decision-making processes, and may sometimes represent their own interests as representative of the group and its interests.

Common property systems have long come under attack by institutions such as the World Bank, the International Finance Corporation and other IFIs, and states have been pressurised to privatise these holdings. This thinking is largely based on the long-discredited ideas of Garrett Hardin's 'Tragedy of the commons' (1968), and a core neoliberal commitment to privatisation as the basis for 'sound' development (Harvey 2011).

Patriarchal and colonial thinking have worked together and separately to undermine women's land rights and their ability to participate in community or group decision-making processes, with women navigating and exercising their creative agency to undermine or 'work' the system as their status permits. Uchendu Chigbu, Gaynor Paradza and Walter Dachaga (2019) note that women's access to land and tenure security is highly differentiated according to class, age, health status, inheritance practices and migrant status.[15]

As Simon Fairlie (2009) notes, the enclosure of common fields, grazing lands and forests in the traditional global North started in Britain during the twelfth century, with full enclosure there more or less concluded by the nineteenth century.[16] Giangiacomo Bravo and Tine De Moor (2008) point out that in Europe, the pace of privatisation was slower and greatly differentiated, but gained traction in the nineteenth century, though common rights remain intact over some areas of pasture and woodland – but under increasing pressure. Common property over land, water, forests and fish in the African context, as well as other parts of the traditional global South, are the living commons to be defended, protected and expanded in transformative ways that enable both the land rights and decision-making rights of women and young people. The commons are the first line of defence against the encroachments of capital upon people and nature, and represent the founding basis of the right of peoples and women to say an emphatic 'no' to extractives-driven development.

Ubuntu – I am because we are
Ubuntu, also referred to as Botho, Hunhu Munhu, Umuntu, Muthu, Bumuntu, Gimuntu, Vumuntu, Omundu and so on in other Bantu languages, is an African philosophy that rests on the belief in a universal bond of sharing that connects all humanity, that is, a person is a person through other people. It derives from an Nguni word, *ubuntu*, meaning 'the quality of being human'.

This philosophy holds that we owe our selfhood to others and calls on us to mirror our humanity for and to each other. It sits contrary to the Western emphasis on individualism and individual human rights, asking instead that we put the interests of the community ahead of the individual. Jacob Mugumbate and Andrew Nyanguru (2013) contend that through ubuntu we recognise the humanity of others and activate behaviour imbued with respect, tolerance, sharing, empathy and love.

Kai Horsthemke (2017) and Danford Chibvongodze (2017) both challenge critiques of ubuntu as being anthropocentric in nature and argue instead that this philosophy consolidates the human, natural and spiritual tripartite allowing Africans to extend the moral obligations they hold to humans to nature, including wildlife. In African religious and spiritual ontology, the humanity and existence of Africans is intertwined with that of plants, animals and rivers. By way of example, the Herero of Namibia regard cattle as sacred and believe that they originate from the same 'tree of life' as human beings. In some African cultures, snakes are believed to symbolise human spirits and may not be killed. Instead, they must be given food and drink when they visit people's homes. In rural parts of Cameroon, the family will often worship at the site of a fig tree, which is a refuge for gods that protect local people from harm. The fig tree cannot be desecrated or felled. Clan names, which play an essential role in African religion, are often derived from the identities and mannerisms of wild animals. These religious beliefs ensure that humans coexist with the environment and animals in respectful and non-exploitative ways (Chibvongodze 2017).

Ubuntu presents us with the values of care, love, empathy, respect and common interest over individualism, which few in progressive social movements would argue does not represent, in part, the type of society, community, Africa and world we strive for. These values represent the prefigurative politics we should strive for in our social formations and movements. However, ubuntu may be critiqued as a philosophy that fails to grapple with power structures and the unequal relations of class, gender, ethnicity, age and so forth, which undermine the enjoyment of these very values. While this may be true, the philosophy and practice of ubuntu is complementary to the structural analysis and confrontations with capital and patriarchy which characterise the struggles of progressive movements.

From a perusal of the Anglophone African literature, ideas of ubuntu have been taken up in the rights of nature work, in the sphere of education, and on the more dubious grounds of environmental management and even tourism, which cynically present ubuntu in marketing materials as an opportunity for tourists to 'enjoy' African hospitality and culture. The extent to which this philosophy and its call to a transformed praxis of resistance has been taken up in African movements and political formations is unclear and a point for further exploration. WoMin, which defines as African and, more recently, as an alliance pursuing pan-African politics, is only now, eight years after its formation, starting to explore ubuntu from an African eco-feminist vantage point. It seeks to understand whether and how this philosophy shapes the daily lives of rural African women and their coping strategies in the midst of multiple crises and integrate this into our political analysis and strategy for confronting patriarchal, extractivist capitalism.

Pan-African politics and movement

Pan-Africanism, an ideology and political movement, has its origins in the struggles of all African peoples against five centuries of enslavement and colonisation. It aims to unify Africans on the continent and in the diaspora, all bound by a common history and destiny, and reclaim African peoples from colonisation, neocolonisation and imperialism. More generally, the pan-African movement aims to 'promote the political, socio-economic and cultural unity, emancipation and self-reliance of Africa and its diaspora' (Adebajo 2020: 4).

Between 1884 and 1885, the infamous Berlin Conference agreed to the balkanisation of Africa into 50 nation-states, laying the basis for colonisation and neocolonisation for well over the next century.[17] This gave greater impetus to the emerging pan-African movement, which met for the first time 15 years later in London, from 23 to 25 July 1900. This was followed by five successive conferences between 1919 and 1945.

According to Adekeye Adebajo (2020), pan-African civil society activism can be traced back to the 1770s in the United States diaspora when Phillis Wheatley, a woman, published a volume of poetry which put forward a positive and empowering image of the 'black world'. Since then, the pan-African lineage of thinkers, philosophers and revolutionaries has embraced a wide range of political orientations and ideas. These include Africa for the Africans, with the learned playing a 'civilising' role towards the 'backward tribes'; Ethiopianism, the spiritual strand of pan-Africanism, which was dominant during the 'high' imperial period; pan-African nationalism; and pan-African socialism, of particular interest to me, and largely advanced by Ghana's Kwame Nkrumah and Burkina Faso's Thomas Sankara.

The Organisation of African Unity (OAU) Charter was adopted in a meeting of 32 African states in Addis Ababa and represented a first effort to institutionalise pan-Africanism by fostering unity and solidarity between African countries. The OAU was weakened by the lack of implementation mechanisms and by the non-binding status of assembly resolutions. More profoundly, the OAU failed to bring down imposed national boundaries, deconstruct nationalities and create a unified African sovereignty. If these actions had been undertaken, they would have unmade the Berlin

37

Conference decisions, and unlocked a powerful process of continent-wide decolonisation as well as a reimagining and remaking of Africa and its peoples.

The more contemporary Pan-African Parliament and African Union have replicated the same disappointments, failing to offer a transformative vision of the continent. Instead, states continue to compete for elusive foreign investment, trade deals and loans, in this way facilitating the continued plunder of Africa's resources on highly unjust terms, and perpetuating Africa's marginalised geopolitical positioning.

While the formal institutionalisation of pan-Africanism has not yielded what the continent and its peoples need for genuine socio-economic, political and cultural liberation (the guiding elements of pan-Africanism), pan-African civil society activism and solidarity within and across the boundaries of the nation-state is vibrant. This organising has adopted divergent politics and taken different forms, including networking and activism targeting the subregional blocs, solidarity campaigns, alliance building within linguistic blocs, and genuine attempts at building pan-African organisation. This informs a new imagination about Africa that its peoples need, drawing from an abundant living praxis, and informed by a rich history of African philosophy, spirituality and movement. A revitalised pan-Africanism must be constructed from below by African citizens, wedded in demand and solidarity across nations, and rooted in their daily practices and relations with each other and with Mother Nature. African women across the continent are at the forefront of mobilisations to stop mega extractives and infrastructure projects, condemn repression and violence, and demand climate justice. These struggles represent a living pan-Africanism, rooted in a long tradition of women's resistances against colonialism, against the privatisation of public services under neoliberalism and against the land and resource grabs of neocolonial capitalism.

Dialogues with women on a just pan-African future

WoMin is collaborating with its partners and allies to undertake dialogues with women resisting extractivism on their dreams and hopes for a different community, society and Africa. This process started in July 2019 at a continental convening of feminists, environmental justice activists and activist academics to explore the idea of eco-feminist just transitions in the African context. In this meeting a set of principles to guide just transitions on an eco-feminist basis were agreed, as was a proposal to collaborate with women impacted by extractivism to dream and imagine a different community, society and Africa. The dialogues were piloted in Madagascar, Guinea (Conakry) and South Africa, and have been rolled out in sites in another ten countries. In this process, women reflect on their familial and communal histories to identify ways of living and producing that have been lost or distorted through colonial and neocolonial processes. They consider the present and what this has meant for women and their communities and, building on past and present, explore their hopes and dreams for radically transformed futures. These dialogues are unfolding, in different forms, at various levels (local, national and subregional) and in collaboration with diverse movements, culminating in a pan-African women's assembly within a planned continental 'Thematic Social Forum on Extractivism, African Sovereignty and Pan African Solutions' in 2024. The dialogues are being systematised by women at the national and subregional levels, and their hopes and dreams are finding expression in writing, stories, as well as in maps, drawings, beadwork and tapestry. This unified solidarity and action of African women across nations dialoguing, imagining and organising, represents an important strand of a renewed living, breathing pan-Africanism.

NOTES

1   Extractivism describes economic activities that entail the removal of substantial amounts of a nation's natural commons (in raw form) for sale on the world market. This includes minerals, gas and oil extraction, plantation forestry, industrial agriculture and fisheries. New forms of extractivism exist in emerging renewable energies. Extractivism also refers to the conditions under which these resources are extracted and whose interests they serve, speaking to a dominant and highly unequal model of development which deeply shapes the nature of the economy, class structures, gender relations, the functioning of the state and public discourse (Acosta n.d.; Aguilar 2012; Gudynas 2010).

2   Social reproduction refers to the activities involved in maintaining and reproducing current workers and their labour power, nurturing future workers, and maintaining members of families and communities who cannot work on a daily and generational basis. It involves 'a range of different kinds of work – mental, manual and emotional' and traverses the provision of food, clothing, shelter, basic safety and health care, alongside the transmission of knowledge, values and cultural practices (Laslett and Brenner 1989).

3   The global South has traditionally referred to nation-states that have been economically disadvantaged by colonisation and neoliberalism, and has replaced the political idea of the 'Third World'. By the notion of a more expansive definition, I refer to territories and peoples negatively impacted by contemporary capitalist globalisation, such that we have the economic Souths in the geographic North and the privileged North in the traditional geography of the global South (Mahler 2017).

4   WoMin is an African eco-feminist alliance, working with partners and allies in 17 countries across sub-Saharan Africa to support women organising and movement building to challenge extractivist mega projects, to evidence their destructive effects and to force (where possible) corporations to internalise the social, environmental, economic and gendered costs. The alliance is accountable to its partners and allies in the 17 countries, but most importantly, places itself at the service of women directly impacted by

extractivism and its fallout, including the climate, ecological and reproductive crises. WoMin, which launched in October 2013, currently has 24 staff and associates (all women), operates a secretariat in Johannesburg and has an annual budget of close to R50 million granted by funders and foundations in Europe, the United Kingdom and North America.

5   In climate change terminology, a feedback loop is like a 'vicious cycle', where something, such as the peat fires in Siberia, triggers a warming trend that accelerates a rise in temperature, termed a positive feedback. A negative feedback, by contrast, would be a cooling trend. See 'What are climate change feedback loops?', *The Guardian,* 5 January 2011, https://www.theguardian.com/environment/2011/jan/05/climate-change-feedback-loops (accessed 9 June 2021).

6   See https://www.opensocietyfoundations.org/voices/how-illicit-financial-flows-drain-african-economies (accessed 23 June 2021).

7   See https://www.pasgr.org/nigeria-haemorrhaging-from-organised-illicit-financial-flows/ (accessed 23 June 2021).

8   WoMin, 'Covid-19 – crisis upon crisis in Africa: An ecofeminist perspective', Press Statement, 8 April 2020, https://womin.africa/covid-19-crisis-upon-crisis-in-africa-an-ecofeminist-perspective/ (accessed 9 June 2021).

9   See Saker et al. (2004); Ord (2020); Walsh (2020); WHO (2014).

10   World Health Organization, 'Fact sheet: Climate change and health', 1 February 2018, https://www.who.int/news-room/fact-sheets/detail/climate-change-and-health; United Nations Economic Commission for Africa, 'Policy brief: Climate change and health in Africa: issues and options' 2013, https://repository.uneca.org/bitstream/handle/10855/23158/b11563965.pdf?sequence=1&isAllowed=y; WHO, 'Climate change increases risk of outbreaks in Africa', 7 November 2018, https://www.afro.who.int/news/climate-change-increases-risk-outbreaks-africa (all sites accessed 9 June 2021).

11   See Soy (2020) and BBC News, 'Coronavirus: Age and climate seen as behind Africa's low cases', 25 September 2020, https://www.bbc.com/news/world-africa-54300855 (accessed 9 July 2021).

12   The Sahel is a vast semi-arid region of Africa which separates the Sahara Desert to the north and tropical savannahs to the south.

13   See Zeilig and Cross (2020); Ian Angus interview by ROAPE (2020); Grain (2020); Shiva (2020).

14   See https://riseagainstrepression.org/ (accessed 13 December 2022).

15   See Chigbu et al. (2019) for a three-country (Ghana, Nigeria and Zimbabwe) study exploring women's land rights.

16   See also Windling (2015) and 'The Enclosure Act', https://courses.lumenlearning.com/suny-hccc-worldhistory2/chapter/the-enclosure-act/ (accessed 9 June 2021).

17   See https://www.uj.ac.za/newandevents/Pages/A-re-awakening-year-for-Pan-Africanism.aspx (accessed 9 June 2021).

REFERENCES

Acosta, A. (n.d.). 'Extractivism and neo extractivism: Two sides of the same curse'. Transnational Institute (TNI). Accessed 9 June 2021, https://www.tni.org/files/download/beyonddevelopment_extractivism.pdf.

Adebajo, A. 2020. *The Pan African Pantheon: Prophets, Poets, and Philosophers.* Johannesburg: Jacana Media.

Aguilar, C. 2012. 'Transitions towards post extractive societies in Latin America'. Accessed 9 June 2021, https://www2.weed-online.org/uploads/transitions_towards_post_extractive_societies_in_latin_america_2012.pdf.

Barkham, P. 2020. '2020 likely to be one of the warmest years on record despite La Nina', *The Guardian*, 29 October. Accessed 9 June 2021, https://www.theguardian.com/environment/2020/oct/29/2020-warmest-year-record-la-nina-climate-crisis.

Bravo, G. and De Moor, T. 2008. 'The commons in Europe: From past to future', *International Journal of the Commons* 2 (2): 155–161.

CADTM (Committee for the Abolition of Illegitimate Debt) and WoMin. 2020. 'Cancel Africa's debt', Statement. Accessed 9 June 2021, https://womin.africa/wp-content/uploads/2020/10/Debt-Statement-Womin_CATDM_EN_13102020-1.pdf.

Chibvongodze, D.T. 2017. 'Ubuntu is not only about the human! An analysis of the role of African philosophy and ethics in environment management', *Journal of Human Ecology* 53 (2): 157–166.

Chigbu, U.E., Paradza, G. and Dachaga, W. 2019. 'Differentiations in women's land tenure experiences: Implications for women's land access and tenure security in sub-Saharan Africa', *Land* 8 (2). Accessed 9 June 2021, https://www.mdpi.com/2073-445X/8/2/22.

Cleary, S. 1989. 'Structural adjustment in Africa', *Trocaire Development Review* 1989: 41–59.

Dantas, T. 2018. 'How climate change affects biodiversity loss', *Medium*, 14 November. Accessed 9 June 2021, https://medium.com/@thalesetd/how-climate-change-affects-biodiversity-loss-d6a93fb1a760.

Fairlie, S. 2009. 'A short history of enclosure in Britain', *The Land* 7. Accessed 9 June 2021, https://www.thelandmagazine.org.uk/articles/short-history-enclosure-britain.

Gevers, A., Musuya, T. and Bukuluki, P. 2020. 'Why climate change fuels violence against women'. *UNDP* blog post, 28 January. Accessed 9 July 2021, https://www.undp.org/content/undp/en/home/blog/2020/why-climate-change-fuels-violence-against-women.html.

Grain. 2020. 'New research suggests industrial livestock, not wet markets, might be origin of Covid-19', 30 March. Accessed 9 June 2021, https://www.grain.org/en/article/6437-new-research-suggests-industrial-livestock-not-wet-markets-might-be-origin-of-covid-19.

Gudynas, E. 2010. 'The new extractivism of the 21st century: Ten urgent theses about extractivism in relation to current South American progressivism'. Accessed 9 June 2021, http://postdevelopment.net/wp-content/uploads/2016/10/NewExtractivism10ThesesGudynas10.pdf.

Hardin, G. 1968. 'The tragedy of the commons', *Science* 163 (3859): 1243–1248.

Hargreaves, S. 2019. 'Addressing crisis and building counter power through new African ecofeminist movement', *International Viewpoint*, 30 August. Accessed 9 June 2021, http://www.internationalviewpoint.org/spip.php?article6200.

Harvey, D. 2011. 'The future of the commons', *Radical History Review* 109 (Winter 2011): 101–107.

Harvey, F. 2020. 'Climate breakdown "is increasing violence against women"', *The Guardian*, 29 January. Accessed 9 July 2021, https://www.theguardian.com/environment/2020/jan/29/climate-breakdown-is-increasing-violence-against-women.

Hausfather, Z. 2020. 'State of the climate: 2020 on course to be warmest year on record', *Carbon Brief*, 23 October. Accessed 6 September 2022, https://www.carbonbrief.org/state-of-the-climate-2020-on-course-to-be-warmest-year-on-record.

High Level Panel. 2015. *Report of the High Level Panel on Illicit Financial Flows from Africa*. Report commissioned by the AU/ECA Conference of Ministers of Finance, Planning and Economic Development. Accessed 8 February 2023, https://au.int/sites/default/files/documents/40545-doc-IFFsREPORT.pdf.

Horsthemke, K. 2017. 'Animals and African ethics', *Journal of Animal Ethics* 7 (2): 119–144.

Keneally, M. 2014. 'How Ebola emerged out of the jungle', *ABC News*, 28 July. Accessed 9 July 2021, https://abcnews.go.com/Health/ebola-emerged-jungle-photos/story?id=24740453.

Laslett, B. and Brenner, J. 1989. 'Gender and social reproduction: Historical perspectives', *Annual Review of Sociology* 15: 381–404.

Mahler, A.G. 2017. 'Global South'. In E. O'Brein (ed.), *Oxford Bibliographies in Literary and Critical Theory*. New York: Oxford University Press. DOI:10.1093/obo/9780190221911-0055.

McQue, K. 2018. 'Did deforestation cause the Ebola outbreak?', *New Internationalist*, 10 April. Accessed 9 June 2021, https://newint.org/features/web-exclusive/2018/04/10/deforestation-ebola-outbreak.

Mkandawire, T. and Soludo, C.C. (eds). 2003. *African Voices on Structural Adjustment: A Companion to Our Continent, Our Future*. Ottawa: International Development Research Centre.

Moszynski, P. 2008. '5.4 million people have died in Democratic Republic of Congo since 1998 because of conflict, report says', National Library of Medicine. Accessed 4 September 2022, https://www.ncbi.nlm.nih.gov/pmc/articles/PMC2223004/.

Muggah, R. and Cabrera, J.L. 2019. 'The Sahel is engulfed by violence. Climate change, food insecurity and extremists are largely to blame', World Economic Forum, 23 January. Accessed 9 June 2021, https://www.weforum.org/agenda/2019/01/all-the-warning-signs-are-showing-in-the-sahel-we-must-act-now/.

Mugumbate, J. and Nyanguru, A. 2013. 'Exploring African philosophy: The value of Ubuntu in social work', *African Journal of Social Work* 3 (1): 82–100.

O'Loughlin, J. and Hendrix, C. 2019. 'Will climate change lead to more world conflict?', *The Washington Post*, 11 July. Accessed 9 July 2021, https://www.washingtonpost.com/politics/2019/07/11/how-does-climate-change-impact-conflict-world/.

Ord, D. 2020. 'Why we need worst-case thinking to prevent pandemics', *The Guardian*, 6 March. Accessed 9 June 2021, https://www.theguardian.com/science/2020/mar/06/worst-case-thinking-prevent-pandemics-coronavirus-existential-risk.

ROAPE (Review of African Political Economy). 2020. 'Ecosocialism or barbarism: An interview with Ian Angus', 24 March. Accessed 9 June 2021, https://roape.net/2020/03/24/ecosocialism-or-barbarism-an-interview-with-ian-angus/.

Saker, L., Lee, K., Cannito, B., Gilmore, A., Campbell-Lendrum, D. et al. 2004. *Globalization and infectious diseases: A review of the linkages*. Geneva: World Health Organization. Accessed 9 June 2021, https://www.who.int/tdr/publications/documents/sebtopic3.pdf.

Shiva, V. 2020. 'Ecological reflections on the corona virus: One planet, one health – connected through biodiversity', Navdanya, 18 March. Accessed 9 June 2021, https://www.navdanya.org/bija-refelections/2020/03/18/ecological-reflections-on-the-corona-virus/.

Soy, A. 2020. 'Coronavirus in Africa: Five reasons why Covid-19 has been less deadly than elsewhere', *BBC News*, 8 October. Accessed 9 July 2021, https://www.bbc.com/news/world-africa-54418613.

Sylla, N.S. 2018. 'Descent into hell', *Development and Cooperation*, 1 August. Accessed 9 June 2021, https://www.dandc.eu/en/article/africa-structural-adjustment-did-not-trigger-fast-growth-had-contractive-impact.

Tomala, L. 2019. 'Siberian peat bogs in the shadow of climate change', *Science in Poland*, 14 August. Accessed 9 June 2021, https://scienceinpoland.pap.pl/en/news/news%2C78240%2Csiberian-peat-bogs-shadow-climate-change.html.

United Nations. 2019. 'Climate change recognized as "threat multiplier", UN Security Council debates its impact on peace', *UN News*, 25 January. Accessed 9 July 2021, https://news.un.org/en/story/2019/01/1031322.

UN Women. (n.d.). 'The shadow pandemic: Violence against women during Covid-19'. Accessed 9 July 2021, https://www.unwomen.org/en/news/in-focus/in-focus-gender-equality-in-covid-19-response/violence-against-women-during-covid-19.

Walsh, B. 2020. 'Covid-19: The history of pandemics', *BBC*, 26 March. Accessed 9 June 2021, https://www.bbc.com/future/article/20200325-covid-19-the-history-of-pandemics.

WHO (World Health Organization). 2014. 'Zoonotic disease: Emerging public health threats in the region'. WHO Eastern Mediterranean Regional Office. Accessed 9 June 2021, http://www.emro.who.int/fr/about-who/rc61/zoonotic-diseases.html.

Wiley, L.A. 2018. 'Community of property in Africa', Brief. Accessed 6 August 2022, https://www.forestpeoples.org/sites/default/files/documents/Brief%202%20-%20Community%20Property%20in%20Africa.pdf.

Windling, T. 2015. 'Enclosure of the commons: The borders that keep us out'. Blog post. Accessed 9 June 2021, https://www.terriwindling.com/blog/2015/09/the-commons.html.

WMO (World Meteorological Organization). 2020. *State of the Climate in Africa 2019*. Geneva: World Meteorological Organization. Accessed 13 December 2022, https://library.wmo.int/docnum.php?explnumid=10421.

WoMin. 2017. *No Longer a Life Worth Living: Mining Impacted Women Speak Through Participatory Action Research in the Somkhele and Fuleni Communities, Northern Kwazulu Natal, South Africa*. Johannesburg: WoMin. Accessed 23 June 2021, https://womin.africa/no-longer-a-life-worth-living-report/.

WoMin. 2020. *Guns, Power and Politics: Extractives and Violence against Women in Sierra Leone*. WoMin Research Paper. Accessed 9 June 2021, https://womin.africa/wp-content/uploads/2020/09/Sierra-LeoneReportFINAL.pdf.

World Rainforest Movement. 2016. 'Defending the body-earth territory: An alternative for social movements in resistance', *WRM Bulletin*, 20 October. Accessed 9 June 2021, https://wrm.org.uy/articles-from-the-wrm-bulletin/defending-the-body-earth-territory-an-alternative-for-social-movements-in-resistance-1/.

Zeilig, L. and Cross, H. 2020. 'Pulverized: Capitalism, Africa and Covid-19'. *ROAPE* blog post, 31 March. Accessed 9 June 2021, https://roape.net/2020/03/31/pulverized-capitalism-africa-and-the-covid-19-crisis/.

2

JINEOLOGY AND THE PANDEMIC: ROJAVA'S ALTERNATIVE ANTI-CAPITALIST-STATIST MODEL

Hawzhin Azeez

INTRODUCTION

The Covid-19 pandemic is one of the worst global health emergencies the world has seen since the last century. In a world that is still staggering from the 2007 global financial crises, the pandemic led to another financial downturn that further highlighted the inherent exploitative and repressive systemic apparatuses within the capitalist-statist system. Specifically, it has devastatingly highlighted the ways in which women are disproportionately impacted, further oppressed and compelled to carry the additional burden of caretaking during the pandemic. The economic downturn, closure of schools and daycare centres, increased childcare needs, intensified gender-based violence and increased poverty, homelessness and mental health issues have all exacerbated gender oppression. Women-dominated industries such as education, hospitality and restaurants have been impacted worse than others, resulting in a disproportionately negative impact on women economically. Experts indicate that the gender disparity will widen as a result of the pandemic, with women in the global South affected disproportionately more. Indeed, some have called the pandemic an utter disaster for feminism (Lewis 2020). Combating Covid-19 is therefore a feminist issue, and one in which women-centred responses, mutual aid, community support, grassroots social organisations and radicalism must fundamentally restructure the current neoliberal system urgently.

Amongst the responses that have emerged globally, that of one group of women has been radically different in its approach: the women in the region known as Rojava, in northern Syria. This is a region where I spent almost four years as part of the post-Islamic State of Iraq and Syria (ISIS) reconstruction effort and as a Kurdish academic observing other Kurdish women's revolutionary efforts.[1] An analysis of the response of Rojava and its women's grassroots organisations demonstrates a robust tendency to fill governance and institutional gaps that a traditional state would usually fill, but also the desire to establish a new society heavily centred on justice. As part of my work in the region I became familiar with the communes, the women's cooperatives and spaces such as Mala Jin (women's houses); in time, several activists, myself included, set up an organisation called Hevi Foundation, which designed the historic women-only village, Jinwar.

However, what women's revolutionary struggles, grassroots efforts, the decentralisation of power and implementation of ecologically sound and gender-liberating policies can achieve is limited within a stateless democracy when the neoliberal capitalist patriarchal system continues to actively hinder recognition, humanitarian support and development in the region. As this chapter highlights, Kurdish women's struggles in the region can fill societal gaps and needs only to a certain degree. When oppressed, dispossessed, silenced, othered and orientalised subjects function within the boundaries of the neoliberal, capitalist-statist hegemony they face manifold structures and forces of erasure and violence. Certainly, the efforts of the women of Rojava are profoundly radical and political – the antithesis of the vision of not only womanhood but also feminism and liberation that the Eurocentric capitalist-statist system sanctions, in other words: liberal feminism. Indeed, even socialist and Marxist-feminist responses in the West, such as the Marxist Feminist Collective, have worked largely within the confines of the patriarchal statist model.[2]

As Helen Lewis (2020) argues in *The Atlantic*, one of the worst aspects of the current pandemic is the 'West's failure to learn from history', including numerous other global health threats such as the 2014 Ebola crises across Africa, the Zika virus in 2015 and various severe acute respiratory syndromes (SARS), as well as bird flu and swine flu outbreaks. This implies that the global order has had ample time to adapt and formulate adequate gender-based responses to the current crises. Previous crises highlighted that the pandemic has disproportionately killed poor working or precariat peoples, people of colour and indigenous peoples, especially the women within these communities.

The question then remains, why has the international system not produced more adequate measures to protect vulnerable groups within societies? The answer is largely based on the implementation of neoliberal, orthodox feminist approaches to the pandemic that act merely as a thin veneer of social justice and equality. This chapter thus critiques liberal feminism and its responses to the pandemic. Any approach tolerated and even accepted by the capitalist patriarchal system cannot produce revolutionary change or justice. While the responses of the women of Rojava are certainly not perfect, they nonetheless serve to demonstrate that alternative, anti-state, radical democratic and ecological responses *can* be formulated. In other words, these responses point out that another way – beyond the violent borders and limits of the capitalist system – is possible. Nevertheless, the majority of the policies and responses implemented within the developing world have relied on liberal feminist practices. It is argued here that liberal feminists are co-conspirators with the Eurocentric, capitalist patriarchal system in their mutual oppression of marginalised peoples and especially women of colour.

This chapter analyses the inherent failures of liberal feminism, which have mandated women in the global South to formulate alternative liberation approaches. The Kurdish women's movement and the ideology of jineology are discussed as examples of such alternative, grassroots approaches to achieve justice and socio-political changes. A critical examination of their successes and challenges suggests that jineology empowered women in the Rojava region to deal with the difficulties created by the Covid-19 pandemic, which may well serve as a model for grassroots radical action in the future.

FEMINISM WITHIN NEOLIBERAL CAPITALIST PATRIARCHY

As the capitalist patriarchal dimensions of the pandemic become ever more pronounced it is clear that a feminist response is necessary to bring about urgent socio-political and economic changes. Many international aid organisations, think tanks and scholars, from Oxfam to the Centre for Feminist Foreign Policy, have called for the necessity of a feminist response to the pandemic, though they have largely failed to ask what kind of feminism is required. Yet it is fundamental that a new socio-political and economic path is formed. Old measures are no longer effective in addressing the widening disparity regarding gender oppression. A new world vision is required if we wish to emerge from the pandemic with a modicum of justice, humanity and equality in place. As Marina Sitrin has argued: 'We are not all in the *same* boat. Structural inequality shows itself in crisis and disaster, and this one is revealing all the ugliness and systemic oppressions and inequalities most of our societies were built upon, and that privilege the very few, and try and pit the rest of us against one another' (Sitrin and Sembrar Commune 2020: xvi). This argument is epitomised by the images of empty shelves with people mass-hoarding toilet paper, cleaning products and essential food items.

Access to health care is a strongly gendered concept. Studies have indicated that women feel that medical professionals discriminate against them due to their gender (Paulsen 2020). Women have a vested interest in being at the forefront of these discussions and the implementation of new policies and paths towards equality and justice. Initiatives by women in the developing world, such as the African Eco-Feminist Collective, have attempted to formulate knowledge and anti-capitalist responses based on ecological and economic changes that are necessary in order to support the most marginalised women. Promotion of food sovereignty as a response to anti-capitalist approaches is one such method explored by the collective (Nyambura 2020). The historical failure of liberal feminism, its Eurocentrism, its bourgeois foundations, its continued efforts to function under a capitalist-statist system and its utter failure to see race and ethnicity as intersections of oppression have resulted in alternative articulations, such as intersectional feminism by black women (1960s) and jineology (2008).

The reaction to the pandemic in the developed world has been one based on neoliberal, individualist, profit-orientated, capitalist policies that reinforce class, gender and racial hierarchies. For instance, articles from well-established research and news organisations indicated that the countries with the best responses to Covid-19 were ones that were led by women. Countries such as Germany, Taiwan, New Zealand, Iceland, Finland, Norway and Denmark were hailed as the most successful in combating the pandemic precisely because they were guided by women leaders. Germany's Angela Merkel, for example, was hailed as one of these visionary women who protected her country early with effective measures. Likewise, New Zealand's Jacinda Ardern was applauded for her quick thinking, clarity and decisive measures. Yet these women, all predominantly white women (with the exception of Taiwan), present problematic domestic and foreign policies which continue to impose war, violence and racial oppression on women. These white women are also in charge of well-organised core industralised and developed states. All of these states are settler colonies or colonial states.[3]

Angela Merkel, for example, approved arms sales worth 25.9 million euros to Turkey once it commenced its anti-Rojava campaign from the period of 10 October 2019 to 22 June 2020 alone (Duvar 2020). Another report indicated that more than one-third of the military exports from Germany go to Turkey (Kokkinidis 2020), with full knowledge of how Turkey utilises these weapons in places like Rojava. Domestically, neofascism, right-wing terrorism and violence, as well as anti-refugee attitudes and Islamophobia are on the rise in the country (see Bartsche et al. 2020). Likewise, Ardern criticised Black Lives Matter protests, calling them unfair during a pandemic, and comparing the protesters to people who had to postpone weddings or funerals (SBS 2020). This is despite the fact that Ardern is much criticised for the ongoing prevalence of anti-blackness and racism against Maori and indigenous peoples, making such protests essential (Browne 2020). These women promote a liberal feminist line, even as they marginalise or ignore racial tensions and oppressions, or as their domestic and foreign politics reinforce imperialist policies.

Liberal feminism is largely the ideological worldview of the bourgeois middle-class woman. It emerged when the bourgeois merchant class sublated the feudal aristocracy. The bourgeois cosmovision veiled the actual, concrete social sphere where real-life active subjects and social groups exist, seeing instead a social structure organised around bourgeois civility, law, etiquette and culture. The state–civil society dynamic was structured as a natural duality and contradiction. The state was a mediating arbitrator overseeing the dynamic 'free' competition between and within different forces in civil society and the market. The liberal feminist worldview is thus based on the promotion of gender equality through empowering women in civil society within and under the rule of state apparatuses. The belief is that the liberal capitalist and statist system is the most advanced form of social organisation. Within this system, improved women's access to better positions in the socio-political and economic spheres becomes the teleological destiny of liberal feminism. According to liberal feminists the dominant status quo within the capitalist system is not inherently bad but, rather, requires reforms to accommodate women. Injustices and prejudices that occur within the system are due to anomalies, not constitutive components of the system. Reforms can occur through legal changes or through using education to change attitudes. Accordingly, the subordination of women under the capitalist system is an aberration in an otherwise just and equal society. Gender-based oppressions can be addressed effectively, according to liberal feminists, if women dominate more spaces in the public sphere. For this reason, there is a heavy emphasis on legal reforms, which includes voting. The fact that 53 per cent of white women voted for Donald Trump in 2016 (Rogers 2016), or that in the 2020 US elections the choice was between two equally problematic and sexist, wealthy cisgender white men with a number of sexual assault allegations against them, speaks for the values that liberal feminism advocates (Powers 2020). Liberal feminists especially believe in the transformative power of the market to open doorways for women's equality (see Kiraly and Tayler 2015). The more women have jobs, the more they breach the wage gap; the more women are active participants and consumers within the economic system, the better off they are.[4]

Even when women from minority groups – whether trans, indigenous, queer, poor, black or refugees – have been able to break through the system and attain high positions, it has not resulted in widespread systematic change and progress for other women. The election of Indian-American senator Kamala Harris as the vice-president of the USA, hailed as symbolic of interracial solidarity, the success of brown women and immigrants and anti-racial politics – when her racist, anti-trans, pro-prison industrial system policies are clearly evident – is a perfect example of this liberal feminist approach. Unsurprisingly, critics have stated that liberal feminism 'appears to empower, while in fact reaffirming power as it already exists' (O'Shea 2020). Consequently, women like Harris function solely to promote the model minority myth, while brown, black, indigenous, poor and immigrant women and gender-diverse people are forced to accept low wages, terrible working conditions, have difficulty accessing adequate housing or can access only social services that are woefully insufficient and underfunded. Moreover, powerful elite women rely on women in the lower classes to maintain their positions within the capitalist system; they become co-conspirators with capitalist-statist patriarchy in oppressing working-class peoples and women of colour. Research indicates that having a limited number of women in positions of high power or capital does little to bring about mass change, progress and equality (Williams 2017: 32; Crenshaw 2017). Anything short of a radical social transformation would be inadequate to allow all women, across races, cultures, religions, classes and orientations, to be able to find a modicum of equality. Yet elite women have too much of a stake in capitalist patriarchy to ever be the revolutionary agents of change and progress women of today so urgently need. This is why liberal feminism can never be the answer to the liberation of the oppressed masses – Frantz Fanon's 'wretched of the earth'. Liberal feminism is, at its core, fundamentally flawed in enacting justice and equality for all women, minorities and oppressed groups. Yet liberal feminism has been endorsed by the ruling bourgeois classes and their subservient comprador circuits as the most effective form of women-centric responses during the pandemic.

It is no surprise that liberal feminists' responses to the pandemic have seen a number of woefully inadequate measures, such as increasing the number of hand-washing stations, distributing feminine hygiene products, relocating the homeless, providing temporary housing, handing out baby wipes and baby formula (Jackson 2020) or making legal changes such as moratoriums on evictions. Other measures have included limited charity to support at-risk women and homeless mothers and their children. Such measures can only be cosmetic, especially when these women are seen as 'clients' rather than as human beings and essential members of communities (see Schwan et al. 2020). This has prompted leftist scholars and activists to label liberal feminism and its policies of aiding women as 'frivolous, cosmetic change, completely divorced from the actual lived experience of most women' (Crispin 2017).

While some intellectuals have called the pandemic the undoing of feminism, Koa Beck (2020) argues that the pandemic 'is not undoing "feminism"' but, rather, 'it is revealing the key fissures in white-feminist ideology, which has always centered white heterosexual women of a certain income level'. The pandemic has demonstrated the gaps and failures in housing, health and social services within the capitalist system. The failure of the capitalist system and its profit-orientated, liberal feminist handmaidens is woefully apparent and continues to oppress the most marginalised and at-risk sectors within societies. This oppression is labelled by Latin American scholar Rita Segato (2016: 619) as the psychopathic 'pedagogy of cruelty' that is nurtured by modern capitalism, and liberal feminism merely promotes and reinforces this cruelty. There cannot be a modicum of justice in a system which continues to promote change and progress within the confines of this violent capitalist system. It therefore cannot be the solution. In the words of the prolific Audre Lorde (1984), 'The master's tools will never dismantle the master's house.'

Of course, Marxist and socialist women's groups and organisations such as the International Women's Alliance and the Barcelona En Comú in Catalonia, amongst many others, have filled important gaps in aid, support, health care, food security, justice, mental health and more, while still working within the confines of the state. However, this process has added a triple burden on women to fill gaps within society that not only the state but also hegemonic liberal feminism has failed to address. A women-centric response should aim to reduce women's hardships instead of *burdening* them to fill urgent gaps. This is where the case of Rojava proves informative.

JINEOLOGY

The vision of Kurdish women's liberation in Rojava is articulated under the ideology of democratic confederalism, developed in 2005. The Kurdish liberation movement, with Marxist–Leninist leanings and led by Abdullah Ocalan, emerged in the late 1970s following decades of state-sponsored terrorism and the incarceration of Kurds in Northern Kurdistan, Turkey. Ocalan was eventually imprisoned and placed in solitary confinement on the Turkish island of Imrali. During this period,

Ocalan was influenced by the works of Friedrich Nietzsche, Immanuel Wallerstein, Maria Mies, Fernand Braudel and Murray Bookchin, and was inspired to produce a new anti-statist, anti-capitalist liberation approach based on direct democracy, environmentalism, feminism, multiculturalism and self-governance. This model entails three pillars: grassroots democracy, gender liberation and ecology. Ocalan was deeply impressed by Bookchin's works, including *The Ecology of Freedom* (1982) and *Toward an Ecological Society* (1980), and his vision of communalism as a response to the destructive hierarchies created by capitalism across society. Anti-capitalism, communalism, environmentalism and anti-hierarchy were all elements of Bookchin's philosophy, the influence of which is evident in Ocalan's democratic confederalism.

Ocalan envisioned Kurdish freedom being based on women's liberation, and more explicitly, on the promotion of justice for women and the social ecology.[5] According to Ocalan, not only were women the 'first colony' but the 'social subjugation of women was the vilest counter-revolution ever carried out' (Ocalan 2013: 28). He therefore 'encouraged the establishment of women's movements and institutions so that women can question and reshape themselves, their lives, men and society' (Ocalan 2013: 8). Ocalan consequently wrote extensively on the liberation of women and his writings were collated into the ideology of jineology, called the science of women, in 2008. Since then the grassroots women's movement and activists have continued to develop this idea based on 40 years of revolutionary struggle, resistance and militarism. Ocalan went so far as to state that to him, 'women's freedom is more precious than the freedom of the homeland' (Ocalan 2013: 8). This is a significant break with the historical trend of subordinating women's liberation to the freedom of the homeland, while traditional revolutionary movements shamelessly utilised woman's energy, mobilisation, bodies and labour in nationalist liberation. The 'Algerian lesson' (see Sadiqi 2016: 3), where Algerian women fought side by side with men only to find themselves, post liberation, in a worse situation politically, socially and economically, is a perfect example. Later, women's participation in the Arab Spring personified this problem even more prominently, with women subjected to sexual harassment, violence, arrest, beatings and virginity tests by both those they were protesting against, and those they were protesting with. The kinds of social changes, institutions and political involvement promoted under democratic confederalism – such as co-leadership, women's communes, cooperatives, women-only spaces, women's houses, women's military protection units and so on – are therefore geared in such a way as to promote the equality and visibility of women, as well as justice for them. A key aspect of this process is to allow women to have visible public, political, economic and self-protection roles in line with their significant contribution to the Rojava Revolution. Anything short of this would be failure to learn from past lessons and would fail to implement justice in the new system.

Rojava's process of justice also involves preventing particular groups of women from dominating other women. According to democratic confederalism, women's subordination of women not only breeds capitalism, but also the nation-state and religion act as avenues of control and institutionalise male dominance. This subordination produces 'relationships that foster inequality, slavery, despotism, fascism and militarism. If we want to construe true meaning to terms such as equality, freedom, democracy and socialism that we so often use, we need to analyse and shatter the ancient web of relations that has been woven around women. There is no other way of attaining true equality (with due allowance for diversity), freedom, democracy and morality' (Ocalan 2013: 11).

Consequently, to achieve this vision and implement lasting change requires political, ideological and social transformation to eliminate male domination. To start with, this process requires the destruction of the 'housewifisation' of women in society. In other words, what is required is the destruction of everything that created the myth of the woman bound to the private sphere, that sexualises her, and that socialises her into a silenced, helpless, voiceless and erased subjectivity, as well as the destruction of whatever oppressive patriarchal institutions and practices dominate and create hierarchies of violence and oppression – whether within the nation-state model or within capitalism. Unlearning what has been inculcated under the violent, capitalist heteropatriarchy and relearning democratic modes of coexistence, of social ecology and of gender liberation are part of the restructuring of society and gender relations in Rojava. This transformation process is therefore also heavily reliant on a pedagogy of liberation founded on the idea that women need to be educated not only about their long-lost history, but also about the crucial importance of ideologically killing the 'dominant' patriarchal male, as well as his attitudes and values, within society (see Jineolojî Academy 2021). In fact, much of the ideological *perwarda* (education) that is held across the communes focuses on the concept of justice and equality, and locating social mechanisms that would promote these concepts. Consequently, ideological education regarding the history and rise of the state and capitalism, patriarchy, democracy and colonialism are all part of the *perwarda* programmes in which all citizens are encouraged not only to participate, but also to continue the (un)learning process in a lifelong commitment to radical change. Indeed, as part of my time as an activist in Rojava, I participated in numerous *perwardas* in which women who lacked any formal education were able to present highly complex critiques of capitalism, the state and the patriarchy.

Thus, the connection between state, capital and gender oppression must be studied and understood if a new, radical society is to be born. In Rojava, civic responsibility, leadership and participation across multiple institutions, communes, cooperatives and civil society organisations are encouraged. The *perwardas* politicise society and arm it ideologically to identify and actively resist the institutionalisation of hierarchies and oppressions. Finally, and crucially, underpinning this transformation process is a constant assertion of the importance of the social ecology in creating a democratic, just and equal society. Where Ocalan explicitly identifies women as the first colony, it is the subjugation of the ecology that has set the ideological, political and economic basis for this colonisation. The liberation of women in Rojava is, therefore, intimately intertwined with the liberation of the ecology from the oppressive clutches of the patriarchal capitalist system.

In Rojava, steps taken to implement change and transformatory progress had a profound influence on how the pandemic was addressed. Women-only communes and spaces within the community, the women-only village of Jinwar, pro-women's ideological *perwarda*, military training, Mala Jin, gender equality quotas and co-leadership all function to promote women's empowerment. Access to women's houses acts as a first step towards women accessing justice, learning further about their human rights and the laws that protect them, all of which are important processes in the sustainable development of freedom for women. Similarly, the economic system implemented in Rojava 'is an alternative economy based on a social communal model' (Azeez 2017). Furthermore, 'the significance of the cooperative system lies in efforts to democratise all sectors of society, including the economy. For this reason, creating alternative avenues that allow traditionally marginalised groups such as women to actively participate is an essential aspect of the radical democratic model' (Azeez 2017).

These steps are infused with women's leadership in the rehabilitation of the ecology and the promotion of environmentally friendly farming, sustainability practices and coexistence with the land. They contribute to the visibility of women's power and role in public spaces, and in exercising influence and decision making. By taking up physical space while also being empowered to protect themselves against capitalist and patriarchal mentalities, women in Rojava have achieved an unprecedented level of participation and decision making in the democratic process. A healthy social ecology is one in which every effort is made to eliminate hierarchies of oppression and power. The women's Assayish forces as well as the YPJ (women's protection units) are two militant and powerful organisations that visibly enforce and protect women's position and power within society. This combination of ensuring women's visibility in public spaces, nurturing the connection of women and the ecology and establishing new institutions and military self-protection creates a strong web of protection for women.

Consequently, we can already envision a social setting in which women are highly empowered and organised to protect one another and their community during periods of crisis. Jineology and its ongoing development serves as an alternative mode of women's organisation and self-protection, with localised forms of mobilisation. Given the failures of Western feminism, from its Eurocentricism to its propensity to accommodate the concerns of elite or white women who are part of the ruling property-owning class while dismissing the collective of brown women's concerns, it is not surprising that women from the developing world are increasingly distancing themselves from the concept and formulating alternatives. Doing so is necessary in order to articulate theories and responses to their specific historical-cultural oppressions. As a result of the vast and multilayered violence and oppressions imposed on them, feminists in the developing world increasingly create and articulate localised knowledge about their oppression – and also about their liberation.

However, capitalist-statist patriarchy has consistently attempted to curb or limit the influence and ideological impact of women in Rojava. Liberal media and academia have articulated the ideological underpinnings of the women's movement through a liberal feminist lens and have focused on sensationalist depictions of the AK-47-wielding women. They have presented these women as 'Ocalan's Angels', reminiscent of the US television series *Charlie's Angels*, or as 'attractive' young women (Tavakolian 2016), or they have tended to overemphasise the ethno-nationalist element of the Kurd's struggle, overshadowing the feminist objectives of these women (see Ozcan 2006). Orientalist, romanticised and often external accounts of these women's anti-capitalist, pro-justice practices gloss over the historical, internal and external socio-ecological and politico-economic conditions that have shaped the type of mobilisation that has emerged.[6] In the process, the agency of women and the subjectivity of their experiences in the developing world are ignored or dismissed. International analysis of Kurdish women's struggles has tended to depoliticise the revolutionary and women-centric aspirations of these women. Its attempt to orientalise, fetishise and sexualise these women, rendering them as merely local women forced to fight a war that has landed on their doorstep and as concerned with their physical appearance as their Western counterparts, has decentred these women's agency. Accounts of Kurdish women and their struggle against ISIS terrorism are often presented as Eurocentric-looking women whose desires align ideologically with Western liberal values and women's rights. Yet Kurdish women have had to fight the conditions of the four intersecting oppressions of patriarchy, capitalism and the nation-state, *and* the 'pedagogy of cruelty' referred to earlier (Segato 2016). Additionally, Kurdish women are subjected not only to localised ethno-religious patriarchal values but also to Western patriarchy and orientalisation, which 'obfuscate a productive understanding of their struggle, limiting opportunities for solidarity and community-building' (Shahvisi 2018: 11).

Through the struggles, self-organising efforts and policies implemented by women in Rojava on an intersectional level, a new form of resistance against the capitalist patriarchy has emerged, shattering the binary of women either being victims of or part of the perpetrator class that often defines identitarian politics. In the process, Kurdish women have dislocated orientalist stereotypes of brown women needing to be saved from brown men by white men (Spivak 1994). The military and socio-political actions not only allowed for a reclaiming of a feminist presence and space in the liberation struggle, but also circumvented colonial practices and ideas of brown women needing to be saved. This new ideology involved the central notion of free coexistence – of women with men, and also as women of a minority group with other ethno-religious groups – being based on the non-negotiable right to self-defence. Such notions have had a lasting impact on women's visions for the future, their involvement in the community and their sense of responsibility and leadership during crises.

What the women have achieved in Rojava has not come easily nor was it produced overnight. Through the four decades of revolutionary experience it became very clear that deep and meaningful social change requires time, practice and effort. Women in Rojava traditionally faced issues such as forced marriages, domestic violence, polygamy, honour killings and more. Traditionally, gender-related discriminations were often dealt with by religious or tribal courts (Gupta 2016). In contrast, the work of the women of Rojava has resulted in the publicisation and awareness-raising of gender-based abuses and violence such that these are now at the forefront of society's consciousness. Although change is implemented slowly, the persistent efforts of women activists, accompanied by ongoing re-education and training of not only women but also men across society, has produced fundamental changes.

The theory and praxis of jineology differs from liberal feminism on multiple fronts. Firstly, unlike liberal feminism, whose primary concern has been with the promotion of equality and liberation on an individual level, jineology is concerned with the collective liberation of women from patriarchy and capitalism. According to Shahvisi (2018: 8) 'the ideology of Rojava centers intersectionality, places value on autonomous spaces, and confronts the challenges posed by masculinity. At its core, jineology envisions and aspires towards a post-capitalist and post-statist model. As such, it is markedly different to the forms of feminism which prevail in mainstream political, economic, and cultural institutions in the West, which are generally focused on atomistic individual identities.'

Where liberal feminism has always been concerned with the plight of individual women and freedom rather than the collective, jineology is an ideology that is concerned with the liberation of all women – across class, ethnicity, race and religion – from the violence of the state. Most importantly, it sees this liberation as firmly grounded in the establishment of a strong and healthy social ecology. For many women living in the developing world, a liberation approach based on an individual basis makes little sense because the lifestyle, mentality and attitudes that determine their lives and communities are a collectivist one. In line with eco-feminism, jineology argues that the patriarchy has established political, social and economic relations and practices which are based on the exploitation of natural resources. This is why so many of the social changes, cooperatives and projects such as Jinwar are geared towards increasing women's reliance on and connection with the ecology rather than capitalism. Indeed, patriarchal capitalist society employs the same exploitative approach to our ecology as it does towards women. It is therefore essential to eradicate all forms of exploitation and all hierarchies of power institutionally, culturally, socially and in every other manner that it manifests within society. For as long as capitalist tendencies remain within the system, perpetuating oppressive hierarchies of power and hence injustice and oppression, there can be no liberation.

KURDISH WOMEN'S RESPONSES TO COVID-19

Much of the success of Rojavan women's response to the pandemic is due to the changes they had implemented systemically since 2012 and even earlier, over the past four decades of women's revolutionary struggle. Kurdish women had developed self-organising institutions in Syria covertly well before the 2011 civil war that sparked the rise of the Rojava Revolution. As far back as 2005, the umbrella women's organisation, 'Yekitiya Star', for instance, was working to train and educate women politically and militarily (Isik 2016). Consequently, when the Revolution occurred in earnest in 2012, women had many years of ideological and military training to defend their communities and not only actively participate but also lead in the construction of new institutions. Jineology, and the necessity of producing a collective form of liberation that saw women's involvement as both a foundational and a non-negotiable aspect of this liberation, has allowed women to produce radical changes. Historical lessons have been learnt, and in their view the Algerian example will not be repeated. An interview with Berivan Issa (Kobane, 30 June 2022), from the Kobane Canton's Humanitarian Affairs Office, revealed that women participated across all institutions, communes and cooperatives to support their community.

In Rojava, women have been empowered to start or to continue their education, have been trained as teachers, engineers, journalists, activists, health-care workers, and comprehensively involved in civil society organisations and in the political and economic spheres. These were significant changes since the Kurdish people were heavily oppressed politically and culturally and had little access to education and other necessary services. Women were encouraged to participate in communes or cooperatives designed to encourage economic independence, self-sufficiency and confidence. These institutions have continued to function during the pandemic and have provided crucial support and aid to the wider community. They have become, in many ways, the backbone of the community connection, support and organisation. They have also been instrumental in providing the community with information regarding the pandemic. Cooperatives involved in bread-making and the production of dairy products, jams and other condiments; textile-based cooperatives and cooperatives involved in planting fruits and olive trees have filled an essential service gap, allowing a war-traumatised society to see a path out of the pandemic.[7]

Emre Sahin and Khabat Abbas (2020: 5), in their analysis of Rojava's response to the pandemic, speak of the hostility of nation-states towards mutual aid or solidarity work since they highlight the inadequacies and failures of their own work. This resulted in the need to formulate alternatives to support the community. Within days of the start of the pandemic, the administration of the cantons established a special committee called the Central Crisis Committee charged with the responsibility of addressing the ongoing health crises. The Committee focused on four specific areas: education, health, local governance and security. Women actively participated in multiple ways at the street, local, neighbourhood and canton levels. They were active in registering the names of their neighbours who needed food packages, fuel for winter or urgent assistance. They participated in the sterilisation of their streets and neighbourhoods and communities. Local voices argued that 'Our main strength is that the society is organised' and that public health is just as important as the economy.

Rojava's distinctive achievement during the pandemic has been not to simply *increase* the burden on women to fill essential gaps, as women in other societies have been forced to do in the absence of the state fulfilling its roles. Instead, in Rojava women are an integral aspect of a well-functioning social ecology in which they do not take on additional burdens but rather work in symbiosis with other civil society groups, organisations, municipalities, communes, cooperatives and other horizontal and grassroot efforts to collectively find solutions to challenges during the pandemic. For instance, when the women's cooperatives changed their usual activities in order to produce face masks for the community, their level of care and work did not change. They simply changed the products they were making. When the developed nation-states failed to provide testing kits directly to Rojava, and instead chose to subordinate a health crisis to the ideal of the state system, the health ministry in Rojava worked to produce its own testing kits, thereby overcoming the necessity of the state-to-state interaction.

Kurdish women's revolutionary struggle[8] has attempted to prevent and stop the reproduction of male supremacy, especially in decision-making spheres, thus promoting power-sharing mechanisms that have benefited collective society. An important example of such collaboration is the measures taken to continue planting trees and to promote the ecology as a means of supporting the community. For instance, displaced people from the region of Afrin, who were forced to leave their homes as a result of Turkish invasion and annexation of the region in 2018, planted 27 500 olive trees and other types of fruit-bearing trees in an effort to make their makeshift camps self-sustaining and to have access to a means of income through agriculture (RIC 2020a). These projects have in turn fuelled cooperatives, giving people access to food where international aid organisations have been weaponised against them. Promoting and educating society about the use of organic and locally grown herbs as alternatives to combat Covid-19 where medicines are unavailable has filled urgent gaps in health care. The visibility and effectiveness of women's security forces help to reduce gender-based violence and oppressions. The Mala Jin act as visible sites of protection, vividly symbolising the rights of women to be protected and to have access to avenues of safety and support. These women also regularly visit the homes of their communities, spreading information pamphlets (Shako, in Sahin and Abbas 2020: 9), informing society about new laws or connecting with families and building relations of trust and support. According to Berivan Issa during our discussion, women of Rojava have contributed to supporting their communities and have participated in the municipal sub-committees engaged in efforts to provide food and gas to struggling families (interview, Kobane, June 2022).

Women's support for each other in Rojava is not an act of charity, which does not empower, grow or encourage radical change but simply creates dependency and hopelessness. Despite their efforts, however, gender-based violence and oppression continue to occur on multiple levels in Rojava. Centuries of gender oppression cannot realistically be eradicated in the space of a few decades. However, physical institutions such as the Mala Jin, the visibility of the YPJ and the ongoing re-education of society across all levels help to encourage organic change. Likewise, the economic model is essential. Indeed, 'cooperatives within the Rojava system allow the community to veer away from traditional capitalist practices such as profit-focused objectives, encourage workers' independence from the traditional bosses and the resulting exploitation, ensure that women participate in the decision-making processes and produce a place where people can organise and develop their ideological consciousness' (Azeez 2017).

Still, there are a number of severe limitations which affect the capacity of these women, communes and cooperatives to provide support to the people. The first case of a Covid-19-related death was not reported by the World Health Organization (WHO) to the health authorities of Rojava until two weeks later (Stocker-Kelly 2020). According to the Rojava Information Centre (RIC), there are only two fully functioning hospitals out of the 11 in the region. The only hospital with testing facilities was destroyed by Turkey during its bombings in October 2019 (see Arafat 2019). The region's population is estimated to be around four million, amongst which 1 650 000 are considered to be in dire need of humanitarian aid. Additionally, there are over 600 000 internally displaced people and refugees in the region, of which 65 000 are the remaining ISIS prisoners and their families. To make matters worse, as a result of further invasions and bombings by Turkey, the region of Hasake has not had water since October 2019. All of these factors have made the effort to support an already war-torn community incredibly difficult, and women have played a crucial role in filling the gap – but that process has naturally come as an additional burden of extra labour.

The response of Rojava's Autonomous Self Administration has been to implement a number of lockdowns in order to prevent the spread of the disease, including closing down border posts. The Committees of People's Health, along with the municipalities, also engaged in sterilisation, cleaning and monitoring services for local areas and markets in order to protect people (Kongra Star 2020). A special hospital of 120 beds was immediately established in Heseke, though it lacks the capacity to handle severely infected patients (RIC 2020a). Other measures have included waiving utility bills, reducing the price of food and organising urgent distribution of food packages to families. At the time of writing, the latest reports indicate that there is a total of 40 ventilators to serve the entire population of the region. This means that there is capacity to treat only 500 cases at any particular time. All schools and public gatherings, including prayers, festivals, sports events and so on, have been banned. Schools and universities went online in an effort to continue the education of students; however, lack of electricity, internet and access to technology for numerous families has affected many students.

The women's cooperatives have taken on an important role in this regard, including the production and distribution of masks and food, and the development of additional cooperatives to fill the necessary gaps. Food packages and bread distribution often involve brochures containing information about the illness and the need to self-isolate, for instance (RIC 2020b). The women's health centre in Jinwar village, called Shifa Jin, helps to educate and inform women regarding basic medicine and herbs as a means of allowing women to protect their families and communities (Women Defend Rojava 2020). The situation of the displaced people from Afrin, now living in the Shehba region, is more precarious. The health authorities of the Autonomous Self Administration have not been able to travel to the region, and when they have been able to do so, they have been faced with significant barriers, tolls and fines imposed by regime forces.

Turkey continues to inflict its colonial aspirations by cutting water supply to the region. The deliberate and ongoing reduction or prevention of water flow from Turkey to Rojava has resulted in at least a million people being without water. Meanwhile, there have been ongoing threats of further invasion, attacks and airstrikes by Turkey and allied jihadists. People continue to suffer and to be displaced. Women are specifically targeted in acts of violence, including sexual violence, sexual slavery and trafficking. Minorities such as the Yezidi community are targeted and terrorised systematically. Turkey has continued to ignore the United Nations' (UN) call for a ceasefire and maintains a protracted multipronged war of terror and ethnic cleansing designed to make life unbearable for the people. Through lobbying from Russia and Turkey, major international organisations such as the UN and WHO are no longer functioning or distributing aid through the region. All supplies are now provided directly to the Assad regime, 'leaving the Autonomous Administration at the mercy of the hostile Assad regime' (Briy 2020). Even worse, the previous UN route from Iraq into Rojava, which previously provided 40 per cent of the medical needs to the region, has been closed. Water and aid continue to be weaponised and used as a source of terror and control over the already traumatised people of the region.

CONCLUSION

The global pandemic has demonstrated that alternative ideologies and mobilisation are necessary as a means of survival for the oppressed. Modern-day, mainstream feminism has become exclusionary in that it takes into account only upper-class, elitist, cosmopolitan women and disregards the plight of poverty-stricken women, rural women, working women, trans women, women of colour, immigrants and refugees. Even Marxist and socialist feminists continue to work within the confines of the state system. Such forms of feminism remain privileged, silent and unperturbed by the situation of the large majority of women who do not fall within the elitist circle of capitalist or state perpetrators. They cannot be the solution that will resolve the multitude of intersecting oppressions facing the vast majority of less privileged women. An alternative is required. Jineology and women's grassroots mobilisation have created a new ideology of women's empowerment and participation in the public sphere. This practice has allowed women to step in and provide essential economic, social and material support to the war-torn and traumatised communities across Rojava. While women of Rojava fought for all women across the world in their fight not only against ISIS but also against violent patriarchal and capitalist institutions and values, liberal feminism responded by strengthening the limited, capitalist and patriarchal interpretations of the revolutionary mobilisation and struggles of these women on the ground. Liberal feminism is a byproduct of the greater disease called capitalist-statist patriarchy and cannot be the solution for a group of people it fails to see or support. Its vision is crippled by its ongoing subservience to a global system that daily promotes and creates conditions of violence, terror, murder and genocide for women. Women cannot envision and enact radical change if they are simply told that working within the boundaries of systemic oppression is enough to liberate them. Not all liberations are equal. Some 'liberations' are in reality counter-revolutionary and promote superficial changes while in reality re-enforcing the chains of oppression and violence that all women experience. The work of women in Rojava, in contrast, can act as an alternative model of resistance, mobilisation and grassroots radical action that contests the capitalist-statist patriarchy. To what degree the model of women's work in Rojava can be transferred externally is debatable and a subject for further research. Nevertheless, libertarian municipalism, social ecology and intersectional, inclusive gender liberation need to be not only a part of the response to Covid-19 but also a response to the ongoing oppression of women in the post-Covid world. Ultimately, women-centric responses to crises must formulate collective solutions that do not increase women's burdens but create lasting, organic social changes that encourage society at large to desire the inclusion and promotion of gender liberation.

NOTES

1   I was also involved in the rebuilding of schools, hospitals and roads during the post-war reconstruction period following Kobane's liberation, and participated in the cantons' and communes' discussions regarding important socio-economic and political decisions.

2   For instance, certain Marxist-feminist organisations, including the Marxist Feminist Collective in the USA, have argued for government closure of prisons, increased government funding for anti-domestic violence services or better pay and working conditions for essential workers (see Thomson 2020). Other research based on a Marxist-feminist perspective in countries such as Pakistan argues that the pandemic resulted in a significant increase in domestic violence towards Pakistani women. Their conclusions involved a call for paid domestic and reproductive labour in order to reduce women's financial dependence on men. Other solutions, such as prudent government strategies and interventions to force the economy back on track towards recovery, as well as the provision of financial incentives to unemployed women, were seen as effective responses (see Memon et al. 2022).

3   Likewise, Taiwan is a semi-periphery state that is held as a buffer zone against 'Chinese incursions'.

4   This conveniently ignores the role that brown, black, Latinx and indigenous women perform in their homes, from childcare to domestic work.

5   In his seminal text, *The Ecology of Freedom* (1982), Bookchin highlights how social evils and problems are connected intrinsically with the destruction and exploitation of the environment. Bookchin traces the core of the issues within society to the destruction of our ecology, and not, as Marx had advocated, to the class struggle.

6   Limitations, internal critiques and lessons learned from past failures are also essential to address here.

7   Despite this, there were of course cooperatives that failed to be launched or had to be shut down as they were not adopted efficiently by the local population. Back in 2016, I held conversations with the women of the 'Yekitiya Star' organisation about which cooperatives were the most successful. These discussions, and those held with members of other communes, indicated that communal bread-making cooperatives, those involved in mass soy bean production and women's sewing cooperatives had failed because they lacked the necessary replacement equipment and supplies. Failures, however, are part and parcel of the ideological and pedagogical *perwarda* on the path to the liberation of society.

8   Ideologically, decades of revolutionary mobilisation and struggle by Kurdish women along with men, the importance of the *perwardas*, the historical fight against ISIS and the liberation of Kobane, among many other examples, have implemented a shift in the collective psyche and attitudes of men and women in the region. What the practice of jineology has attempted to implement is the notion that women should not be defined by their bodies, or as simply mothers or as carriers of the nation's honour and dignity, but rather that they should be seen as equal and capable agents of change and progress.

REFERENCES

Arafat, H. 2019. 'Turkish airstrikes target hospitals in Syria, allied militants abduct medical team', *Kurdistan24.com*, 13 October. Accessed 2 September 2020, https://www.kurdistan24.net/en/news/b10ddedc-72b6-4f07-90d9-f970b1fc0b11.

Azeez, H. 2017. 'Women's cooperatives: A glimpse into Rojava's economic model', *The GreenLeft* Issue 1127, 27 February. Accessed 19 June 2022, https://www.greenleft.org.au/content/women%E2%80%99s-cooperatives-glimpse-rojava%E2%80%99s-economic-model.

Bartsche, M., Baumgärtner, M., Diehl, J., Gebauer, M., Gude, H., von Hammerstein, K., Höfner, R., Jüttner, J., Knobbe, M., Latsch, G. et al. 2020. 'Exploring right-wing extremism in Germany's police and military', *Spiegel International*, 13 August. Accessed 25 August 2020, https://www.spiegel.de/international/germany/the-dark-side-of-state-power-exploring-right-wing-extremism-in-germany-s-police-and-military-a-0600aa1e-3e4e-45af-bfc9-32a6661e66ef.

Beck, K. 2020. 'Don't call the pandemic a setback for feminism', *Time*, 23 December.

Bookchin, M. 1980. *Toward an Ecological Society*. Montreal: Black Rose Books.

Bookchin, M. 1982. *The Ecology of Freedom*. Palo Alto, CA: Cheshire Books.

Briy, A. 2020. 'Rojava: Statelessness in a time of pandemic', *Open Democracy*, 19 May. Accessed 20 August 2020, https://www.opendemocracy.net/en/north-africa-west-asia/rojava-statelessness-time-pandemic/.

Browne, S. 2020. 'Racism in New Zealand runs deep', *Newsroom.co.nz*, 28 July. Accessed 29 August 2020, https://www.newsroom.co.nz/racism-is-endogenous-to-new-zealand.

Crenshaw, K. 2017. *On Intersectionality: Essential Writings*. New York: The New Press.

Crispin, J. 2017. 'The failure of mainstream feminism', *Newrepublic.com*, 13 February. Accessed 26 August 2020, https://newrepublic.com/article/140248/failures-mainstream-feminism-misogyny-doom-hillary-clinton.

Duvar. 2020. 'Germany approves 25.9 million euros worth of arms exports to Turkey after Syria operation: Report', 3 August. Accessed 29 June 2021, https://www.duvarenglish.com/diplomacy/2020/08/03/germany-approved-25-9-million-euros-worth-of-arms-exports-to-turkey-after-syria-operation-report/.

Gupta, R. 2016. 'Rojava revolution: It's raining women', *Open Democracy*, 26 April. Accessed 29 June 2021, https://www.opendemocracy.net/5050/rahila-gupta/rojava-revolution-it-s-rainingwomen.

Isik, R. 2016. 'Kurdish women struggle for a next system in Rojava', *The Next System Project*, 30 March. Accessed 18 November 2020, https://thenextsystem.org/kurdish-women-struggle-for-a-next-system-in-rojava-kurdistan-northern-syria.

Jackson, J. 2020. 'As the pandemic rages on, homeless women and children are facing a dire future', *Refinary* 29, 4 August. Accessed 25 August 2020, https://www.refinery29.com/en-us/2020/08/9941797/covid-homeless-women-mothers-children-risk.

Jineologî Academy. 2021. 'Killing and transforming the dominant man', Andrea Wolf Institute. Accessed 1 June 2022, https://jineoloji.org/en/wp-content/uploads/2021/02/Killing-and-Transforming-the-dominant-man-booklet-en-compressed compressed-1.pdf.

Kiraly, M. and Tayler, M. 2015. *Freedom Fallacy: The Limits of Liberal Feminism*. Queensland: Connor Court Publishing.

Kokkinidis, T. 2020. 'More than one third of German military export go to Turkey', *EU Greek Reporter*, 23 June. Accessed 25 August 2020, https://eu.greekreporter.com/2020/06/23/more-than-one-third-of-german-military-exports-go-to-turkey/.

Kongra Star. 2020. 'Ongoing initiatives to make muzzles under curfew', 7 April. Accessed 1 September 2020, https://eng.kongra-star.org/2020/04/07/ongoing-initiatives-to-make-muzzles-under-curfew/.

Lewis, H. 2020. 'The Coronavirus is a disaster for feminism', *The Atlantic*, 19 March. Accessed 20 June 2022, https://www.theatlantic.com/international/archive/2020/03/feminism-womens-rights-coronavirus-covid19/608302/.

Lorde, A. 1984. 'The master's tools will never dismantle the master's house'. Accessed 13 December 2022, https://collectiveliberation.org/wp-content/uploads/2013/01/LordeThe MastersTools.pdf.

Memon, A., Kamal, M., Aijaz, U. and Ali, S. 2022. 'A Marxist feminist approach to violence against women during Covid-19 pandemic in Pakistan', *Webology* 19 (3): 3430–3450.

Nyambura, R. 2020. 'African feminist and anti-capitalist responses to Covid-19: Labor, health and ecological questions', *Anchor.fm*, African Ecofeminisms. Podcast, 2 April. Accessed 23 August 2020, https://anchor.fm/african-ecofeminisms/episodes/African-Feminist-and-Anti-Capitalist-Responses-to-COVID-19-Labor--Health-and-Ecological-Questions-eca7o6.

Ocalan, A. 2013. *Liberating Life: Women's Revolution*. Cologne: International Initiative Edition. Accessed 29 June 2021, http://www.freeocalan.org/wp-content/uploads/2014/06/liberating-Lifefinal.pdf.

O'Shea, L. 2020. 'How liberal feminism fails women', *Redflag*, 10 March. Accessed 18 November 2020, https://redflag.org.au/node/7051?fbclid=IwAR1v5DjHGbn7sAx-LfSym1ndnLLNqBcOmpwQ8Eds5uyCwiVkEWZkC3UzL4.

Ozcan, A.K. 2006. *Turkey's Kurds*. New York: Routledge.

Paulsen, E. 2020. 'Recognizing, addressing unintended gender bias in patient care', *DukeHealth*, 14 January. Accessed 18 June 2022, https://physicians.dukehealth.org/articles/recognizing-addressing-unintended-gender-bias-patient-care.

Powers, K. 2020. 'Biden denies sex assault claim. If you don't believe him, should you vote for him anyway?', *USA Today*, 1 May. Accessed 23 August 2020, https://www.usatoday.com/story/opinion/2020/05/01/2020-choice-trump-outstrips-biden-sexual-assault-accusations-column/3056601001/.

RIC (Rojava Information Centre). 2020a. *Annual Report of the Autonomous Self Administration of North and East Syria*. Accessed 13 April 2023, https://rojavainformationcenter.com/2020/07/annual-report-of-the-autonomous-administration-of-north-and-east-syria/.

RIC. 2020b. 'The regime blockade suffocates this region: Health workers on corona virus crises in Shehba region', 9 September. Accessed 9 September 2020, https://rojavainformationcenter.com/2020/09/the-regime-blockade-suffocates-this-region-health-worker-on-coronavirus-crisis-in-shehba-region/.

Rogers, K. 2016. 'White women helped elect Donald Trump', *The New York Times*, 9 November. Accessed 3 September 2020, https://www.nytimes.com/2016/12/01/us/politics/white-women-helped-elect-donald-trump.html.

Sadiqi, F. (ed.). 2016. *Arab Spring, North Africa*. New York: Palgrave Macmillan.

Sahin, E. and Abbas, K. 2020. 'Communal lifeboat: Direct democracy in Rojava (NE Syria)'. In M. Sitrin and Sembrar Commune (eds), *Pandemic Solidarity: Mutual Aid during the Covid-19 Crisis*. London: Pluto Press, pp. 3–17.

SBS (Special Broadcasting Service, Australia). 2020. '"It was not right": Jacinda Ardern criticizes NZ Black Lives Matter protestors over Coronavirus risk', *SBS News*, 2 June. Accessed 26 August 2020, https://www.sbs.com.au/news/it-was-not-right-jacinda-ardern-criticises-nz-black-lives-matter-protesters-over-coronavirus-risk.

Schwan, K., Versteegh, A., Perri, M., Caplan, R., Baig, K., Dej, E., Jenkinson, J., Brais, H., Eiboff, F. and Pahlevan Chaleshtari, T. 2020. *The State of Women's Housing Need and Homelessness in Canada: A Literature Review*. Toronto, ON: Canadian Observatory on Homelessness Press.

Segato, R.L. 2016. 'Patriarchy from margin to center: Discipline, territoriality, and cruelty in the apocalyptic phase of capital', *South Atlantic Quarterly* 115 (3): 615–624.

Shahvisi, A. 2018. 'Beyond orientalism: Exploring the distinctive feminism of democratic confederalism in Rojava', *Geopolitics* 26 (4). DOI:10.1080/14650045.2018.1554564.

Sitrin, M. and Sembrar Commune. 2020. *Pandemic Solidarity: Mutual Aid during the Covid-19 Crisis*. London: Pluto Press.

Spivak, G.C. 1994. 'Can the subaltern speak?'. In P. Williams and L. Chrisman (eds), *Colonial Discourse and Post-Colonial Theory: A Reader*. Hertfordshire: Harvester Wheatsheaf, pp. 66–111.

Stocker-Kelly, J. 2020. 'Politics hampers humanitarian response in Rojava', *Rudaw.com*, 22 April. Accessed 24 August 2020, https://www.rudaw.net/english/middleeast/syria/coronavirus-rojava-humanitarian-aid-22042020.

Tavakolian, N. 2016. 'Ocalan's angels are waging war against ISIS', *Huck Magazine*, 27 April. Accessed 3 September 2020, https://www.huckmag.com/perspectives/reportage-2/kurdish-female-fighters/.

Thomson, K. 2020. 'A Marxist-feminist response to Covid-19', *Revisesociology.com*, 20 April. Accessed 12 April 2021, https://revisesociology.com/2020/04/20/a-marxist-feminist-response-to-covid-19/.

Williams, J. 2017. *Women vs. Feminism: Why We All Need Liberating from the Gender Wars*. Bingley, UK: Emerald Publishing.

Women Defend Rojava. 2020. '"There is nothing which is healing more than freedom": Şifa Jin new healing center in Jinwar', 5 April. Accessed 23 August 2020, https://womendefendrojava.net/en/2020/04/05/there-is-nothing-which-is-healing-more-than-freedom-sifa-jin-new-healing-center-in-jinwar/?fbclid=IwAR-2BLx0G-gO-AaZKLxR8Z9TAzIyFduX8fl1zOS5urdHS4i4rHdiWl3qMQ.

ECOLOGY AND TRANSFORMATIVE WOMEN'S POWER IN SOUTH AFRICA

3

DOING ECO-FEMINISM IN A TIME OF COVID-19: BEYOND THE LIMITS OF LIBERAL FEMINISM

Inge Konik

INTRODUCTION

Feminism, in any of its manifestations, can be regarded as a positive development since it aims to validate and serve the interests of that half of human beings, namely women, who have historically experienced subordination based on their socio-sexual differences from men. Sexual discrimination against women remains a constant challenge, and is experienced by many women, from a multiplicity of contexts and cultures, throughout their lives. That said, at this socially and ecologically precarious juncture, feminism must deliberately address itself to myriad complex problems facing women – and indeed human civilisation as a whole – including unprecedented phenomena such as Covid-19. But not all is equal among feminisms when it comes to meeting this demand, as the limits of liberal feminism at this point are clearly showing. This chapter attempts to demonstrate as much through contrasting liberal feminism with materialist ecological feminism, paying special attention to differences between their epistemological frameworks, as these differences speak to their differing capacities for facilitating multidimensional emancipation today.

The feminist movement is said to have started during the French and American Revolutions of the late 1700s, continuing through the emergence of first-wave feminism in the 1920s among suffragettes and others, and resulting in second-wave feminism that began in the 1960s. And of the various types of feminism that have emerged since then, 'liberal feminism is the most widely known form of feminist thought … often seen as synonymous with feminism *per se*' (Beasley 1999: 51). It is also 'the most commonly borrowed … approach in the feminist pantheon' (Beasley 1999: 53). This is possibly 'because liberal feminism is the most moderate feminist ideology, [since] adherence to its basic principles serves as a minimal criterion to assess whether an individual is a feminist' (Carroll 1994: 140). Broadly conceived, this type of feminism seeks to dispel the myth that women are less capable than men of assuming influential roles in the public and private sectors. Indeed, over time, liberal feminists, as well as women generally, have amply demonstrated their capacity for and ability to be 'equivalent' to men in governance, business, education, and so on. Increasingly, too, women have been making their own opportunities in such contexts instead of waiting for institutional backing or any man's 'permission' to do so, including in some cases using their sexual power to gain ascendency over men (McGee 2012: 228, 230).

On the other hand, ecological feminism, while similarly emphasising women's struggles, has different roots, epistemological commitments and aims from those of liberal feminism. Rather than growing out of middle-class liberal feminism, eco-feminism originated as a grassroots movement among women focused on environmental problems. This focus constitutes its organic starting point, implying that subsequent academic attempts to explain it as a 'feminism' can be at least partially attributed to theorists feeling obliged to refer to existing paradigms. Further, like liberal feminism, eco-feminism is a variegated movement as it 'draws on many feminisms' (Mellor 1992: 45). Thus, 'eco-feminists [can] range from New Age thinkers to socialists', and the movement might be read 'as embodying variants of cultural or radical feminism [or constituting] … a neo-Marxian socialism' (Mellor 1992: 45; see also Salleh 1991: 130). The version of eco-feminism under discussion in this chapter is a 'materialist' one – a socialist form of this movement. Yet, unlike socialism, materialist eco-feminism is rooted in embodied materialism. It 'is "embodied" because it enfolds into the analysis of production, an ethic of care-centred reproductive labour … And it is "materialist" because it argues that "the subordination of women and the degradation of the natural world are historically and materially related"' (Odih 2014: lxxiii–lxxiv).

In this chapter, it is advanced that eco-feminism's pragmatic grounding in everyday contexts profoundly influences its epistemology – giving the movement greater capacity than liberal feminism for dealing with contemporary challenges such as Covid-19. The South African feminist scholars and activists Khayaat Fakier and Jacklyn Cock touch on this, arguing that 'exploring alternatives and developing analytical and strategic capacities for collective action grounded in the material and daily realities of working-class people is where a revolutionary potential lies' (Fakier and Cock 2018: 42). Keeping the trajectory of this argument in mind, it is time to consider liberal feminism in more detail, including materialist eco-feminists' and others' criticisms of it. This will provide a clear silhouette of eco-feminism, allowing the reader to begin to sense how the two movements differ. Moreover, it could help dispel any negative associations that some people might have with anything labelled feminist precisely *because of* liberal feminism, which is, with good reason, regarded as promoting a 'competitive, individualistic ethic' and 'protecting and advancing the interests of [largely] white, middle-class women' (Fakier and Cock 2018: 50).

THE LIMITS OF LIBERAL FEMINISM

Accounts of the emergence of liberal feminism vary but at base, 'liberal feminism is grounded squarely on an acceptance … [that i]f individuals are rational in the required sense, their physical structure and appearance are unimportant', and women accordingly should be afforded the same opportunities as men, *as* rational human beings (Jaggar 1983: 37). While this is a valid point, what is problematic is that 'the liberal conception of rationality is … conceived as a property of individuals rather than of groups' (Jaggar 1983: 28). This sees liberal feminism ineluctably caught up in the logical unfolding of the capitalist ideology of liberal individualism. Indeed, liberal feminism's continued complicity with the capitalist status quo is forcefully criticised by the German materialist eco-feminist Maria Mies: 'While many of us would agree that our enemy is capitalist patriarchy as a system, and not just men, we cannot deny that many feminists do not even talk of capitalism … Others only want more equality with men, … and do not even aspire to transcend capitalist patriarchy as a system' (Mies 1986[1998]: 1). But not only eco-feminists have commented on liberal feminism's uncritical attitude towards capitalism: the sociologist Christopher Thorpe, for example, similarly suggests that liberal feminism lacks genuinely emancipatory potential. He maintains that 'in the continuum of forms of feminist thought, liberal feminism is the least radical … [as t]he aim of liberal feminists is to eradicate gender inequalities through reform rather than revolution – reform of existing patriarchal structures and institutions, political policies and cultural forms' (Thorpe 2018). In other words, liberal feminist women tend to follow in the well-trodden tracks of the existing politico-economic framework, seeking power and equal opportunity in highly exploitative institutions and entities embedded in the neoliberal system. Why this is not seen as problematic to a liberal feminist, is because 'liberal feminism … does not link female oppression directly to the institution of private property and/or the nature and functioning of advanced capitalism' (Valentich and Gripton 2016: 1–2).

Related to the latter is another limitation of liberal feminism: it fosters single-issue pluralism insofar as liberal feminists tend to treat their politics as separate from worker struggles, environmentalism and black politics, for example. Accordingly, they are prone to what American feminist and critical theorist Nancy Fraser describes as 'identity politics' – something which 'scarcely fosters social interaction across differences [and] on the contrary … encourages separatism and group enclaves' (Fraser 2000: 113). Such dynamics, Fraser adds, 'serve not to promote respectful interaction within increasingly multicultural contexts, but to drastically simplify and reify group identities' (Fraser 2000: 108). This goes some way towards explaining why the eco-feminist Ynestra King holds that 'the version of feminism least able to appropriately address ecology is liberal feminism[:] … a [predominantly] white middle-class movement, concerned with the extension of male power and privilege to women like themselves, not the fate of women as a whole' (King 1990: 119). King adds that 'to the extent that they address ecological concerns, liberal feminists will be "environmentalists" rather than "ecologists"', in an 'environmental management' sense of the term, where the aim is 'to make sure that … [natural] resources are not depleted to a degree that slows human productivity' (King 1990: 120).

A primary aim of liberal feminism, then, is to facilitate women's full participation in the existing economic system rather than undermining it on the grounds of its unadulterated exploitation of workers, the environment, most women and the disenfranchised peoples of this world, whom Marxist urban theorist Mike Davis refers to as 'surplus humanity' (Davis 2006: 174). So like men, women too can and do play exploitative roles in the existing capitalist patriarchy and see this as a sign of their own empowerment *as* women. British eco-feminist Mary Mellor is, therefore, quite correct to argue that the principal archetype of our time, economic man or *homo economicus*, is not necessarily male. Mellor explains that, just like career men, career women turn away from an ethics of care because, like their male counterparts, they 'have to operate according to the principles of male/bourgeois individualism, that is, they must deny any domestic responsibilities or pass them on to someone else (usually another woman)' (Mellor 1992: 55; see also Fakier and Cock 2018: 49). They thereby end up embedded in 'a masculine-experience economy … that has cut itself free from the ecological and social framework of human *being* in its widest sense' (Mellor 2009: 254).

A final issue to be considered here in relation to liberal feminism, is the cultivation of a consumer feminist image that traps women in the capitalist-consumerist cycle. This 'liberated woman' archetype relates to the post-World War Two emergence of a liberal 'commodity feminism' (Goldman et al. 1991: 333) spurred on by businesses' aggressive marketing campaigns targeting women not as housewives but as consumers in their own right (Osgerby 2001: 51–52). Arguably, the very idea of women's liberation became enfolded in the capitalist-consumerist cycle at this point, since the liberation *of* women became at least partially articulated in relation to self-care through competent, individualistically orientated consumerism (Osgerby 2001: 331–351). Notably, this tendency transcended race. Because of urbanisation, women of colour moved from a subsistence orientation, through a household provisioning role, to commodity feminism and careerism as markers of both sexual and racial empowerment (Walker 2009: 400–401).

This framing of women's liberation as something obtainable through individualistic consumerism and the career which affords the latter, is regarded as a debilitation of feminism by some. New Zealand media theorist, Hilary Radner, explains why: a consumer-orientated liberal feminism 'seems to reply to the women's movement precisely by containing its demands', as it involves 'the inscription of this position … within an institutional structure that remains largely patriarchal and the representation of this position as the capacity to act as a consumer' (Radner 1995: 2–3). In her turn, the eco-feminist Mies warns women about this capitalist-consumerist trap. She writes: 'As the capitalist commodity market creates the illusion that the individual is free to fulfil all her … desires and needs, [and] that individual freedom is identical with the choice of this or that commodity, the self-activity and subjectivity of the person is replaced by individual consumerism' (Mies 1986[1998]: 40). From a more critical viewpoint, then, liberal feminism is little more than an economic ruse. Its epistemological commitments, and its resulting approaches to the women's struggle, do little to facilitate emancipation from the system that parasitises women, workers, other marginalised peoples and wider nature alike. Moreover, the complicity of liberal feminism with the capitalist patriarchal status quo hamstrings it when it comes to responding to the socio-ecological crises of our time, such as Covid-19. From this, one gains the sense that liberal feminism and materialist eco-feminism are almost diametric opposites except for their shared interest in uplifting women – something that will become clearer in the wake of a more detailed discussion of eco-feminism itself.

MATERIALIST ECO-FEMINISM AS AN EMANCIPATORY PRAXIS

What is now known as a *materialist* ecological feminism emerged in the 1970s as a grassroots movement of women – one that, crucially, included within its ambit of concern other oppressed and disenfranchised members of the world community.

73

This movement is also holistic and inevitably so, since it emerged out of women's real-world challenges and concerns, deriving from their experience of breakdown relating to societal and environmental health. Thus, central to eco-feminism of this kind, is a solid understanding that humans form part of a dynamic yet fragile eco-system, and that their actions should comport with this reality so that, in the long run, people themselves do not become compromised. Australian eco-feminist Ariel Salleh provides some examples of this 'barefoot epistemology' (Salleh 1997[2017]: 196) in action:

> Eco-feminism is found in initiatives like women's legal challenges to giant nuclear corporations in the USA and tree-hugging protests against loggers in north India. These actions express a materially embodied standpoint grounded in working women's commonsense understanding of everyday needs. Despite cultural differences between women around the world, this … politics reflects a common intuition that somehow the struggle for a feminine voice to be heard is joined to the struggle for a nurturant, protective attitude towards our living environment. (Salleh 1997[2017]: 38)

Fakier and Cock, too, discuss this barefoot epistemology in their reflections on eco-feminist organising in South Africa. While explaining that women's work – 'social reproduction … the complex tasks that ensure the production and reproduction of the population on a daily and generational basis' – is what is parasitised by capitalism, they argue that these labours of social reproduction are at the same time epistemologically catalytic ecologically (Fakier and Cock 2018: 44; see also Fraser 2017: 147, 152). They elaborate that 'women's unpaid work in their communities to protect the air, water and land necessary to social reproduction, [also] exposes how much environmental damage is due to the externalization of costs by capital' (Fakier and Cock 2018: 44).

Eco-feminism's critical focus on capitalism, which differs radically from liberal feminism's complicity with this system, has understandably resulted in eco-feminism being associated with socialism – if not regarded as a variant of it. Certainly, materialist eco-feminism and eco-socialism, for example, are 'complementary … political strands' (Salleh 1991: 129), but generally socialism differs from eco-feminism by being less critical of productivism and of technology's role therein. Also, while certain forms of socialism, such as eco-socialism, do incorporate concern for the environment, socialist theorists routinely steer clear of factoring into their analyses the parallel exploitation of women and the environment under capitalism. Mellor lays bare the enormous consequence of this attitude when she writes that 'it will prove impossible to construct an eco-socialist/feminist revolutionary theory and practice unless we can finally break out of the laager of economic analysis to embrace women and nature, not as objects of the economic system but as subjects in their own right' (Mellor 1992: 43).

Indeed, caregiving women, as a hyper-exploited group (Fraser 2017: 147) and specifically through their sex–gender-allocated labours, recognise both their embodiment within and people's dependence on the overall health of the physical environment. This, eco-feminists argue, catalyses an emancipatory epistemology and praxis – something corroborated by social reproduction theorists. That is, in social reproduction theory focus might not fall specifically on ecological matters, as it does in eco-feminist theory, but resonant claims are made for the catalytic potency of caregiving: it has 'distinctive normative and ontological grammars of [its] … own [such as] … ideals of care, mutual responsibility, and solidarity' (Fraser 2017: 152). Still, some early eco-socialists criticised materialist eco-feminism for supposedly 'privileg[ing] "body" over mind' (Salleh 1991: 133) given their focus on embodied caregivers – something that in their view detracted from the business of analysing the problem of capitalism. This does not change the fact that women's epistemological perspectives and materially embedded labours *are* crucial to factor into analyses of capital. Women need to be heard because they are at the forefront of concerns relating to women's and nature's parallel exploitation under capitalism. Indeed, womanist resistance movements articulating such matters emerged more or less 'spontaneously' in the 1970s: not only in France but 'in other "centers" too – Sicily, Japan, Venezuela, Australia, Finland, [and] the U.S.' (Salleh 1991: 132). And today, the WoMin African Alliance likewise underscores and works against women's and nature's parallel exploitation. As WoMin leader Samantha Hargreaves states in chapter 1 of this volume, 'WoMin works on the frontiers of extractivism in the African context and the costs this model of capitalist accumulation externalises to women, their bodies and their labour.'

In effect, 'women don't need a pre-packaged social philosophy in order to see that their labor and sexuality are "resourced" by men in ways that match the instrumental exploitation of "nature"' (Salleh 1991: 132). The sociologist Shannon Bell expands on this point: there seems to be an 'identity correspondence between [women's] … personal identities and the collective identity of the environmental justice movement because many view their activism as an extension of their roles as protectors of children, community, culture, and heritage' (Bell 2016: 86). Women's caregiving in the home and their related efforts to protect wider nature might go unmonetised and unrecognised but constitute, in actuality, 'another kind of activity that could be identified as economic' (Salleh 1991: 134) and that thus requires serious treatment. New Zealand liberal feminist politician Marilyn Waring has also forced caregiving into view as an undeniably economic activity without which the capitalist system could not exist. In a powerful critique of the United Nations System of National Accounts, she makes a detailed economic analysis of the costs borne by women internationally due to the 'non-monetised' status of caregiving, premised on the false ideas that the '"average housewife" does not work, and the household is not a productive enterprise' (Waring 1988[1999]: 112–113). That capitalism owes a colossal debt to these caregivers, to others outside of the formal economy and to wider nature, is something that many strands of Marxism and socialism nonetheless continue to neglect in their focus on workers.

Debt owed to caregiving women is thus a concern shared by materialist eco-feminists and liberal feminists such as Waring at least. But there is an important difference: liberal feminists might push for an *economic* value to be attributed to such labours, but materialist eco-feminists shed light on the intrinsic *epistemological* value of such labours. This is because these caregiving labours shape perceptions and behaviours for the better, counteracting the dominant exploitative ethos of capitalism. Mellor, for instance, speaks of the 'immediate altruism' that accompanies women's caregiving work – it 'is carried out for only incidental personal gain (the pleasure of close personal relationships) and ... is immediate in the sense that it cannot be "put off" or slotted into a work schedule' (Mellor 1992: 54). Falling within the ambit of social reproduction, 'the needs to which women respond are demands that cannot be ignored; if they are ignored the social fabric of society begins to disintegrate' (Mellor 1992: 54). And most significantly, Mellor correlates caregiving with a complex, holistic epistemology because 'women's lives as reflected in domestic and caring work represent the embodiedness of humanity, the link of humanity with its natural being. Women's work represents the fundamental reality of human existence, the body's life in *biological time*[:] the time it takes to rest, recover, grow up and grow old' (Mellor 2009: 255). The Indian materialist eco-feminist Vandana Shiva likewise observes that 'women produce and reproduce life not merely biologically, but also through their social role in providing sustenance. All ecological societies of forest-dwellers and peasants, whose life is organised on the principle of sustainability and the reproduction of life in all its richness, also embody the feminine principle' (Shiva 1989: 42). Salleh again explicitly links women's caregiving activities and indigenous people's labours with reproduction of the humanity–nature metabolism and cultivation of 'a characteristic epistemology and practice, one that can be articulated as a people's science' since it derives from these people's 'experience of reproducing nature's metabolic cycles' (Salleh 2010: 207).

The eco-feminist insistence on the importance of caregiving labour to the reorientation of contemporary societies – an insistence shared by social reproduction theorists – diverges most markedly from '*power liberal feminism*' (Bhandary 2020). In this recent incarnation of liberal feminism, explains feminist ethicist Asha Bhandary, focus falls 'on women's greater professional advancement, increased financial gain, and freedom *from* caregiving responsibility' (Bhandary 2020, emphasis added). In the eyes of such feminists, 'caregiving is accompanied by disadvantages, and its nature is burdensome and mundane'; it is clearly seen as 'an obstacle to women's maximal self-development and equality of opportunity' (Bhandary 2020). As a result, such 'liberal feminism makes everyone as insensible to the needs of the vulnerable as privileged persons (men)' (Bhandary 2020). In effect, dismissal of care ethics, and lack of connection to exploited Others beyond a specific demographic of women, undermines liberal feminism's capacity to address multifaceted crises such as Covid-19. By contrast, eco-feminism's stress on humanity–nature care work and epistemological holism gives this movement an advantage in diagnosing and remediating such crises, as the subsequent analysis aims to illustrate.

COVID-19 THROUGH A MATERIALIST ECO-FEMINIST LENS

Salleh and her co-editors of *Pluriverse: A Post-Development Dictionary* (Kothari et al. 2019), in an opinion piece on Covid-19, state that 'the Corona pandemic ends a universe of false promises', because it exposed that 'economic globalization has not brought universal prosperity but ecological devastation, social disruption and inequality' (Kothari et al. 2020). But this is not news to caregiving labourers, indigenous meta-industrials and eco-feminists. Indeed, the fundamental inequalities characteristic of capitalism, which entail injury to women, other oppressed persons, non-human others and wider nature, are what materialist eco-feminists have tried to respond to from the start. And this sensitivity to *multiple* overlapping dominations and the need for their simultaneous address is what makes materialist eco-feminism genuinely emancipatory as a movement. In fact, 'it carries forward four revolutions in one. Ecofeminist politics is a feminism in as much as it offers an uncompromising critique of capitalist patriarchal culture from a womanist perspective; it is a socialism because it honours the wretched of the earth; it is an ecology because it reintegrates humanity with nature; [and] it is a postcolonial discourse because it focuses on deconstructing eurocentric domination' (Salleh 1997[2017]: 282–283). And the Covid-19 pandemic, in laying bare the dominations referred to in the above-mentioned four discourses, offers a chance to right historical wrongs – the abuse of our earthly home and of marginalised societies, the very people who will suffer most from this pandemic. This viral outbreak is a sign that by going too far in exploiting the rest of nature, the dominant globalising culture has undone the planet's capacity to sustain life and livelihoods. The unleashing of micro-organisms from their animal hosts means that they must latch on to other bodies for their own survival. (Kothari et al. 2020)

This is a view common to various chapters in this book, and can also be seen in certain press reflections on Covid-19, such as the one offered by the South African ambassador to Ireland and former African National Congress MP, Melanie Verwoerd. Uncannily echoing Kothari et al's (2020) opinion piece some two months after its publication, Verwoerd argues that 'Covid-19 has … highlighted the huge inequalities that exist in our world – our country being one of the most unequal in the world' (Verwoerd 2020). But questioning matters, she adds, is 'not something that has been encouraged in the consumerist, growth-driven economic model that the post-World War II generation has grown up in … This epidemic has shown more than ever how intertwined we are as human beings' (Verwoerd 2020). Such texts consistently thematise the now highly evident wrongs in the world, arguing that the globalising capitalist-consumerist model is responsible and that Covid-19 has revealed – albeit most cruelly – the interrelation of everything and everyone. All of this should imply that the Covid-19 pandemic cannot but have a monumental epistemic impact on people, one perhaps yet to be fully realised. One epistemo-logical misstep badly in need of exposure is the longstanding Eurocentric dualis-tic construct of man/nature, framing people as separate from, independent of and impervious to the happenings in wider nature. It is certainly the case that Covid-19 has served to undermine the man/nature dualism to a degree, insofar as through this pandemic, people were summarily ripped out of any disembodied view they might have harboured, joining the rest of the planetary ecosystem as just another vulnerable organism.

The foregoing suggests that what eco-feminists theorise is what many women, and men committed to a caregiving or subsistence ethic, often fig-ure out independent of any theoretical education. This is evidently because these issues emerge out of lived experiences (Salleh 1991: 132). And, sig-nificantly, argues Hargreaves in chapter 1 of this volume, these are expe-riences that help meta-industrials to shape 'the living and breathing' alternatives so urgently required in her home continent of Africa. But these experiences have often gone ignored by socialist theorists preoccupied with the productive economy, who in the process 'fail … women, peasants, and indigenes – labor outside of the factory', not to mention wider nature itself (Salleh et al. 2010: 188). Even so, socialism is critical of capitalism whereas liberal feminism does not even get that far. The latter's complicity with capitalism hinders it from being able to offer more to women than a hollow version of liberty – a weakness underpinned by 'the partial absorption of Second Wave feminism by capitalist patriarchal objectives [which] has blurred many women's political focus' (Salleh 1997[2017]: 281).

Nonetheless, because of Covid-19 the need for systemic change is being raised increasingly – and in relation to myriad issues. One powerfully vocalised issue is that women in South Africa and abroad still shoulder much of the care-giving workload, something that was worsened during Covid-19 through government-mandated lockdowns across the world. In this context, not only the continued naturalising of women's caregiving under patriarchy but women's own immediate altruism as caregivers (Mellor 1992: 54) deprived many women of any respite. As a woman academic interviewed by *The Guardian* stated: 'Research has fallen by the wayside', because even though 'it's important and I want to do it, … it's not as urgent as supporting my students. My students and my children have to be my priority' (Fazackerley 2020). This in an article reporting that during the UK's Covid-19 lockdown period, women's research dropped off completely, whereas for certain journals men's research submissions increased by as much as 50 per cent. In a similar vein, a South African woman, in a letter submitted to the *Parent24* news division, articulates the impasse she was facing as a mother *and* a worker during the South African Covid-19 lockdowns. Known only as 'working mom of two', she contended: 'I … feel dread at the thought of being torn between being a mother and being a good employee. I mean, how can we be fully committed to either when we are split between the two? My husband assists where possible, but I bear the brunt of the responsibility' (Parent24 2020). Yet, while these important concerns regarding the division of labour under capitalist patriarchy were being raised, neoliberal pundits were prescribing economic (capitalist) policy-related solutions to Covid-19, which they deemed simply another war that capitalism has to weather (Dell'Ariccia et al. 2020). For them, the objective, ironically, was to save the very system criticised and attacked by Verwoerd and others. The economistic, masculinist 'war talk' that emanated from International Monetary Fund (IMF) quarters in relation to a virus, disconcertingly corroborates the view that the capitalist paradigm entrenches 'the domination of masculine power over life-affirming feminine care' – something deplorably embodied today 'in a heavily militarised global neoliberal capitalist (dis)order' (Kothari et al. 2020). Like the *Pluriverse* team cited earlier, Verwoerd associates the current socio-economic model with aggression and excess, and calls for a radical alternative. She proposes that 'inherent in these inequalities are a cruelty and an unkindness, a deep-seated injustice, that diminishes all our humanity. As we start to think about a post-Covid world we have to collectively find the moral courage and outrage to change this' (Verwoerd 2020). This is especially so in the context of poor- and working-class South African women, who before, during and even after the Covid-19 lockdowns, remain trapped in a 'failing economy infused with patriarchal and corrupt politics [which] places undue burdens on households and fuels domestic violence' (Fakier and Cock 2018: 48).

Ultimately, perhaps the greatest epistemological chasm between liberal feminism and materialist ecological feminism is that in the eco-feminist view, caregiving is promoted as a potent catalyst for change whereas in liberal feminism, it remains framed as an impediment. Another point worth mentioning, which broadens eco-feminism's emancipatory reach, is that materialist eco-feminists advance the project of caregiving as highly inclusive, such that an eco-feminist theorist might speak of 'mothering practices' when specifically discussing women caregivers but also employ a broader, 'more generic term *holding* which lets us talk about kinds of sustaining labour regardless of gender role' (Salleh and Hanson 1999: 210). Materialist eco-feminism as four revolutions in one constitutes nothing short of a civilisational critique, central to which is rejection of capitalist patriarchy and its dominant values, which liberal feminists seek merely to reform and to nuance to the advantage of select women. Liberal feminism carries the 'underlying assumption that "male is better"' and so in practice, this type of feminism is relatively unconcerned with 'the fate of women as a whole' (King 1990: 119). Very importantly, what has also been lost in such incarnations of feminism is 'the original radical feminist project of changing how men … work, think, love and rule' – a project retained by eco-feminists such that their 'politics converges with the men's movement wish to free "masculinity" from deforming social structures' (Salleh 1997[2017]: 282). Men and women need to cultivate a care-based societal ethic countering capitalist mores together, and this is not an impossible task because caregivers, many of them women, already preside over 'the organic basis of this paradigm shift' (Salleh 1984: 339). Humanity–nature bridging labours, be they caregiving or subsistence, involve participants adopting roles 'that run … counter to the exploitive technical rationality which is … the requisite masculine norm' (Salleh 1984: 342). By implication, when people begin to value and take on such roles, they are embracing a feminine value constellation (Fraser 2017: 152–153). This liberation of what might be styled 'the feminine' is key to civilisational emancipation:

The suppression of the *feminine* is truly an all pervasive human universal. It is not just a suppression of real, live, empirical women, but equally the suppression of the feminine aspects of men's own constitution … [Deep, radical transformation] will not truly happen until men are brave enough to rediscover and to love the woman inside themselves. And we women, too, have to be allowed to love what we are, if we are to make a better world. (Salleh 1984: 344–345)

Eco-feminism sounds forth a call to care, for all people and for nature. In the wake of the further exposure of capitalist patriarchal violence through the Covid-19 pandemic, it is surely a matter of urgency for us all to heed this call, now.

REFERENCES

Beasley, C. 1999. *What is Feminism? An Introduction to Feminist Theory.* London: Sage Publications.

Bell, S.E. 2016. *Fighting King Coal: The Challenges to Micromobilization in Central Appalachia.* Cambridge, MA: The MIT Press.

Bhandary, A. 2020. *Freedom to Care: Liberalism, Dependency Care, and Culture.* New York: Routledge, Kindle edition.

Carroll, S.J. 1994. *Women as Candidates in American Politics* (second edition). Bloomington, IN: Indiana University Press.

Davis, M. 2006. *Planet of Slums.* London: Verso.

Dell'Ariccia, G., Mauro, P., Spilimbergo, A. and Zettelmeyer, J. 2020. 'Economic policies for the COVID-19 war'. *blogs.imf.org*, 1 April. Accessed 10 May 2020, https://blogs.imf.org/2020/04/01/economic-policies-for-the-covid-19-war/.

Fakier, K. and Cock, J. 2018. 'Eco-feminist organizing in South Africa: Reflections on the feminist table', *Capitalism Nature Socialism* 29 (1): 40–57. https://doi.org/10.1080/104 55752.2017.1421980.

Fazackerley, A. 2020. 'Women's research plummets during lockdown – but articles from men increase', *The Guardian*, 12 May. Accessed 25 May 2020, https://www.theguardian.com/education/2020/may/12/womens-research-plummets-during-lockdown-but-articles-from-men-increase?CMP=sharebtnfb&fbclid=IwAR2ZFOp8MqVbgJrh7XeX-CGSFdb1Mp1tNgHwuKaH-tLSofGGbvv05Qqv4-E.

Fraser, N. 2000. 'Rethinking recognition', *New Left Review* 3 (May/June): 107–120.

Fraser, N. 2017. 'Behind Marx's hidden abode: For an expanded conception of capitalism'. In P. Deutscher and C. Lafont (eds), *Critical Theory in Critical Times: Transforming the Global Political and Economic Order.* New York: Columbia University Press, pp. 141–159.

Goldman, R., Heath, D. and Smith, S.L. 1991. 'Commodity feminism', *Critical Studies in Mass Communication* 8 (3): 333–351. https://doi.org/10.1080/15295039109366801.

Jaggar, A.M. 1983. *Feminist Politics and Human Nature.* Totowa, NJ: Rowman & Allanheld Publishers.

King, Y. 1990. 'Healing the wounds: Feminism, ecology, and nature/culture dualism'. In A.M. Jaggar and S.R. Bordo (eds), *Gender/Body/Knowledge: Feminist Reconstructions of Being and Knowing.* New Brunswick: Rutgers University Press, pp. 115–141.

Kothari, A., Escobar, A., Salleh, A., Demaria, F. and Acosta, A. 2020. 'Can the Coronavirus save the planet?', *Open Democracy*, 26 March. Accessed 9 May 2020, https://www.open-democracy.net/en/oureconomy/can-coronavirus-save-planet/.

Kothari, A., Salleh, A., Escobar, A., Demaria, F. and Acosta, A. (eds). 2019. *Pluriverse: A Post-Development Dictionary*. New Delhi: Tulika Books.

McGee, K. 2012. 'Orientalism and erotic multiculturalism in popular culture: From Princess Rajah to the Pussycat Dolls', *Music, Sound & the Moving Image (MSMI)* 6 (2): 209–238. https://doi.org/10.3828/msmi.2012.14.

Mellor, M. 1992. 'Eco-feminism and eco-socialism: Dilemmas of essentialism and materialism', *Capitalism Nature Socialism* 3 (2): 43–62. https://doi.org/10.1080/10455759209358486.

Mellor, M. 2009. 'Ecofeminist political economy and the politics of money'. In A. Salleh (ed.), *Eco-Sufficiency and Global Justice: Women Write Political Ecology*. London: Pluto Press, pp. 251–267.

Mies, M. [1986]1998. *Patriarchy and Accumulation on a World Scale: Women in the International Division of Labour*. London: Zed Books.

Odih, P. 2014. *Watersheds in Marxist Ecofeminism*. Newcastle upon Tyne: Cambridge Scholars Publishing.

Osgerby, B. 2001. *Playboys in Paradise: Masculinity, Youth and Leisure-Style in Modern America*. Oxford: Berg.

Parent24. 2020. '"We're expected to work like we aren't mothers and mother like we don't work"', 27 May. Accessed 29 May 2020, https://www.parent24.com/Family/Parenting/were-expected-to-work-like-we-arent-mothers-and-mother-like-we-dont-work-20200527.

Radner, H. 1995. *Shopping Around: Feminine Culture and the Pursuit of Pleasure*. New York: Routledge.

Salleh, A. 1984. 'Deeper than deep ecology: The eco-feminist connection', *Environmental Ethics* 6 (Winter): 339–345. https://doi.org/10.5840/enviroethics1984645.

Salleh, A. 1991. 'Eco-socialism/eco-feminism', *Capitalism Nature Socialism* 2 (1): 129–137. https://doi.org/10.1080/10455759109358432.

Salleh, A. [1997]2017. *Ecofeminism as Politics: Nature, Marx and the Postmodern*. London: Zed Books.

Salleh, A. 2010. 'From metabolic rift to metabolic value: Reflections on environmental sociology and the alternative globalization movement', *Organization & Environment* 23 (2): 205–219.

Salleh, A., Canavan, G., Klarr, L. and Vu, R. 2010. 'Embodied materialism in action: An interview with Ariel Salleh', *Polygraph* 22: 183–199.

Salleh, A. and Hanson, M. 1999. 'On production and reproduction, identity and nonidentity in ecofeminist theory', *Organization & Environment* 12 (2): 207–218.

Shiva, V. 1989. *Staying Alive: Women, Ecology and Development*. London: Zed Books.

Thorpe, C. 2018. *Social Theory for Social Work: Ideas and Applications*. Abingdon: Routledge, Kindle edition.

Valentich, M. and Gripton, J. 2016. 'Introduction'. In M.Valentich and J. Gripton (eds), *Feminist Perspectives on Social Work and Human Sexuality*. Abingdon: Routledge, pp. 1–5.

Verwoerd, M. 2020. 'Post lockdown: Two important questions', *News24.com*, 27 May. Accessed 29 May 2020, https://www.news24.com/news24/columnists/melanieverwoerd/melanie-verwoerd-post-lockdown-two-important-questions-20200527-2.

Walker, S. 2009. 'Black dollar power: Assessing African American consumerism since 1945'. In K.L. Kusmer and J.W. Trotter (eds), *African American Urban History Since World War II*. Chicago, IL: University of Chicago Press, pp. 376–403.

Waring, M. [1988]1999. *Counting for Nothing: What Men Value and What Women Are Worth*. Toronto: University of Toronto Press.

4

'OUR EXISTENCE IS RESISTANCE': WOMEN CHALLENGING MINING AND THE CLIMATE CRISIS IN A TIME OF COVID-19

Dineo Skosana and Jacklyn Cock

INTRODUCTION

'How do you protect yourself against a hail of bullets through your kitchen and bedroom windows after dark where your children are in bed asleep?' writes the Global Environmental Trust (2020a), following a series of attacks on communities who resist the expansion of mining by Tendele Coal Mining Pty Ltd, a subsidiary of Petmin. Later that year, the news hit the country that Fikile Ntshangase, a prominent activist who resisted the mining-induced relocations in Ophondweni, and a committee member of the Mfolozi Community Environmental Justice Organisation (MCEJO), was gunned down in her kitchen in front of her 11-year-old grandson by three unidentified men. The incident took place on 22 October 2020. Little did she know that her words, 'I refused to sign. I cannot sell out my people. And if need be, I will die for my people' (Global Environmental Trust 2020b), would become a reality.

This chapter investigates women's struggles and resistance in two coal-mining-affected communities in the Highveld, as well as in Somkhele, which lies northwest of Richards Bay in KwaZulu-Natal. Their activities suggest that many African working-class women living in such communities in South Africa are expressing radical eco-feminism in their actions and practices. Their lived resistance to the shocks of both the Covid-19 pandemic and the more extreme weather events of climate change could promote a unifying narrative in the form of an African eco-feminism. The effects of the Covid-19 pandemic and accelerating climate change are both experienced most intensely by poor/working-class African women. This is evident especially in South Africa, which is a major source of the carbon emissions that are driving the rising temperatures, droughts and other extreme events of the climate crisis.

Both the Covid-19 pandemic and the climate crisis are forms of what Rob Nixon (2011) terms 'slow violence', meaning violence which is relatively invisible, often unrecognised and, in this case, involves different forms of pollution – of bodies in the case of the pandemic and of water and air by carbon emissions in the case of climate change. Both are lethal processes. It has been suggested that 'the growing but largely unrecognised death toll from rising global temperatures will come close to eclipsing the current number of deaths from all the infectious diseases combined if planet-heating emissions are not constrained' (Heywood 2020). Both the climate crisis and the pandemic are violating ecological limits: in the case of climate change, caused by the pollution of air and water and the degradation of soils, and in the case of the Covid-19 pandemic, largely caused by the destruction of wildlife habitat and large-scale industrial animal husbandry, which contribute to the spread of the virus. This 'factory farming' involves operations that house thousands of animals (such as chickens, pigs, turkeys and cows) under appalling conditions, designed to maximise production while minimising costs (Genoways 2014).

AFRICAN WOMEN'S ROLE IN SOCIAL REPRODUCTION

Under these conditions, African women's role in social reproduction has become to carry the burden of the two interlinked crises. This chapter suggests that both the climate crisis and the Covid-19 pandemic, as well as the lockdowns resulting from the latter, have exacerbated gender inequality, especially in mining-affected areas. Inequality is understood not in the economistic terms of assets and income, but as 'existential inequality', defined by Göran Therborne as 'a violation of human dignity; it is a denial of the possibility for everybody's capabilities to develop' (Therborne 2013: 10). The chapter suggests that these violations are 'gendered' in the sense that black working-class women experience them differently from men and more intensely due to the gendered division of labour – women are responsible for the provision of food, energy and water resources.

In this chapter we do not call the women we cite 'eco-feminists', because that is not necessarily how they describe themselves. Makoma Lekalakala, the director of the environmental justice organisation Earthlife, has warned against imposing any ideological labels such as 'feminist' or 'activist' because they 'undermine solidarity' and 'an ideological consensus is not necessary'. She stresses that 'there is a lot of different action on climate change, and they are all connected to environmental justice, but we all speak different languages'.[1]

We suggest that, although they do not identify as 'eco-feminists', through their lived experience and practices in relation to the Covid-19 crisis and the climate crisis, black working-class women in mining-affected areas are doing important eco-feminist work in four respects:

- Their role in social reproduction, meaning unpaid care work in the daily work performed in their households and communities, particularly in relation to childcare and the procurement of food, energy and water. Unlike the households of the dominant classes where this work is often commodified in extremely exploitative social relations, there is frequently an ethic of sharing and mutual support.
- The spirit of solidarity which informs this work focuses on collective rather than individualised needs, on changes to the benefit of all.
- A respect for nature that goes beyond the expansionist logic of capitalism, which reduces nature to a store of resources for profit.
- Their role in taking responsibility for and caring for the sick, particularly Covid-19 and pollution victims in their homes, hospitals and communities, and educating the public both as nurses and as community health workers.

With at least 102 568 deaths from the Covid-19 pandemic, South Africa was rated the most infected country in Africa and it experienced one of the strictest lockdowns (World Health Organization 2022). The state's response emphasised restrictions: many businesses in the informal sector, such as taverns and hair salons especially, as well as educational institutions were closed, and three million formal sector workers lost their jobs (two million of whom were women). There were strict controls of public activities and people were urged to remain at home. At the same time, there was some public education about Covid-19 such as the need to maintain physical distance from other people, to wash hands thoroughly and to wear face masks. However, there was no consultation with marginalised groups and both these aspects of the state response completely disregarded the situation of the millions of poor, black South Africans, especially those in informal settlements and rural areas lacking housing and access to clean water and proper sanitation, which made it impossible for them to self-protect.

This disregard was exacerbated for the thousands living close to the operative coal-fired power stations and open-pit working or abandoned mines. They were already experiencing the direct loss of their health due to air pollution, dispossession, forced removals, social dislocation, loss of their land-based livelihoods such as cattle, goats and chickens, threats to food security, limited access to clean water, violation of their ancestral graves and inadequate consultation on the awarding of mining licences (Hallowes and Munnik 2016, 2017, 2019; Skosana 2021).

'Gender' is a relational concept which pays attention to the power involved in all social relations and in this chapter, the focus on women is approached through an intersectional analysis which recognises the interrelation of different forms of oppression.[2] Black working-class women are the 'shock absorbers' of the impacts of both the climate crisis and the pandemic lockdown.

WOMEN AS THE SHOCK ABSORBERS OF CRISES

The research that was conducted in the Highveld and at Somkhele revealed that black, working-class women are the most vulnerable to the shocks of the climate crisis in the form of increasing extreme weather events. The shock absorbers of the pandemic and its consequent lockdowns are the women who lack access to the means for protecting themselves and their families, such as clean water, protective masks, sanitisers, relevant information about the pandemic and nutritious food.

Furthermore, black working-class women constitute the majority of community health workers who expose themselves to contamination, and of nurses who work with Covid-19 patients in poor conditions and often without the necessary protective equipment. According to the health minister, as of 4 August 2020, 1 300 health workers had died of Covid-19 and 27 360 had contracted the virus. Women made up the majority of the cases (see Bischoff: chapter 9 of this volume). The National Education, Health and Allied Workers' Union (Nehawu) threatened a strike as health-care workers continued to face inadequate supplies of protective equipment. Moreover, months into the lockdown instituted in March 2020, a resident of Kwa-Guqa, a township located 16 kilometres west of Emalahleni in Mpumalanga, maintained that the community 'had not seen a food parcel or a community health worker, and had not received any information about the pandemic' (Faith, interview, July 2020).[3] She also reported that 'our only access to water is from a polluted stream. We are out of water since September last year … lots of people in our area use pit toilets, so we are struggling to get water to drink or wash our hands'. Zanele, from Somkhele in KwaZulu-Natal, shared this experience: 'We have struggled for water for years now and Covid-19 has placed us under more threat' (Zanele, interview, July 2020).

Food was also a problem because many of the local spaza shops were closed due to stringent lockdown regulations in Kwa-Guqa. Faith divulged that 'we have to get a taxi to the nearest shop which is more expensive because taxi fares have increased'. Furthermore, she reported price profiteering in the local shops during lockdown, some of which related to staple foods such as maize meal, flour, sugar and canned foods. For a resident who is unemployed and survives on a social grant, as do 44 per cent of the population in Mpumalanga (Action Aid 2018: 12), this made access to food during the lockdown difficult. Faith also emphasised the challenge of accessing clinics in their area because at various points during the various stages of the lockdown, clinics and police stations in different parts of Mpumalanga were closed, and in many places there is no ambulance service to carry patients to a hospital – ten kilometres away, in the case of Kwa-Guqa (Faith, interview, July 2020). The Amajuba hospital is one of those in the country which was closed for several days when the hospital manager was diagnosed with Covid-19. Linda, who lives in Arbor, a peri-urban mining area, shared the difficulty of access to health care: 'In our area, we have a mobile clinic which only comes once every fortnight. This means that we can't get ill before then or after. The mobile clinic has only one doctor. We had difficulty accessing health care before Covid-19, despite the respiratory illnesses most of us have due to coal mining, blasting, dust from trucks transporting coal, and coal-fired power stations in our area. Covid-19 has placed our community's health under more risk' (Linda, interview, July 2020). Furthermore, like Faith, she also mentioned that the lockdown and lack of access to water compelled them to buy foods from supermarkets in towns such as Witbank, Ogies and Delmas, instead of growing their own. She maintained that 'the taxi-fare and staple foods such as bread have increased at least by R5'. In communities whose only source of income is social grants, this increase has dire consequences for households (see Morgan and Cherry: chapter 5 of this volume). Price-hiking during the Covid-19 pandemic was a national problem. The Competition Commission received over 800 complaints about food pricing after the beginning of the lockdown and prosecuted 30 companies within the first few months (Gedye 2020). The Commission found, for example, that between April and June 2020, staples such as

25 kg bags of white mealie meal increased from R129.99 to R159.99, and others by the following percentages: rice (29%), cake flour (7%), cooking oil (13%) and bread (14% to 16%). The price of affordable sources of protein was also increased: eggs (18%), pilchards (3%), sugar beans (18%) and amasi (9%).

In addition, the closure of police stations had terrible consequences for women, who experienced increased gender-based violence during the lockdown. Records show that the gender-based violence hotline received 2 300 calls in the first five days of lockdown – nearly three times the rate prior to lockdown (Harrisberg 2020). The general sentiment of those who live in coal-affected areas was that the lockdown was 'a nightmare' and most stress that their living conditions, always adverse, worsened during the lockdown. The only positive outcome of the lockdown that was noted was that air pollution and dust decreased with fewer mines operating and fewer trucks transporting coal on the road. As a result, community-based researchers observed an improvement in their health. Linda (interview, July 2020) revealed, 'I coughed less during the lockdown, my bronchitis got a little better.'

Women bear the brunt of multiple crises. Both the accelerating climate crisis and the Covid-19 pandemic mean women are having to work harder to perform all the tasks of social reproduction, such as having to walk further to obtain clean water, growing food on degraded land, making meagre amounts of money stretch further to buy necessities, dealing with increased domestic-based violence and caring for those ill from exposure to toxic pollution or the Covid-19 virus. This unpaid care work involves intense levels of anxiety and overburdening. As one woman said, 'We are the rock. We have to deal with everything.' The collective nature of much of this work is significant: women sharing the onerous task of clearing land for planting, hanging their washing together, collecting water or firewood as a group. In other words, the caring work of social reproduction involves strong affective bonds, and the emotional demands are acknowledged and discussed.

The concept of social reproduction directs us to the importance of this work in the class-based, material realities of everyday life (Luxton 2006; Bezanson and Luxton 2006; Fakier and Cock 2009). Furthermore, the concept makes visible the 'value' of unpaid domestic work, which is often trivialised or ignored. It provides us with a powerful critique of capitalism and its relation to patriarchy, and exposes the savage inequalities on which it is based. It points us to alternative social forms and provides a validation of, and links to, other struggles.

In mining-affected communities many working-class struggles are moving beyond the point of production to the terrain of social reproduction. Much collective action, usually framed as protests about service delivery, is confronting the lack of access to the material environmental conditions necessary for social reproduction, such as access to clean air, water, adequate housing and land for subsistence agriculture. Women often constitute the majority of people in these struggles confronting the threats to their health, land and livelihoods. This is because their role in social reproduction means that they deal most directly with the damaging effects of polluted air and water, crop failures and the more extreme weather events associated with climate change. The struggle to meet some of the social responsibilities that women have in their communities saw some in Somkhele take to the streets in 2018, over water. This struggle began 15 years ago, with the Tendele anthracite open-cast coal mine exacerbating the water crisis in the area. Before the water crisis, the feminist organisation WoMin had facilitated participatory action research to bring awareness of how the presence of the mine impacted the community's access to water. The women presented their research findings to the local government where they were promised action, but the problem was not addressed (WoMin 2019). In 2019, at least 29 women were arrested for property violation and were subsequently released on bail.

The explanation for women's preponderance in these environmental struggles is not essentialist. It is not based on any natural affinity which women have with nature, which some people claim. On the contrary, writes Carolyn Merchant, 'any analysis that makes women's essence and qualities special ties them to a biological destiny that thwarts any possibility of [their] liberation' (Merchant 1990: 102). The explanation lies in the gendered division of labour; the unpaid care work which women are doing both in the home and in the community in relation to the climate and pandemic crises. As Vandana Shiva writes, 'Women are most directly involved with subsistence work and are the safeguards of the natural resources needed to sustain the family and community' (Shiva 2014: 165).

Not only does this work involve protecting nature from pollution and destruction by consuming natural resources minimally and respectfully, it also promotes a new narrative about our relationship with nature; a revaluing of nature as something more than a store of natural resources for economic activity, to be utilised for short-term gain without concern for long-term survival. Under capitalism, nature is still mainly viewed as external, as a store of natural resources, allowing what Max Oelshinger (2002) has termed 'resourcism', often used by capital instrumentally to externalise production costs. Naomi Klein has decried the 'expansionist extractive mindset which has so long governed our relationship to nature … we need a new civilizational paradigm, one grounded not in dominance over nature, but in respect for natural cycles of renewal and acutely sensitive to natural limits' (Klein 2011). The environmental imaginary of some of the residents of Somkhele takes this even further, stressing our shared connections in an ecological community and affirming the value of participatory democracy and accountability. In eFuleni (KwaZulu-Natal), a group of women who formed their organisation, Thandolwethu, in 2018 explained, 'The organisation was formed as we were attending meetings as mine-affected communities. We realised that mines have specific effects on women ... being part of the organisation has changed our lives because whatever we harvest, we share. And when we sell our vegetables, we can feed our children and pay for their transport for school' (Thandolwethu, interview, June 2019).

The role of 'shock absorber' implies a certain vulnerability or exposure that could fade into a sponge-like passivity and perpetuate the notion of women as predominantly victims. But these women are also protecting their communities by challenging social and environmental injustice.

BUILDING RESISTANCE

Before the pandemic, in many mining-affected communities women were forming new grassroots organisations, building social networks, formal or informal alliances and a collective identity through an emphasis on shared everyday experiences. Many of these grassroots organisations draw on notions of climate justice, food sovereignty and energy democracy, which are building blocks for an eco-feminist society. However, after the start of the pandemic, all resistance efforts in mining-affected communities in provinces such as Mpumalanga and KwaZulu-Natal faced considerable obstacles. The lockdown restrictions on maintaining a physical distance from other people translated into a social distance, thus eroding social bonds. The restrictions banned gatherings of more than 40 people. The state not only blocked organisation, but also used violence to enforce its rules, arresting a group of women violating lockdown regulations in a collective protest about the lack of access to water and confiscating the goods of women traders when such economic activity was banned (Majavu 2020). As one resident said, 'It is difficult to practise solidarity in our communities, now each one is on her own ... we used to help our neighbours with their difficulties but now it is hard' (Faith, interview, July 2020). The individualisation of the struggle is not simply a Covid-19 problem. In Somkhele the women shared how mining threatens resistance by providing job opportunities only to a few and vulnerable individuals (Thandolwethu, interview, June 2019).

Material dependence on coal for heating and cooking, and for providing employment as well as a market for local informal sector activities, produces a certain ambivalence in especially women's resistance to coal. In Mpumalanga there are complex patterns of ambiguous resistance. For example, Mildred is active in the grassroots organisation Mining Affected Communities United in Action (MACUA) and participated in the mass march of 5 000 people organised by MACUA at the giant coal power station, Kusile, but she sells *vetkoek* outside the mine in order to survive. Several informants expressed an ambivalence about coal because of this dependence. A member of a local organisation which describes itself as 'anti coal mining' has a contract as a cleaner at a local mine. Some communities, such as Arbor and the informal settlement around the Black Wattle colliery in Middelburg (Mpumalanga), regularly receive a wheelbarrow of inferior-quality coal from the mine and many depend on coal as a source of energy because either they are not connected to the electricity grid or 'there are no trees here to provide wood to cook and warm our houses' (exchange workshop, Kwa-Guqa, 11 July 2019). No alternatives to coal as a source of energy were mentioned. Many stressed that 'coal is good because it gives us electricity. With coal you can cook and keep warm'. Similarly, various 'developmental' initiatives by different mining corporations, such as schools and a mobile clinic, are used extensively. For example, one of the community-based researchers, Linda, works as a tailor in a container shelter which was supplied by Ntshovelo Mining in Arbor. The women also make a living by sewing overalls for coal-mine workers.

Coal thus provides the possibility of employment and coal-mine workers provide a market for extensive informal sector activities. These forms of livelihood are crucial in South Africa, as in the global South, especially for women. Selling fruit and vegetables, 'russian' sausages, chicken parts, fish and chips, alcohol and cigarettes and herbal medicine; providing services such as panel beating and vehicle spraying, shoe repairs, clothes washing, hairdressing and cooking food; operating driving schools and servicing taverns were some of the informal livelihood activities identified in a scoping exercise on this dependence. Others let backyard rooms to migrant coal miners, wash clothes and cars, drive the coal trucks and do cleaning work.

In Arbor, one woman described how letting a backyard room to a coal miner brought in an income of R800, which provided 'food for the household'. The food items consumed were 'tea, sugar and mealie meal'. She was a participant in exchange workshops and among the 120 informal traders and coal workers interviewed in three different Mpumalanga communities – Arbor, Vosman and Phola. Many were opposed to the closure of coal mines for a range of reasons. Another woman asked, 'If the mine closes how will I get compensation for the damage to my house from blasting?' The most common reason cited for opposing mine closures was increased unemployment. The possibility of these closures generated some degree of anxiety. 'It is unclear what will happen to us if the mines close. What about the people who are starving out there?' During one exchange workshop, instead of understanding a just transition as a space for positive change, it was even claimed that 'this just transition will kill us'. There were frequent appeals for information. Most said during the workshops, 'This just transition is very confusing. We people on the ground are not informed. And anyway, the damage has already been done.'

All these forms of dependence create what Victor Munnik calls a 'captive imaginary' which makes it difficult to conceptualise a just transition to a world without coal. In answer to the direct question, 'What would a world without coal look like?', most answered in catastrophic terms. For example: 'a world without coal would be dark and bad with no electricity, fewer jobs and more crime'; 'it will be the death of my business. It will mean going back to live like our forefathers, no electricity, no petrol, no development'; 'it would be a dark and dangerous world full of crime and hunger'.

However, there were exceptions. For example, one participant commented during an exchange workshop that a world without coal would 'be healthier, because there will be no dust, our streams will be clean, our trees will be safe, no one will cut them down for mining operations. It will be a greener world without coal. A world without coal would be a beautiful world, no sinkholes, no dust, no pollution, no dangers from all the coal trucks'. Another coal worker said during the workshop, 'A world without coal will be better, less sickness, clean water and available land. Also, we will be healthy ... our generation is a sick generation.'

Besides these complex connections to coal, both formal and informal, there is often a normalisation of toxic pollution as natural and inevitable in these Mpumalanga communities. The causal connection between the more extreme weather events of accelerating climate change and carbon emissions is not directly obvious, and more extreme weather events are not always connected to climate change in the popular media. In several community workshops in Mpumalanga, it was evident that climate change – the bedrock of the argument for a transition from coal – was not fully understood and seemed remote and abstract to desperately poor communities concerned with immediate survival.

Material dependence is not the only factor inhibiting resistance. There is also increasing repression, violence and intimidation from supporters of mining. The proponents of extractivism include chiefs and headmen who are the executives of the local economy in the former bantustans. Many are notorious for the authorisation of mining deals without the consent of the affected communities (Capps 2012; Skosana 2012). The unresolved role of traditional authorities in South Africa, as well as their historical role in the administration of land, has positioned chiefs as the agents of dispossession in mining areas. In Somkhele, over 100 households have been relocated by Tendele Coal since beginning open-cast mining in 2007. During the pandemic, Tendele launched an application in the Pietermaritzburg High Court to force the remaining 24 of 145 families to move from the Ophondweni and Emalahleni area, in line with plans to expand the mining operations at the border of the Hluhluwe-iMfolozi Park. Both affected areas are under the authority of the Mpukunyoni Traditional Council, whose signatures, which authorised mining and the relocations, appear on Tendele's affidavit.

The traditional council in the area not only controls the land, but also exercises a close surveillance of villagers. One of the anti-coal militants in Somkhele had an armed man point a gun at him for resisting removal from his home (Ramabina 2020). Another activist revealed that his car was burned and that he faced multiple forms of intimidation from people in the traditional authority office (Lethabo, interview, June 2019). Activists face various other threats such as banishment, torching of their houses and defamation suits for criticising the mine, chiefs and the local government. One informant said, 'Organising in Somkhele and Fulani is difficult because people are afraid of the chiefs. They fear for their lives. Even pickets and marches are becoming dangerous' (Lethabo, interview, June 2019). In tribal areas, organising a march requires permission from the office of the traditional authority, the police, as well as the local municipality. This bureaucratic permit process is put in place to halt all kinds of resistance.

Another young woman at a workshop stressed the power of the chief and his indunas (headmen) to allocate land and impose fines. She attended a public meeting in Fulani, organised by the mining corporation. 'The mining men told us that the traditional council gave them the authority to mine, but no one ever came to my house and asked my permission.' After the meeting, an induna visited her home and said, 'I don't like what you are saying. If you continue to say that mining might be bad, you and your family will be banned from this village, and you will have to pay a fine.' Asked why she never reported this to the police, she commented, 'No, you cannot go to the police station. You have to deal with it in a traditional, cultural way.' In the same workshop another participant commented, 'With their powerful traditional authority the chiefs rely on fear and intimidation to maintain power and control.' There are fears in mining-affected communities that the police collude with the chiefs; that they are bribed by the mine, instead of protecting residents. In Somkhele, Tendele Mining management instigated violence indirectly through linking resistance to job losses and bonus payments. In their affidavit to the High Court, Tendele mentioned that failure to relocate the 24 families from Ophondweni and Emalahleni would result in the loss of jobs. This is a form of domination which could generate submission and acquiescence. However, one woman leader in Makhasaneni said, 'We are not scared of dying, we even sleep with doors unlocked. If they kill us it will be known that we died fighting the mine' (cited by Yeni 2018: 16).

The support of coal-mining corporations by local authorities generally – not only in KwaZulu-Natal – is another major obstacle to resistance. For example, in justifying his decision to grant approval for coal mining to Atha-Africa Ventures in the Mabola Protected Environment, a government official maintained that the severely impoverished local communities 'would benefit directly both socially and economically from the mine' (cited in Bega 2017).

ECO-FEMINISM

Eco-feminism is a contested notion. It is claimed that 'eco-feminism is by no means a position or a theory but implies a wide-open field of enquiry' (Rigby 1998: 144). While encompassing a diversity of approaches, it opposes all forms of hierarchy and domination, stresses the exploitation of women and nature and frequently claims that women have a specific relationship to nature because the oppression of women and the exploitation of nature are intertwined. It is not embraced as a label, or a set of political beliefs, but as a form of solidarity with other women, a way of life, a way of practising a commitment to collective action for change, change which goes beyond the narrow conception of gender equality that characterises liberal feminism within the existing social order. Whereas few women we encountered during our research claim the identity of 'feminist', their lives demonstrate this commitment, their support for other women and their challenge to the individualising elitism of liberal feminism. They are concerned with collective empowerment rather than individual advancement.

Driven by a desire for survival, do these women's eco-feminist values and practices – a respectful, reciprocal relationship with nature and caring and solidarity – represent a form of resistance? Are they expressing in their actions and practices an understanding of radical eco-feminism? As Greta Gaard writes, 'Ecofeminism has been a theory and movement largely articulated by the activists themselves' (Gaard 2010: 648). It has been argued that 'it might seem reasonable for western academics to label some movements [of poor women in the global South] as feminist on the basis of their discourses, actions and values – despite the fact that not any of them identify as feminists. In many countries in the global south, it is not an easy or simple choice for movements to declare or define themselves as feminists' (Seppala 2016: 14). This is for a number of reasons that are relevant in Africa, such as increasing state violence, surveillance and intimidation, and because feminism often carries negative connotations.

The organisation WoMin operates in these mining-affected areas and promotes an explicitly eco-feminist agenda. WoMin is an NGO which operates throughout Africa with its main mission being 'to support the building of women's movements to challenge destructive extractivism and propose development alternatives that respond to most African women's needs'. The organisation has strong connections with grassroots organisations, especially in Mpumalanga and KwaZulu-Natal. Its logic is that African working-class and peasant women are the shock absorbers of the climate crisis and need to be involved in defining just solutions for people and the climate at a continental scale. They maintain that 'the African climate justice movement is weak and fragmented'. For this reason, they are committed to a char-ter-building and dialogue process. 'We see this as a key to support the strengthening of the climate movement and bringing women's voices and demands into the centre of thinking about the just transition as a development alternative.' They are com-mitted to struggling against the extractivist model of development, which extracts profits from scarce non-renewable resources, because, they note, extractivism is deeply patriarchal and racist.

In a recent document, 'Women building power', WoMin call for 'a gendered just transition' because 'the current energy system is unequal and unjust, leads to energy poverty and has to change' (WoMin 2016: 41). WoMin is presently mobilising for a Just Transition Charter with grassroots women throughout Africa. A meeting of a group of eco-feminists in July 2018 resulted in a draft of 26 principles titled 'The Mogale Declaration', which 'provides a working frame and a clear set of political demands', including:

- Ecological balance – a harmonious coexistence with nature
- Social and economic justice for all
- Food sovereignty
- Socialised renewable energy which benefits women
- Clean air and water
- Valuing and reclaiming African traditional knowledge
- Living ubuntu in our relations with each other and nature
- Land held as commons.[4]

The content of the charter will be built in a participatory process which involves asking women questions such as, 'What is the world you want?' This contrasts sharply with the values of neoliberalism, such as possessive individualism and acquisitiveness. For many eco-socialists, the goal is 'living well' rather than striving to live better at the expense of others. What is problematic is that the 'living' often ignores women's care work. This is why the preamble to the Mogale Declaration states, 'together we will define what just development and a fair transition from capitalist patriarch to a different social and economic order would look like' (WoMin 2019: 2). Too many charters and manifestos are not grounded in grassroots participation and many are gender blind.

WoMin is committed to participatory action research which 'enables women to carry out social investigations into their own issues and articulate the problems from their own perspectives' (WoMin 2017). They run annual feminist schools throughout the African continent and are organising in different ways, for example, a week-long camp of 80 women from mining-affected communities at Ogies in Mpumalanga. Sharing her experience of the camp, Beverley said, 'There were women of all ages from mines all over the country and we learned about things like climate change and renewable energy.' The camp involved women cooking their own food, sharing limited water and sleeping on the floor of a local church, because 'people are so poor in this area, we wanted to organise differently which didn't involve staying in expensive hotels ... instead we were practising simplicity and sharing' (Beverley, WoMin organiser, interview, July 2018).

There are flashes of a formal, organised commitment to eco-feminism in other initiatives. For example, another feminist organisation, the Rural Women's Assembly (RWA), formed in 2009, brings together some 500 community-based organisations working on food and land issues and is deeply committed to a just transition. It describes itself as 'a self-organised network or alliance of national rural women's movements, assemblies, grassroots organisations and chapters of mixed peasant unions, federations and movements across eight countries in the SADC [Southern African Development Community] region.'[5] Their strategies include running feminist schools, organising exchange visits throughout the region and promoting alternatives such as agroecology and seed saving as key components of a just transition. In their statement marking ten years of operating throughout southern Africa, the RWA stated, 'in this great diversity of language, culture, sexuality, histories and experiences, we have managed to forge unity and solidarity'. They are 'very committed to an eco-feminist methodology' which respects emotional work as part of social reproduction and 'demand that our connectedness to nature is respected ... all life should thrive. Everything is connected in the web of life' (RWA 2020). WoMin and RWA both operate feminist schools for local women which involve deepening local understandings of concepts such as climate justice and emphasise women's solidarity (see Azeez: chapter 2 of this volume).

This not only means collective empowerment rather than the individual advancement of women but also involves a redefinition of 'nature' in two senses: firstly, a rejection of 'nature' as the source of gender identities which subordinate women by 'naturalising' qualities of submission, and secondly, a rejection of the dualistic view of 'nature' as a discrete entity separate from society. The latter is not 'new' in that it draws on an integrated understanding of the nature–society relation as integral to many 'traditional' African cultures. However, in the instrumentalist, expansionist logic of neoliberal capitalism, nature is separate from humans, a store of resources for economic activities and a sink for waste products.

CONCLUSION

This chapter describes a context in which black working-class women are bearing the burdens of social reproduction intensified by climate shocks and the Covid-19 pandemic, as well as numerous injustices, violence and patriarchal power. They are also contesting these patterns of domination and exclusion, but there are many constraints. The zones of exclusion in which they live are replete with threats to their known worlds. They experience a multidimensional insecurity caused by both health threats from the pollution of soil, water and air by the coal mines and coal-fired power stations in the areas where they live, and now by the added threats of the Covid-19 pandemic. It is a level of insecurity both material – anxiety about where the next meal is coming from – and existential, about their futures with the closing of the coal mines and/or the spread of the pandemic. The physical distancing required by the state lockdowns has eroded social bonds, making mobilisation more difficult and blocking any sense of effective agency. This is the moment when a unifying narrative such as an African eco-feminism is needed.

Much environmental activism by these women is not framed as eco-feminism. But their struggle to survive in mining-affected communities represents an expression of an eco-feminism as a set of practices rather than as an identity. The eco-feminist values and practices of caring, a respectful, reciprocal relationship with nature, solidarity with other women, and commitment to transformative change and collective empowerment rather than individual advancement represent a form of localised resistance. As has been said of a different context, 'our very existence is the resistance'.

NOTES

1   University of Johannesburg Roundtable on Action against Climate Change, Johannesburg, 2 September 2020.
2   Social identities are multiple and oppression overlaps. It is important to understand how relations of domination reinforce one another but also are experienced differently, for example how black women experience racism differently from black men. However, the current usage of the notion of intersectionality is problematic because it potentially distracts from the class relations which shape the material conditions of the everyday.
3   All interviewee names used in this chapter are pseudonyms.
4   See https://womin.africa/mogale-declaration-living-the-future-now/.
5   See https://www.landportal.org/organization/rural-women%E2%80%99s-assembly-southern-africa.

REFERENCES

Action Aid. 2018. *Mining in South Africa: Whose Benefit and Whose Burden: Social Audit Baseline Report.* Johannesburg: Action Aid.
Bega, S. 2017. 'MEC facing court over mine approval', *Saturday Star*, 2 December. Accessed 22 August 2022, https://www.pressreader.com/south-africa/saturday-star-south-africa/20171202/281586650921299.
Bezanson, K. and Luxton, M. (eds). 2006. *Social Reproduction.* Quebec: McGill-Queen's University Press.
Capps, G. 2012. 'Victim of its own success? The platinum mining industry and the apartheid mineral property system in South Africa's political transition', *Review of African Political Economy* 39: 63–84.
Fakier, K. and Cock, J. 2009. 'A gendered analysis of the crisis of social reproduction in contemporary South Africa', *International Feminist Journal of Politics* 11 (3): 353–371.
Gaard, G. 2010. 'New directions for eco-feminism: Toward a more feminist ecocriticism', *Interdisciplinary Studies in Literature and Environment* 17 (4): 643–665.
Gedye, L. 2020. 'SA companies cash in on Covid-19', *New Frame*, 24 August. Accessed 8 June 2021, https://www.newframe.com/sa-companies-cash-in-on-covid-19/.
Genoways, T. 2014. *The Chain: Farm, Factory and the Fate of Our Food.* New York: HarperCollins.
Global Environmental Trust. 2020a. 'A threat more deadly than Covid-19', 2 May. Accessed 8 June 2021, http://globalenvironmentaltrust.org/a-threat-more-deadly-than-covid-19/.
Global Environmental Trust. 2020b. 'The killing of Somkhele environmental activist, Fikile Ntshangase', 23 October. Accessed 8 June 2021, http://globalenvironmentaltrust.org/the-killing-of-somkhele-environmental-activist-fikile-ntshangase/.
Hallowes, D. and Munnik, V. 2016. *The Destruction of the Highveld. Part 1: Digging Coal.* Pietermaritzburg: Groundwork.
Hallowes, D. and Munnik, V. 2017. *The Destruction of the Highveld. Part 2: Burning Coal.* Pietermaritzburg: Groundwork.
Hallowes, D. and Munnik, V. 2019. *Down to Zero: The Politics of Just Transition.* Pietermaritzburg: Groundwork.
Harrisberg, K. 2020. 'Murders of South African women surge as 9-week lockdown eases', *Global Citizen*, 23 June. Accessed 8 June 2021, https://www.globalcitizen.org/en/content/gender-violence-covid-19-lockdown-south-africa/.

Heywood, M. 2020. 'Covid-19 emergency and lockdown: What went wrong and what will it take to fix it?', *Daily Maverick*, 29 July. Accessed 23 June 2021, https://www.dailymaverick.co.za/article/2020-07-29-covid-19-emergency-lockdown-what-went-wrong-and-what-will-it-take-to-fix-it/.

Klein, N. 2011. 'Capitalism vs the climate', *The Nation*, 9 November. Accessed 23 June 2021, https://www.thenation.com/article/archive/capitalism-vs-climate/.

Luxton, M. 2006. 'Feminist political economy in Canada and the politics of social reproduction'. In K. Bezanson and M. Luxton (eds), *Social Reproduction*. Quebec: McGill-Queen's University Press.

Majavu, A. 2020. 'Police respond to rural water protests with bullets', *Mail & Guardian*, 14 July. Accessed 8 June 2021, https://mg.co.za/news/2020-07-14-police-respond-to-rural-water-protests-with-bullets/.

Merchant, C. 1990. *The Death of Nature*. New York: HarperCollins.

Nixon, R. 2011. *Slow Violence and the Environmentalism of the Poor*. Cambridge, MA: Harvard University Press.

Oelshinger, M. 2002. *The Idea of Wilderness: From Prehistory to the Age of Ecology*. New Haven: Yale University Press.

Ramabina, M. 2020. 'Coal mine's bid for KZN land puts compensation criteria to test', *Daily Maverick*, 26 May. Accessed 8 June 2021, https://www.dailymaverick.co.za/article/2020-05-26-coal-mines-bid-for-kzn-land-puts-compensation-criteria-to-test/.

Rigby, K. 1998. 'Women and nature revisited', *Arena Journal* 12: 144–178.

RWA (Rural Women's Assembly). 2020. 'Statement: Rural Women's Assembly: 10 years on'. Accessed 23 June 2021, https://alicenews.ces.uc.pt/?lang=1&id=28314.

Seppala, T. 2016. 'Feminizing resistance, decolonizing solidarity: Contesting neoliberal development in the global South', *Journal of Resistance Studies* 1 (2): 12– 47.

Shiva, V. 2014. *The Vandana Shiva Reader*. London: Zed Books.

Skosana, D. 2012. 'Why are chiefs recognised in South Africa's new democracy? Issues of legitimacy and contestation in local politics: A case study of chiefly and local government in Vaaltyn', unpublished MA thesis, University of the Witwatersrand, Johannesburg.

Skosana, D. 2021. 'Grave matters: Dispossession and the desecration of ancestral graves by mining corporations in South Africa', *Journal of Contemporary African Studies* 4 (1): 47–62.

Therborne, G. 2013. *The Killing Fields of Inequality*. Cambridge: Polity Press.

WoMin. 2016. *Women Building Power: Towards Climate and Energy Justice for Women in Africa*. Accessed 27 December 2002, https://womin.africa/download/women-building-power-towards-climate-energy-and-justice/.

WoMin. 2017. *No Longer a Life Worth Living*. Johannesburg: WoMin.

WoMin. 2019. *The Mogale Declaration: Living the Future Now*. Johannesburg: WoMin.

World Health Organization. 2022. *Global Health Observatory 2022*. Geneva: Word Health Organization.

Yeni, P. 2018. *Traditional leadership, violation of land rights, and resistance from below in Makhasaneni village, KwaZulu-Natal*. Working Paper, Mapungubwe Institute for Strategic Reflection, Johannesburg.

WOMEN AND FOOD SOVEREIGNTY: TACKLING HUNGER DURING COVID-19

Courtney Morgan and Jane Cherry

INTRODUCTION

Beyond the immediacy of hunger and the practical challenge of providing food to communities who have been denied access, hunger must also be interrogated through a Marxist and eco-feminist lens. Imperialism, colonialism and globalisation have all contributed to the destruction of the planet as well as indigenous culture and practice. In this chapter we look at how hunger is a manifestation of that capitalist destruction, and thus how food sovereignty as an alternative not only addresses hunger directly but also contributes to a movement against these systems.

The hunger crisis in South Africa, exacerbated by the 2014 drought, climate shocks and, more recently, the Covid-19 pandemic, has deepened powerlessness amongst communities, particularly women. However, food sovereignty responses to the crisis are providing a strong and viable alternative to the current food system, enabling communities to reclaim their power. As we show in this chapter, these responses by women in South Africa are inherently eco-feminist (a strand of emergent emancipatory feminism), because they challenge patriarchal capitalism while building their own emancipatory food pathways.

We begin the chapter by introducing food sovereignty and the unique way in which it has been translated locally by the South African Food Sovereignty Campaign (SAFSC). We then highlight the links between food sovereignty and eco-feminism and thereafter outline the ways in which women experience crises in society, the (gendered) powerlessness of hunger, and the effects this has on social reproduction. To illustrate the transformative potential of food sovereignty, we show how food sovereignty interventions and actors in South Africa are responding to the hunger crisis (pre- and during Covid-19) to build an alternative food system by wielding symbolic, direct, movement and structural power. We also show how food sovereignty is giving power to women farmers or activists in the SAFSC, as they are in turn developing, informing and deepening food sovereignty pathways in South Africa.

Despite numerous challenges, women interviewed in this chapter are building grassroots power through food sovereignty and in doing so are gradually dismantling the racialised, patriarchal and neoliberal food system through their transformative practices. This approach is in contrast to elite, liberal feminism, which assumes gender equality can be achieved in the existing neoliberal economic and food system. The approach can further be described as eco-feminism because food sovereignty is deeply cognisant of nature's processes, and the practice of agro-ecology (working with rather than against nature to produce food) is central to these women's practices and to the food sovereignty approach in South Africa and internationally.[1]

THE FOOD SOVEREIGNTY ALTERNATIVE

The emergence of food sovereignty

Food sovereignty emerged as a response to the multiple crises facing society, including inequality, hunger, obesity, landlessness, unemployment and environmental and social crises. In particular, food sovereignty arose as a counter-movement and alternative to the globalisation of the neoliberal model of agriculture and the crisis-laden corporate-controlled food regime (Akram-Lodhi 2013: 2; De Schutter 2015; Desmarais 2003; Rosset 2008; McMichael 2014). The history of the international food sovereignty movement can be traced back to 1993, from both the mobilisation of campesinos in Costa Rica and the protests of small-scale farmers in Karnataka, India (De Schutter 2015). However, it was in 1996 that La Via Campesina (the way of the peasant), an international peasant and farmer movement of now over 200 million members from 182 organisations,[2] termed their counter-approach to the existing food system 'food sovereignty'. La Via Campesina defines food sovereignty as 'the right of peoples to healthy and culturally appropriate food produced through ecologically sound and sustainable methods, and their right to define their own food and agriculture systems. It puts the aspirations of those who produce, distribute and consume food at the heart of food systems and policies rather than the demands of markets and corporations' (Nyeleni Forum for Food Sovereignty 2007: 1).

La Via Campesina emerged in 1993 towards the end of the Uruguay Round of the General Agreement on Tariffs and Trade (GATT) where the Trade Related Intellectual Property Rights (TRIPS) agreement was signed. This agreement would gradually erode farmers' rights and power by prioritising corporate interests in developing countries. This began neoliberal efforts to push the vulnerable to the edges of society, increasingly leaning on globalised models of production. As a response, peasants and farm organisations vowed to collectively resist the globalisation of agriculture and ensure that the voices of small-scale food producers of the world would be heard. Most importantly, resistance included developing and strengthening viable alternatives (Desmarais 2003), which would involve restructuring food production and consumption at the local, national and global levels (Rosset 2008) and building a new food system through food sovereignty at the local level.

Food sovereignty in South Africa
Calls made almost 30 years ago by rural peasants are echoed all over the world as the food system becomes more and more globalised, and as a result, volatile, inaccessible and unsustainable. This has become particularly clear during the Covid-19 pandemic. In South Africa the state's responses have not been sufficient to address the deepening hunger crisis (and associated powerlessness) that is haunting millions of the population. As a result, these calls for food sovereignty are gaining traction – but they are not new. Even prior to Covid-19 there were a number of localised and national food sovereignty interventions. In this chapter we focus on the SAFSC and some of its activists.

Since its launch as a national campaign in 2015, the SAFSC has been campaigning consistently to oppose the state and capital's false solutions to hunger and confront them with the systemic roots of hunger and the climate crisis. At the same time, it has been advancing food sovereignty alternatives from below in communities, villages, towns and cities. It has also provided a unified platform for communities, movements and organisations to champion food sovereignty and has produced a number of activist tools,[3] including a People's Food Sovereignty Act[4] to guide campaigns.

The conception of food sovereignty emerging from SAFSC practice is unique in that it brings together the solidarity economy, agroecology, worker cooperatives, democratic planning and a strong thrust for climate justice; it builds on local knowledge and experience and actively strengthens and builds examples of food sovereignty, particularly in the form of food sovereignty hubs, demonstration sites and agroecological community and household food gardens. Most of these initiatives are led by women in their communities and the SAFSC has amplified their practices and voices. Such efforts to build and strengthen movements around alternatives and collective struggle are an integral part of reclaiming power through food sovereignty (Satgar and Cherry 2019: 6). The SAFSC's conception of food sovereignty is thus locally shaped and builds transformative pathways which lay the basis for a food sovereignty system that deepens the just transition to sustain life in a climate-driven world (Satgar and Cherry 2019: 2).

RECLAIMING POWER: ECO-FEMINISM AND FOOD SOVEREIGNTY

Food sovereignty as power

Through struggle, food sovereignty has evolved over the years and taken different forms, spreading from the international to the local, and the urban to the rural (De Schutter 2015). In practice, food sovereignty is place based and tailored to the local context. Food sovereignty presents a counter to the dominant 'food security' paradigm to address hunger, which includes limited nuances about the lived experiences of people, especially those with differentiated socio-economic situations due to historical dispossession and exploitation. Food security also does not address power in the food system, but merely patches up a broken system with entitlements (Patel 2012).

Food sovereignty can be viewed not only as practical, everyday access to food but also as a decolonising process. Although food sovereignty is relevant to everybody, it is particularly relevant for indigenous peoples around the world, who have used food, agricultural practice and harvesting methods as a tool for decolonisation. It also provides an opportunity for indigenous communities to address destructive processes of colonialism and globalisation, by restoring cultural practices, defending indigenous land rights and honouring cultural practices of passing down recipes, seed and methods of growing from generation to generation. It has the power to work against systems such as globalisation and imperialism, which disempower and destroy cultures and languages, undermining local knowledge and tradition, in order to maintain and restore indigenous methods of living, through food (Ferguson et al. 2022). While we cannot go into the intricacies of it here, it must be noted that the links that colonialism and globalisation have, through the capitalism model, to the restructuring of society have shifted the way that communities operate. This also has interesting implications for work and labour, and for how indigenous communities, through food sovereignty, push against and interact with the globalised, capitalist system (Ferguson et al. 2022). There is a deep link between the expropriation and dispossession of land through capitalism, and the theft of indigenous cultures and food systems. Food sovereignty, in the way that it reconstructs power and questions patriarchal and capitalist definitions of work, time management and productivity, undercuts this and opposes oppressive systems (Tilzey 2017).

Eco-feminism and food sovereignty

Eco-feminism, much like feminism itself, has many strands and has been co-opted by a number of elite groups who often neglect the more nuanced perspective of the concept, held by those who are most vulnerable. The strand of eco-feminism used in this chapter is an emancipatory eco-feminism that connects the domination of women and the domination of the environment (Banerjee and Bell 2007) and recognises the interconnectedness of gender, class and race. This understanding takes from the environmental movement that the human population has transformed the environment, and borrows from the feminist movement that society subjugates women; it then understands that these two forms of domination are linked, both existing in a patriarchal, racialised and neoliberal system. A radical, inclusive form of eco-feminism, a socialist eco-feminism rejects the liberal interpretation of eco-feminism that sees women as being spiritually and biologically linked to the earth as life-giving beings, but rather sees the exploitation of both as a result of an exploitative and masculinist capitalist system (Gaard 2015). The concept is particularly relevant to food and food sovereignty, given that women make up around 60 to 80 per cent of food producers in the global South, but are often not recognised as an integral part of the food system. Food sovereignty forms part of a longer, more entrenched movement of resistance building power against colonisation and other oppressive systems. In providing a space for the questioning of oppressive systems, it is also seen as an eco-feminist tool. Due to some of the obstacles spoken about later in the chapter, food sovereignty efforts have to recognise the agricultural roles that women play, as well as intentionally attempt to dismantle the structures that oppress women, including the globalised food system. Essentially, a feminist approach to the food system reveals the power dynamics that exist in the global system, but an eco-feminist approach provides a pathway to dismantle that system and build an entirely new one, where women's roles in the agricultural system are valued and encouraged with food sovereignty at its centre (Ellinger-Locke 2011). In the same way that food sovereignty reconstructs power dynamics in a capitalist system that profits off the human experience, it reconstructs power dynamics for women in indigenous communities, in an equally patriarchal system. The food sovereignty movement not only creates different forms of ownership within the food system, thus building sovereignty, but also intersects with other efforts to build power and sovereignty through gender, land, water and access struggles. The reconstructions of definitions of autonomy by communities continue to push back at the exclusions of the patriarchal and globalised system (Patel and Grey 2015). Eco-feminism also relates to food sovereignty because of the way in which both emerge as alternative and decolonial practices. In the face of capitalism, which aims to alienate humans from nature, eco-feminism seems to reinforce human–nature connections; similarly, in a food system that alienates people from food production, food sovereignty seeks to reconnect people to it.

As Vandana Shiva (2004) points out, food sovereignty is also a rights matter: it addresses the fundamental human right to food, it secures the rights of farmers to work, and it affirms land rights and the right to water as the commons. Securing the rights of vulnerable groups is also fundamental to the feminist movement. Food sovereignty and the right to food is thus intricately linked to other feminist struggles, including the crisis of social reproduction and how it relates to hunger.

HUNGER AND THE CRISIS OF SOCIAL REPRODUCTION BEFORE AND DURING COVID-19

Social reproduction theory

Social reproduction is a question that feminists have been grappling with for decades. Throughout history there has been debate as to how the feminist movement should move forward and how best to achieve equality. Early understandings of feminism thought that the answer was to open up the labour market to women. While this is important, socialist feminists saw a more nuanced answer to this, arguing that it was not just a matter of moving women from the household to the workplace but rather, that labour itself needed to be reorganised and that work within the household should be recognised as labour (Ferguson 2020). From a political economy perspective, the work that women do within the household contributes to the overall wealth of society and therefore is eligible for compensation – this is the foundation of social reproductive feminism and contributes to capitalist reproduction. Fundamentally, there needs to be a link between capitalism and gender inequality, and this task should be taken up by socialists. One of the first things that needs to be done is to denaturalise household work as women's work; there needs to be an understanding that any work that exerts a skill, the mind or muscles contributes to the production of society. This includes cleaning, child rearing and, particularly relevant to this case, the growing, collection and preparation of food.

The gendered nature of hunger

There is a misconception about hunger: often, it is less about a total shortage or lack of food production and more about access and the claim that people have over the food that is available (Patel 2012). When analysing the hunger crisis, it is important to not just look at the availability of food itself, but to analyse it in the context of social and political conditions which construct power dynamics in society, which then extend to food and access to it. Once the link between power and hunger is clearly made, the link between gender and hunger also becomes clear, given the patriarchal nature of our society. If a gendered approach to hunger is not taken, and a band-aid approach of simply handing out food is pursued, the disempowerment that comes with hunger is not addressed. Food sovereignty in practice and theory is more effective in addressing disempowerment because it calls for people to hold the power to create their own food systems.

Women are fundamentally linked to disempowerment, and in fact make up around 60 per cent of the undernourished. Thus a truly democratic process around the hunger crisis must include women's rights (Patel 2012: 2). Women's rights are important, not only because women make up the majority of the undernourished, but because they are also structurally disadvantaged in the food production process, facing barriers to owning land and farming facilities, particularly in the traditional setting.

The current system and the development paradigm, according to Vandana Shiva, has caused environmental decline as well as poverty, particularly for women (Graham 1996). Women are integrally linked to food, through managing seeds, working the ground and often harvesting the food. Women are also usually the ones who prepare the food, which means that traditionally, women are deeply connected to food from its growth to its consumption (Navin 2015).

How does food sovereignty address the crisis of social reproduction?

La Via Campesina is a campaign that has inspired millions of peasant farmers and, equally importantly, it takes gender justice seriously. Even in their foundational conceptualisations of food sovereignty, a feminist orientation was taken – this is illustrated in La Via Campesina's three main thrusts, all of which seek to give power to and centre the needs and rights of women.

Because so many people rely on food directly from the earth and because this has largely been the responsibility of women, the discussion around food sovereignty and gender justice cannot just be theoretical; the lived experience of people on the ground must be prioritised.

Food and hunger is also a deeply political issue, particularly in South Africa, given its history of land dispossession and spatial planning under the apartheid regime. In South Africa, there are around 2.87 million agricultural households, 2.62 million of which belong to black Africans growing food in backyard gardens (Ngcoya and Kumarakulasingam 2017). From afar it may seem that black Africans in South Africa dominate the agricultural system but, as in many other parts of the South African society, there is a dual system. South Africa has a highly technical, well-funded, commercial agricultural sector that is dominated by a small group of white farmers, which is a legacy from apartheid. This dual system is dominated by racialised and patriarchal forms of land ownership, access and opportunity. Food sovereignty provides a necessary opportunity for transformation because it calls for 'an alternative food system based on economically viable, ecologically sustainable, farmer-driven agriculture grounded in the metaphysical and social worlds of those who work the soil' (Ngcoya and Kumarakulasingam 2017: 485). Examining lived experience is helpful in understanding food sovereignty because it can reflect the nuances of its practices happening locally on the ground, particularly among women. This allows a more finely grained understanding of hunger.

Women in crisis: Hunger and Covid-19 in South Africa

During the national lockdown in South Africa, which was a response to the Covid-19 pandemic, the roles of women in communities became more difficult.[5] The Pietermaritzburg Economic Justice and Dignity (PMBEJD) group conducted research around this, using the household food basket as a basis. This basket was developed with women in the community and consisted of various basic food items such as rice, cake flour, white sugar, sugar beans and so on. From March 2020 to March 2021, the price of the basket rose from R3 321 to R4 039 – an increase of R718 or 21 per cent, which is significant when compared to the increase from March 2019 to March 2020, which was just 3.6 per cent (PMBEJD 2020, 2021). The basket was made up of items that families were buying, which did not necessarily meet nutrition requirements – in fact, the disparity between what families were buying and what families should buy in order to meet nutrition requirements created a price difference of over R800. In the context of the lockdown, with many precarious workers losing income and opportunities for additional income very difficult to find, the hunger crisis worsened.

But the hunger crisis is just one aspect of the difficulties created by the Covid-19 pandemic. There is also a gender aspect, in that women are bearing the brunt of these difficulties, along with those of other crises. Because of the traditional gender roles which many households still abide by, women are responsible for buying and preparing the food, and with prices increasing and household income decreasing, women are under more stress to make sure there is food on the table. This manifests in a number of ways: firstly, because workers and children were home more during the lockdown, women had to buy more food than they used to because food ran out faster than it usually did (PMBEJD 2020). Secondly, because of travel restrictions, women could not go to a number of shops looking for deals and sales; they were forced to buy all their goods from one store, driving up the price. Thirdly, this increased spending meant that women were unable to save and actually got into debt just to be able to purchase monthly groceries. Less money for food also means that women make tough food choices, for themselves and their families, by buying foods that are filling rather than nutritious, further compromising the health of families. Furthermore, in addition to the food basket, there was also the increased cost of household hygiene products such as additional soaps and bleach required to prevent the spread or contraction of Covid-19. This responsibility of reproducing the household falls on women, and often, when food is scarce, they will go hungry, compromising their own health and increasing their vulnerability (Gaard 2015). Clearly, the Covid-19 pandemic has exposed many of the inequalities in South Africa, and in many cases has exacerbated them, as illustrated by the PMBEJD research.

Unemployment was also impacted by the Covid-19 pandemic, according to the National Income Dynamics Study-Coronavirus Rapid Mobile (NIDS-CRAM) survey, which found that an approximate three million people had lost their jobs in the months from February to April 2020. Of those, two million were women, even though women had made up less than half of the workforce before the lockdown, in February (Spaull et al. 2020: 5). What this means is that women are not only already at a disadvantage, holding a lower proportion of the job market, but also experienced a larger proportion of the job losses as a result of the Covid-19 pandemic. The NIDS-CRAM report terms this a 'double disadvantage' (Spaull et al. 2020: 5). This decrease in employment for women also impacts hunger in households. Forty-seven per cent of the respondents surveyed in the report stated that in April 2020, their households had run out of money for food, which is significantly higher than the 21 per cent of households who reported the same thing the year before. Wave 2 of the NIDS-CRAM research showed a 27 per cent decline in hunger among the respondents (Spaull et al. 2020). Although this shows an improvement, the level of hunger is still significantly higher than pre-Covid-19 levels. A report by the Institute for Economic Justice (IEJ), also in relation to the Covid-19 pandemic, states that there is a need for South Africa to make an equitable reopening and recovery that gives the necessary support to vulnerable groups in society, including women. The recommendation is to reopen the economy in a way that mitigates the vulnerability of social groups in a number of ways (Smith et al. 2020). One of these ways is to alleviate the stress on women by increasing incomes of frontline workers, providing income support, increasing the child support grant as well as creating safer spaces for childcare. Support for women also requires that gender-based violence is addressed. The IEJ is clear that vulnerable communities, and women specifically, are 'victims of the social crisis engendered by the Covid-19 outbreak' (Smith et al. 2020: 6), yet women are vulnerable to both the social and economic crises. Women often take on extra responsibilities in the household, including care work, and this becomes more of a burden during a pandemic when care and education facilities are closed. Hunger and the Covid-19 pandemic are both examples of crises which have affected women disproportionately.

BUILDING ALTERNATIVE FORMS OF POWER

The SAFSC's hub and pathway approach during Covid-19

The SAFSC is a national campaign that works at local levels. One of its key strategic thrusts is to promote and strengthen local-level food sovereignty pathways in communities, villages, towns and cities to show that another food system is possible. A number of SAFSC partners have actively been deepening their local food sovereignty practices by setting up agroecology gardens and demonstration sites, supporting local food systems and sharing experiences and lessons with one another. Some organisations have also focused on establishing food sovereignty hubs, for example the Wits Food Sovereignty Centre pilot site. This is a project initiated by the Co-operative and Policy Alternative Centre and the Wits Citizenship and Community Outreach programme, and comprises agroecological gardens; a farmers' market; an eco-demonstration site, including renewable energy and water harvesting; a communal kitchen and a food sovereignty training and learning space. The vision of the pilot site is to end hunger at the University of the Witwatersrand (Wits), but also to serve as an example to other leading institutions of how food sovereignty can be achieved. Part of the strategy proposed by the SAFSC is to replicate this hub model across the country in order to support small-scale household food gardeners and community farmers, thus redistributing power in the corporate-owned food system.

With the urgency of sustenance needs presented by the Covid-19 pandemic, the SAFSC used the moment to build on its past successes and strengthen its strategic emphasis on pathways, hubs and commoning (making food and land, seed and water for food production more freely accessible). The SAFSC also deepened partnerships with like-minded organisations with the aim of strengthening the climate justice and food sovereignty movements in South Africa. There are a number of inspiring initiatives and food sovereignty actors in South Africa who were well placed to respond to the hunger crisis during the Covid-19 pandemic. One example is the Philippi Horticulture Area Food and Farming Campaign's efforts. The campaign is embedded in the community of Philippi, Cape Town, and is aware of who the vulnerable are. Through its networks, it invited donations from the public so that the campaign could purchase food from local agroecological food growers and give it to those in need. Other examples include Elsies River youth who set up a community food garden to feed the hungry in their community, including the elderly. Ukuvuna Harvests, an organisation based in Johannesburg, works with a number of projects in South Africa and has formed a network of 2 300 farmers, with clusters and hubs in the districts where they work to offer demonstrations and share knowledge and seedlings where possible. The Southern Centre for Land Change is active in the Karoo and works with communities and small-scale farmers to assist with setting up communal gardens, among other campaigns. The organisation scaled up its work during the Covid-19 pandemic and has also initiated a number of food sovereignty hubs in the communities it works with.

However, many initiatives and partners in the SAFSC have faced numerous challenges such as lack of water for growing food (as a result of the recent drought and government mismanagement), or restricted movement during lockdown level 5, which prevented them from visiting the farm or community site, for example. It is thus clear that food sovereignty approaches are not yet fully integrated into an alternative food system and have suffered setbacks as a result. Furthermore, an alternative food sovereignty pathway vision cannot be achieved overnight; its success is dependent on a supportive, accountable and democratic state and a host of other preconditions, including people's power.

A food sovereignty vision for South Africa, presented to the Solidarity Fund[6] by the SAFSC (2020) and the National Food Crisis Forum (which the SAFSC established in the early months of the Covid-19 pandemic), proposes a solidarity partnership between the state, the Solidarity Fund and grassroots organisations. One key strategic element of this vision is 'unlocking the food commons and scaling up food sovereignty pathways' (SAFSC 2020: 3). This, according to the SAFSC, is a key precondition for a transition to food sovereignty in South Africa. More specifically, 'food sovereignty pathways and hubs that advance agro-ecological practice, commoning, demonstrate socially owned renewable energy, zero waste and solidarity economy practices are crucial. This would ensure eco-centric production and consumption are connected for localised, people-centred food sovereignty systems' (SAFSC 2020: 3–4). The strategy proposes setting up 1 000 hubs that would be well equipped to respond with resilience to future shocks as communities would be able to feed themselves, make decisions and manage resources and potential shortages democratically.

A democratic, localised food system is an important response to a heating world as it promotes ecocentric agricultural practices through agroecology. As climate change ushers in new living conditions, local farmers (particularly women) who have adapted their growing processes through the use of local and indigenous knowledge and indigenous seeds that are more resilient to shocks will feed our communities, not food corporations in a crisis-ridden food system, and not a centralised government which is already failing us.

Responding to the crisis: Women practising food sovereignty

For this chapter, we conducted seven telephonic or electronic interviews with women who are involved in food sovereignty practices, many of whom are members of the SAFSC. Some of the women are small-scale farmers, some grassroots and community activists, and some have only recently started out in the food sovereignty space.[7] We profile five of these women below.

Magda Campbell is a small-scale farmer operating in the Mitchells Plain area of Cape Town. She runs a food garden at Beacon School for learners with special education needs (LSEN). She has also done extensive work in the area creating more spaces like the Beacon School food garden to ensure that the community has a space for teaching and learning about food gardens, health and business, in addition to having access to nutritious food. Her life changed drastically after she started her involvement with the SAFSC: she became aware of what is happening in the global food system, and her role as a food producer is making a difference to the current unjust system. She is passionate about her vision to change people's mindsets and to empower the community, and she is doing just that as she makes meaningful change in her community. She, in turn, feels empowered by all the knowledge, support and networks she has gained through engaging in this work. During the Covid-19 pandemic and various stages of the resultant lockdown, she had limited access to her food garden and witnessed her community struggle with increased hunger. This inspired her to run workshops with the people in her area, helping them to start their own home gardens that would provide their community with fresh vegetables, and offering skills development through food sovereignty.

Thembi Nxumalo is a small-scale farmer in Johannesburg; she focuses on organic vegetables and herbs, and also has a nursery and grows fruit trees. Once she became involved in the food sovereignty space, she was able to feed her family and also sell surplus produce to the community. Since her involvement in growing food, her family has also become involved and she is able to make an additional living from their food garden. She feels empowered by her work because she is able to support herself, earn a living and knows she is food secure. However, the Covid-19 pandemic and lockdown affected her farm and the market for her produce. It became difficult to procure resources for planting and to enter the market to sell her produce to restaurants, which had closed down, as well as to community members who had lost their income. She unfortunately lost a lot of income from the farm during this time, but she was still able to donate fresh produce to those in need. She also helped homes in the area to start their own food gardens during the pandemic.

Nosintu Mcimeli is a community organiser and founder of Abanebhongo Persons with Disabilities, an NGO which offers care, education, support and advocacy for persons with disabilities in the rural areas of Nqamakwe, Eastern Cape. Amongst other things, Nosintu started an enviro-gardening project in her village. She has drastically changed her life through food sovereignty practices as she is now able to access fresh produce from her garden, and as a result has reduced travel (and associated) costs to town, where she would usually buy fresh produce. She has sparked an interest in the community about food sovereignty, to the extent that they are increasingly becoming involved in projects and she feels empowered as a result. Nosintu suffered greatly during the Covid-19 pandemic, losing training opportunities, as well as engagements and interactions with others in the space, due to restricted travel. She also saw a massive impact on her community, where families were unable to work or help the community, and were also affected by food price increases. Despite the harsh conditions, she was able to start and maintain a community soup kitchen during the lockdown and managed to distribute some groceries to needy households.

Davine Cloete is a community organiser, activist and small-scale farmer in Lutzville on the West Coast. She initiated the West Coast Food Sovereignty and Solidarity Forum in 2015 and has since been actively campaigning for food sovereignty, as well as mobilising to push back harmful mining activities at the coastal areas nearby. Davine has been working with women in her community to develop women's groups to address gender-based violence in her area and women's fisher-folk groups to promote agroecology, food sovereignty and to establish food gardens. During the pandemic Davine and the Forum scaled up their work in the community, campaigning to bring awareness about the drought, water scarcity and climate change and, through community forums, encouraging people not to be used by political parties (for example by giving the parties votes during elections in exchange for promises that never materialise) but rather to focus on growing agroecologically for the next time a pandemic hits. The Forum also reached out to other groups in the nearby communities, such as the Doringbaai women and youth fisherfolk, to provide training in and raise awareness about agroecology and food sovereignty with their members. Davine is also a member of the Landless People's Movement in South Africa, and part of the global La Via Campesina network. In 2017 she was elected onto the coordinating committee of La Via Campesina Eastern Africa Region and she is also part of the Climate Justice and Agroecology Collective of La Via Campesina.

Dorah Marema is a community activist in Johannesburg who supports small-holder farmers through building capacity, providing training and other skills development. Her life has changed since her work began in the food sovereignty space, because she feels she is now more aware of what she is consuming and is able to understand and teach others about the various roles that people play in the food system. She is also more aware of the challenges and practices of small-scale farmers, and because of this she tries to consume more from small-scale producers. She feels empowered not only personally as a consumer, but also because she is able to empower others with the knowledge she can share. Due to the Covid-19 pandemic and lockdown, Dorah was unable to continue with the training workshops she conducts, but she found herself focusing on other aspects of her work, such as mentoring and training smallholder farmers to be part of the solution, namely, to continue production and provide food for communities in need. She was able to organise and mobilise extensively for food to reach communities, as well as for these communities to receive seedlings along with groceries and hot meals. She also made other provisions for teaching and training, assisting households and churches to set up food gardens, visiting small-scale farms and holding training sessions under Covid-19 guidelines.

Women wielding power

The women that we interviewed, as individuals, food producers, activists in their communities or as partners in the SAFSC, are not only advancing their own freedom from the capitalist food system and providing much-needed relief and long-term solutions to hunger in their communities. Their food sovereignty approach has a broader scope. To them, food sovereignty is about the right to create an alternative food system, freedom to produce their own nutritious food and to be in control of their health. Yet, more than that, 'it is an undeniable right to be in control of one's food, and therefore, have control over one's own life … once one starts to actively explore and question the systems at play that directly intersect with one's life – as opposed to an interaction of neutral acceptance – one can start to engage with a greater responsibility as part of a society and a democracy' (Isabella Potenza, interview, August 2020); and simply put 'it means justice' (Mutshidzi Ratshibvumo, interview, August 2020). As we show below, these women are questioning and confronting the systems that shape their lives, promoting justice and emancipation, and are further wielding different types of power, namely movement power, structural power, direct power and symbolic power.[8]

Movement power is about creating a space for convergence amongst a broad base of actors working towards achieving a specific vision (COPAC 2015: 41). As members of the SAFSC, these women are contributing to movement power, and furthering this in their communities. The SAFSC is a loose alliance that enables initiatives from various participating organisations and activists all working in their own spaces to converge on necessary issues and to catalyse food sovereignty alliances. Its focus during the Covid-19 pandemic, in particular the focus on strengthening and building food sovereignty pathways, was also an approach to strengthen the movement. Food sovereignty encouraged these women to understand the political implications of their actions and to share their knowledge with their families and communities, establishing local food sovereignty networks and thus deepening the national movement as a whole. During the Covid-19 pandemic, the SAFSC constituted the National Food Crisis Forum which, at the beginning of lockdown, met once a week to discuss the hunger crisis and associated campaigns. This was a key moment, when important solidarities were built with those giving food relief, those who were involved in food commons projects and communities affected by water issues. It was a space of debate and mobilisation where the group, in its messaging through press releases, consistently called for the democratisation of the Disaster Management Act, the establishment of food sovereignty hubs, support for local struggles and a universal basic income grant. The women who have historically been key to the food sovereignty campaign played an equally important role in the National Food Crisis Forum by involving their communities in the processes (such as mapping water issues), as well as reporting back on local struggles.

Structural power is about building, from the grassroots, alternative pathways for production, consumption, markets, financing and ways of living (COPAC 2015: 41). By wielding structural power, women can show that in practice they are able to meet their needs through food sovereignty practices, such as growing their own food, saving seeds, managing water, providing local markets for selling produce and also scaling these up (Satgar and Cherry 2019: 15). The women we interviewed are doing this in their communities as they meet their needs through growing fresh produce, and strengthen capacity through mentoring and teaching others in their communities how to do the same, thus building alternative food sovereignty pathways. The lockdown has revealed the need and potential for alternative food sovereignty avenues and systems. For example, farmers interviewed were initially forbidden to travel to their farms, and were not able to access markets; however, as the lockdown eased and they were able to visit their farms, they had to set up alternative avenues for markets. In addition, their usual customers were unable to buy their food due to loss of income, or in some cases, they were restaurants that were unable to trade during lockdown and had no need to purchase produce. Alternative avenues included setting up systems for donors to purchase from small-scale farmers to supply food relief efforts, or promoting food commons, where farmers would donate excess produce to share and redistribute amongst their communities. In addition, there has been a surge in the establishment of small-scale gardens and community food gardens. Food gardens are increasingly being viewed as a means to become independent from the current food system, with its increasing food prices. Many of the women we interviewed are directly involved in food relief, but go further to assist community members, family members, churches, community centres and so forth to set up food gardens. These localised food production sites have served to aid the broader community, particularly in rural areas, as people are able to access nutritious fresh produce in their communities without having to travel far to retailers in the towns. Despite the very real challenges that the pandemic and lockdown have brought to individuals, families and communities, such as financial and psychological suffering, job losses, hunger, closure of businesses and so forth, all the women interviewed now have a positive outlook. They are humbled and at the same time proud of community members' selfless responses to the crisis. There is a strong sense of community and solidarity as people have come together to implement short- and long-term solutions to the various crises that are ravaging communities. In communities of need, Dorah sees great potential in the food sovereignty systems she is helping promote. She argues that 'people's lives will be much better post-Covid if they can just be supported through this now' (Dorah Marema, interview, August 2020). Through the SAFSC and the National

Food Crisis Forum, other structural interventions, often led by women, were also undertaken during the pandemic. The South African Informal Traders Alliance, led by Rosheda Muller, became an ally with the campaign when they called on the City of Cape Town to unlock the commons and allow trade in a well-known open space. This was crucial, not only for those traders who had lost their livelihood, but also for consumers, mainly women who had previously relied on this informal market to meet their families' food needs. With informal spaces and the commons being closed off, the ability of women to reproduce the household became more difficult, as was illustrated by the PMBEJD in their research reports.

Direct power includes the methods used to ensure that food sovereignty gains traction among the public. This can be done through mass campaigns, marches, education and awareness-raising (COPAC 2015). However, mass campaigns are not the only means to influence public awareness. The Covid-19 pandemic and lockdown exposed weaknesses in the existing food system, and food sovereignty has emerged as a viable alternative during this time. The SAFSC and National Food Crisis Forum also consistently called for prioritisation of the hunger crisis, most felt by women, highlighting the need for food relief to be supported on the ground; they established a food commons map to locate and profile existing and new food commons initiatives across the country;[9] they hosted assemblies with communities who had listed their communities as 'water stressed' on the SAFSC crowd-sourced map[10] and consistently campaigned for a universal basic income grant, a financial intervention that could further empower women to not only reproduce their household but also create financial independence in a patriarchal system that often encourages dependency. These interventions generated media interest and coverage, which further increased the reach of food sovereignty ideas and alternatives. In addition, the SAFSC hosted eight free online workshops and seminars on how to establish one's own food garden using minimal input and agroecological methods.[11] All these initiatives were integral to building direct power during the pandemic. Many women and other vulnerable groups attended these online workshops and were empowered by the knowledge exchange. This was integral because it contributed to the empowerment of groups that are often excluded from formal spaces of learning. The women we interviewed are strengthening direct power in their spaces of work through promoting food sovereignty and speaking out about current injustices and the need for alternatives. These women have also become spokespeople for those in need, and are proving to their communities that the supply of hand-outs is insufficient. Their approaches of strengthening local food systems and working with communities is bringing this alternative to light. Their successes are telling the food sovereignty story, in some ways, more powerfully than a mass campaign would. In the process, they are sharing and deepening the principles of food sovereignty, thus also promoting symbolic power.

Symbolic power is about the values, principles, vision and practices that an ideal represents. It is about symbolic actions that provide glimpses of these values and provide hope, but also about living examples to show that an alternative food system based on the foundations of food sovereignty, including democratic control of the food system, is possible (COPAC 2015: 41). The women whom we interviewed have promoted symbolic power as they share the values and ideals of solidarity and a sense of community, develop an understanding of the decommodification of food, make use of and promote agroecological practices, and take control of their food system (production, distribution, consumption) in their efforts to feed themselves, their communities and those in need, particularly during the Covid-19 pandemic and lockdown. These values are not new, but have been strengthened during the Covid-19 pandemic as women have realised that the commercial food system is not structured to meet their needs. In this context, women have started envisioning new systems, 'dreaming and listening to their dreams' and 'rebuilding South Africa' (Dorah Marema, interview, August 2020). According to Dorah, 'These are the things that make people want to stand up and rebuild.'

A number of initiatives that the women interviewed have been involved in can be characterised as models of symbolic power. Two notable interventions are the People's Food Sovereignty Act and the Climate Justice Charter for South Africa.[12] The Act was created through a process of consultation and later adopted at a People's Assembly. Although the Act does present a tangible expression of an alternative food system, it is more significant symbolically as is reflects people's power. Similarly, the Climate Justice Charter presents concrete examples of alternative societies but is also an illustration of people's power through its inception, consultation process (with various groups including eco-feminists), writing and editing. The Climate Justice Charter is not just about the physical document; it is also a representation of the grassroots movement behind it that has continued through its creation. The launch of this document took place at an eco-feminist event, where participants heard from leading eco-feminists in South Africa.[13] Some of the sentiments shared by the eco-feminists at the launch were that women are the shock absorbers of the various crises that come with the climate crisis and that particularly black rural women are highly exploited and also burdened with providing for their families, which makes them even more vulnerable to the uncertainties around climate change. These are consistent with the perspectives of those involved with writing the charter and eco-feminist discourse in general. The consultations and viewpoints that informed the writing of both the Act and the charter had significant contributions from eco-feminists and other grassroots feminist forces. All these interventions and realities on the ground reinforce the notion that women are not just passive victims of the system, but are also active and crucial actors in communities, providing and shaping solutions at the local and national levels.

CONCLUSION

Through both the practices of these women in South Africa and the experiences of La Via Campesina globally, it is clear that women have an integral role to play in the food system, and beyond. We have illustrated that under a number of crises – the crisis of hunger, of unemployment, the Covid-19 pandemic and even climate change – women are not only affected deeply and in most cases doubly impacted, they are also conscious and active agents of change who are committed to building alternative systems. Women in the South African Food Sovereignty Campaign are not only leading the call for alternatives, but also addressing the powerlessness that comes with hunger by providing vulnerable groups with food, as well as further empowering themselves and their communities with knowledge and training to sustainably take control of their food situation. This enables communities to establish alternatives with long-term impacts while still addressing the short-term need for food. We have also illustrated how, through the reconstruction of power, the centring of local and indigenous culture and practice and through the questioning of patriarchal capitalist social relations, food sovereignty provides an emancipatory feminist alternative from below.

NOTES

1   Not only is this chapter about eco-feminism, it is also a practice of eco-feminism as we seek to amplify the voices of grassroots women. Both authors, at the time of writing, are organisers in the SAFSC. Through our work we have actively been promoting food sovereignty pathways locally by offering support in the form of training and educational resources, documenting and mapping food relief initiatives and food commons practices, promoting the food sovereignty hub-building approach and supporting many of the grassroots pathways discussed in this chapter. The women we interviewed have journeyed with us and the SAFSC, shared their insights at various online events, and we have learned from them in the process. As we tell their stories and share their insights, we hope that other women will be inspired to tackle patriarchal systems that are oppressing them. It should be noted that while we are organisers in the very movement we are researching, and fellow activists of the women we profile here, we recognise that it does pose some methodological challenges such as bias and taking for granted our prior knowledge. This being said, studying 'sideways' allows us to have an insider

view and a uniquely positioned perspective which can also enrich the study, particularly due to the familiarity with the participants. The purpose of this chapter is to profile the work the women are engaging in and show the role that they have been playing in the transition to food sovereignty. As such, we have been careful to avoid bias as much as possible, while using our insider knowledge to select participants and research questions. It should also be noted that although these women are part of the movement, they are also independent actors and each has her own story, practice and food sovereignty strategy. The SAFSC is a platform that offers support and voice to initiatives like theirs in order to achieve food sovereignty in South Africa.

2   See https://viacampesina.org/en/la-via-campesina-organisational-brochure-edition-2016/.

3   See www.safsc.org.za for activist tools on food sovereignty, seed saving, water sovereignty, land justice and so on.

4   See https://www.safsc.org.za/wp-content/uploads/2017/11/FS-Act-no.1-of-2018.pdf.

5   The South African response to the Covid-19 pandemic included five levels of a national lockdown with varying degrees of restrictions, level 5 being the strictest. Women experienced the most difficulty during level 5 and then level 4, when travel restrictions were imposed and employment became even more precarious than it always had been.

6   The Solidarity Fund is a public benefit organisation, established during the Covid-19 pandemic with a mandate to support the national health response, contribute to humanitarian relief efforts and mobilise members of the public in the fight against the pandemic. See https://solidarityfund.co.za/about/. The Fund established a food intervention for short-term food relief and partnered with a range of organisations that distributed food parcels through established networks.

7   These seven women were selected as part of our study through a purposive sampling method, which takes into account the researcher's personal expertise and knowledge of the spaces in which participants are selected. Through our experience, we chose these women because they are actively championing food sovereignty alternatives in their areas of influence/work. They are either long-time SAFSC members or have come onto our platforms because of the work they have been doing during Covid-19. These specific women were selected because we wanted to profile a range of different women in the food space, including grassroots activists, farmers, students, NGO workers and community members.

8   These forms of power, elaborated in COPAC's (2015) activist training resources, point to the grassroots origins of thinking about power. They have been tested and conceptualised in a grassroots praxis and are evolving. COPAC is a South African NGO that has been working in the development space for over two decades, promoting grassroots development, developing activist resources and championing various grassroots campaigns, including the SAFSC and the Climate Justice Charter Movement.

9   See https://www.safsc.org.za/food-commons-map/.

10   See https://www.safsc.org.za/water-stressed-communities-map/.

11   See https://youtube.com/playlist?list=PLqVUxDeeDDmlEiMt52nHKXwLjOfy1oO7 for phase 1 of setting up a food garden and https://youtube.com/playlist?list=PLqVUx-DeeDDmkjB9VuKq8JguqkjaimUJBV for phase 2 of closing the loop, and https://youtu.be/OSCo5TZauso for an animation on how to set up a food garden.

12   See https://cjcm.org.za/the-charter/en.

13   See https://www.youtube.com/watch?v=dg246Zu94yg&abchannel=COPACSA for the full video of Ecofeminists Speak: Launch of the Climate Justice Charter.

REFERENCES

Akram-Lodhi, A.H. 2013. 'How to build food sovereignty'. Paper presented at the Food Sovereignty Conference, 14–15 September, Yale University, New Haven, CT.

Banerjee, D. and Bell, M.M. 2007. 'Ecogender: Locating gender in environmental social science', *Society and Natural Resources* 20 (1): 3–19.

COPAC (Co-operative and Policy Alternative Centre). 2015. *Food sovereignty for the right to food: A guide for grassroots activism.* Johannesburg: COPAC. Accessed 28 December 2022, http://safsc.org.za/wp-content/uploads/2015/09/Food-Sovereignty-for-the-Right-to-Food-Activist-Guide-compressed.pdf.

De Schutter, O. 2015. 'Food democracy South and North: From food sovereignty to transition initiatives', *Open Democracy*, 17 March. Accessed 28 June 2020, https://www.opendemocracy.net/olivier-de-schutter/food-democracy-south-and-north-from-food-sovereignty-to-transition-initiatives.

Desmarais, A.A. 2003. 'The Via Campesina: Peasant women at the frontiers of food sovereignty', *Canadian Women's Studies* 23 (1): 140–145.

Ellinger-Locke, M. 2011. 'Food sovereignty is a gendered issue', *Buffalo Environmental Law Journal* 18 (2): 158–198.

Ferguson, C.E., Green, K. and Swanson, S. 2022. 'Indigenous food sovereignty is constrained by "time imperialism"', *Geoforum* 133: 20–31.

Ferguson, S. 2020. *Women and Work: Feminism, Labour and Social Reproduction.* London: Pluto Press.

Gaard, G. 2015. 'Ecofeminism and climate change', *Women's Studies International Forum* 49: 20–33.

Graham, H.R. 1996. 'Maria Mies and Vandana Shiva's ecofeminism', *Women in Action* 1: 44–45.

McMichael, P. 2014. 'Historicizing food sovereignty', *The Journal of Peasant Studies* 41 (6): 933–957.

Navin, M. 2015. 'Food sovereignty and gender justice: The case of La Vía Campesina'. In J.M. Dieterle (ed.), *Just Food: Philosophy, Food and Justice.* New York: Rowman and Littlefield, pp. 87–100.

Ngcoya, M. and Kumarakulasingam, N. 2017. 'The lived experience of food sovereignty: Gender, indigenous crops and small-scale farming in Mtubatuba, South Africa', *Journal of Agrarian Change* 17 (3): 480–496.

Nyeleni Forum for Food Sovereignty. 2007. *Declaration of the forum for food sovereignty.* Accessed 27 July 2022, https://nyeleni.org/IMG/pdf/DeclNyeleni-en.pdf.

Patel, R.C. 2012. 'Food sovereignty: Power, gender, and the right to food', *PLoS Med* 9 (6): 1–4.

Patel, R. and Grey, S. 2015. 'Food sovereignty as decolonization: Some contributions from indigenous movements to food system and development politics', *Agriculture and Human Values* 32 (43): 431–444.

PMBEJD (Pietermaritzburg Economic Justice and Dignity). 2020. 'Food hunger and Covid-19'. Accessed 30 January 2023, https://pmbejd.org.za/wp-content/uploads/2020/03/March-2020-Household-Affordability-Index-PMBEJD.pdf.

PMBEJD. 2021. 'Pietermaritzburg household affordability index: March 2021'. Accessed 30 January 2023, https://pmbejd.org.za/wp-content/uploads/2021/03/March-2021-PMB-Household-Affordability-Index 31032021.pdf.

Rosset, P. 2008. 'Food sovereignty and the contemporary food crisis', *Development* 51 (4): 460–463.

SAFSC. 2020. 'Covid-19 and the hunger crisis: Towards a food sovereignty and community driven solidarity partnership: Government, Solidarity Fund and grassroots organisations'.

Accessed 28 June 2020, https://www.safsc.org.za/wp-content/uploads/2020/05/Partnership-FrameworkHunger-Crisis_16-May-2020with-endorsements.pdf.

Satgar, V. and Cherry, J. 2019. 'Climate and food inequality: The South African Food Sovereignty Campaign response', *Globalizations* 17(2): 317–337. DOI:10.1080/14747731.2019.1652467.

Shiva, V. 2004. 'The future of food: Countering globalisation and recolonisation of Indian agriculture', *Futures* 36: 715–732.

Smith, M.N., Coleman, N. and Isaacs, G. 2020. 'Towards a safer, more equitable opening of the economy'. Covid-19 Response Policy Brief No. 2, Institute for Economic Justice.

Spaull, N., Roussow, L., Oyenubi, A., Patel, L., Kerr, A., Benhura, M., Maughan-Brown, B., Leibbrandt, M., Ardington, C., Mohohlwane, N. et al. 2020. 'An overview of results from NIDS-CRAM Wave 2', National Income Dynamics Study-Coronavirus Rapid Mobile Survey. Accessed 8 February 2023, https://cramsurvey.org/wp-content/uploads/2020/10/1.-Spaull-et-al.-NIDS-CRAM-Wave-2-Synthesis-Report.pdf.

Tilzey, M. 2017. 'Reintegrating economy, society, and environment for cooperative futures: Polanyi, Marx, and food sovereignty', *Journal of Rural Studies* 53: 317–334.

INTERVIEWS

Davine Cloete, January 2021, Lutzville, West Coast

Dorah Marema, August 2020, Johannesburg

Isabella Potenza, August 2020, Johannesburg

Magda Campbell, August 2020, Mitchells Plain

Mutshidzi Ratshibvumo, August 2020, Johannesburg

Nosintu Mcimeli, August 2020, Nqamakwe, Eastern Cape

Thembi Nxumalo, August 2020, Johannesburg

ECONOMIC TRANSFORMATION, PUBLIC SERVICES AND TRANSFORMATIVE WOMEN'S POWER IN SOUTH AFRICA

6

QUIET REBELS:
UNDERGROUND WOMEN MINERS
AND REFUSAL AS RESISTANCE

Asanda-Jonas Benya

INTRODUCTION

Industrial mining in South Africa goes back to the late nineteenth century, with platinum mining starting later, in 1924. From the early industrial mining period until 2002 women were prohibited from doing underground production work. The exception to this rule was asbestos mines, which had women cobbers and sorters between 1893 and 1980 as a result of an explicit exemption of asbestos mines from the Mines and Works Act No. 27 of 1956 (McCulloch 2003, 2010). That means for over 150 years only men worked in underground occupations. It was only in 2004, almost 80 years after platinum mining began, that mining houses started hiring women to work full-time underground. Most of these women went into mining not because they had aspirations of being miners, but due to unemployment, economic pressures and the deepening crisis of social reproduction – as elaborated by Sonia Phalatse and Busi Sibeko (chapter 8), Christine Bischoff (chapter 9), Inge Konik (chapter 3), Courtney Morgan and Jane Cherry (chapter 5) and also Dineo Skosana and Jacklyn Cock (chapter 4) in this volume. Similarly, mines employed them not because they wanted women, but because legislation forced them to have at least ten per cent women in their complement of mining staff. For women this attitude meant working in an environment not ready or fully prepared to embrace them, a world governed by androcentrism – from its norms, to how production was structured, to conceptions of safety, and occupational cultural scripts and practices. To survive, women, who are on the margins underground, have had to learn to negotiate not only mining spaces, but masculinity, regardless of their bodies being seen as 'foreign' in underground spaces. Drawing from my ethnographic fieldwork conducted in 2008 and between 2012 and 2014, when I worked with mineworkers underground and lived with them in their residences for close to a year, in this chapter I elaborate on what I see as organic and emancipatory ways in which women mineworkers, the quiet rebels of the underground world, resist despotic logics that facilitate exploitative forms of working and exploitative relations. I also draw from interviews[1] and observational data collected between 2011 and 2014 to unpack how these women miners enact resistance through 'refusals' at work, how their everyday ways of working and being are essentially about refusing to become part of a male-centred division of labour; refusing to do minework like male workers; refusing to do masculinity, which is often mobilised to get workers to be more productive. In other words, they were refusing patriarchal, and to some extent, capitalist ways of being and working, thus redefining *being* and *working* underground. Women resisted the pervasive masculine mining script with its gendered norms when *doing* minework. They charted their own paths, using scripts that were considered unorthodox for the masculine and industrial capitalist underground world. Others, however, negotiated and reconstructed the masculine script and its terms of engagement.

What I observed while working underground is that being an 'alien' availed particular resistance registers to women that were not available to – nor could they be taken up by – men without risking being labelled 'less manly'. I suggest that we read these actions as refusals that enable women to disrupt occupational norms and introduce new registers of resistance underground and in mining generally. As such, women access and perform alternative ways of being and doing underground and ultimately construct different gendered worker subjectivities. By tapping into their marginality and 'alien' status underground, they are inviting us to reimagine everyday resistance and are broadening frames of resistance. In line with bell hooks' conception of marginality, the marginality of these women miners can be seen as 'a site of radical possibility, a space of resistance' and 'a site of freedom, liberation, resistance and empowerment' (hooks in Idahosa and Vincent 2014: 61). Therefore, this is not a marginality one wants to give up or willingly lose, but one to cling to because 'it nourishes one's capacity to resist' (hooks 1990: 149–150).

CONTROVERSIAL INCLUSION

Doors for women in mining officially opened in 2002 with the promulgation of the Mineral and Petroleum and Resources Development Act No. 28 of 2002 (MPRDA) followed by the Mining Charter in 2004, which explicitly stated that mines should have ten per cent women employed in their workforce within specific timeframes. Both the MPRDA and the Charter supplanted old prohibitive mining laws such as the Mines and Works Act No. 12 of 1911 and the South African Minerals Act No. 50 of 1991. In 2020, the Minerals Council White Paper on Women in Mining was released, outlining the industry's strategy on the inclusion of women.

To date, 58 000 – that is 12 per cent – of the mining workforce in South Africa are women. When women joined the mining workforce, they began doing work historically done by men, such as drilling, pounding blasted rock, winching ore to the surface, installing support technologies (such as timber-based support and jackpots, resin-grouted rock bolts, steel bolts and so on) and water and ventilation pipes. Their inclusion has been met with both celebration and controversies.

Liberal feminists and politicians celebrated women's inclusion in mining and saw it as a progressive step indicating a collapse of the stubborn gender barriers that have previously barred women from the mines. Their argument has been that the inclusion of women in mining signifies progress towards equality (see Hawzhin Azeez in chapter 2 and also Dineo Skosana and Jacklyn Cock in chapter 4 of this volume for critiques of the liberal feminist notion of equality). Conservatives, on the other hand, including men in mining, have denounced the inclusion of women, arguing that mining is a snub to women's femininity. In their attempts to keep women out of mines, they argue that mine work is men's work, and women's work is outside the mine gates. Their arguments seek to maintain and reproduce Victorian ideas about women's work and their bodies, as they attempt to 'protect' women by encouraging 'appropriate' gender roles. They see the inclusion of women in mining as 'unnatural' and likely to cause great social imbalance, which will negatively affect the working environment, especially production underground (Mercier and Gier 2009; Macintyre 2006; Benya 2009). These views have been used to legitimise the ten per cent quota on women and to justify the low retention rate and high attrition of women that some mines have noted. Environmentalists and radical feminists, too, have denounced the inclusion of women in mining – but for different reasons. They argue that no one should be in mining and the demand should not be to achieve equality by including women in a sector that destroys the environment, lives and livelihoods, but to reform mining entirely by doing only the mining neces-sary to maintain life and by stopping the extraction of natural resources for profits.

Another critical perspective, which does not pronounce whether women should or should not be in mining but analyses what their inclusion in mining means for gender relations, argues that women's inclusion in masculine workplaces such as mining is a disruption of the status quo and dominant 'gender regimes' (Connell 2002: 53). Women's entrance is seen as troubling masculine normativity and hegemony, but not necessarily altering the gender order and hierarchy (Kvande 1999; Jorgenson 2002; Sasson-Levy 2003; Pyke and Johnson 2003; Czarniawska 2013). The idea here is that women's entrance disrupts gendered occupational norms even if it does not necessarily dislodge the order and the hegemony of masculinity. The question then is, if occupational norms are disrupted, might that present a window of opportunity to think differently and creatively about work, work relations and, by extension, resistance? In this case of women in mining, I demonstrate the ways in which women negotiate and also resist the masculine mining occupational culture. I suggest that we read some of their gendered spatial negotiations underground as refusals that enable them to disrupt occupational norms and introduce new registers of resistance underground and in mining generally. Through their resistance actions they are also showing us alternative ways of being and doing underground and ultimately constructing different gendered worker subjectivities that enable us to revisit everyday resistance for workers.

EVERYDAY REFUSALS AND RESISTANCE

To make sense of women's resistance practices and performances of work and gender underground, I draw from James Scott's (1985, 1992) theory of 'everyday resistance' and emphasise the productive potentialities of everyday non-violent, non-confrontational, uncoordinated and informal resistance practices – what I see as resembling Sara Ahmed's (2016) feminist refusals. In this instance, resistance is conceived as 'subaltern practices', social attitudes that 'challenge, negotiate and undermine power' though not necessarily in a visible way, nor articulated in formal, political and intentional ways (Hollander and Einwohner 2004; Baaz et al. 2016: 142). The resister or receiver need not conceive of actions as resistance, though when present, that conscious recognition is advantageous. In other words, while intention and reception or recognition are important, they are not the final deciding factors of whether or not an action constitutes resistance. Instead, as Mikael Baaz et al. (2016) argue, the consequences of actions, the actors and their position to power in a particular context are what matters.

In the case of women miners, they opt for these strategies mainly because they do not have traditional forms of power in a mining environment, which has historically been dominated by men and has valorised masculinity. Women are not heard or listened to and some of their grievances are not taken seriously or prioritised by employers and unions, while men on the other hand enjoy the control of and access to unions to resist or bargain. Women's strategies, therefore, are a response to exclusion and marginalisation from underground life. Like the women in chapter 4 of this volume, those interviewed for this chapter too, under great constraints, are challenging oppression, exploitation and exclusion.

While still greatly constrained and by no means radically changing the system, their practices or performances are, as I see it, chipping away at and disrupting the masculine practices and culture underground, unsettling the logics of work and incessant capitalist demands on workers. They are introducing new and creative registers of resistance for mineworkers. Underground is an unforgiving space; it remains a masculine preserve. To act out of script, therefore, and to do so in ways that challenge the masculine occupational culture is no small feat, particularly since there are sanctions for those who do not fully observe the prescribed modus operandi.

Some of the experiences I highlight in this chapter may seem to sugggest that women do not know how to do mine work or are unable to do so, and may seem to reinforce masculine hegemony, or play into heteronormative and normative masculine and capitalist orders. This might seem to contradict what one imagines liberatory practices to look like. It is therefore important to centre women's own perceptions and conceptions of their actions *and* consequences thereof, and appreciate their multiple potentials, some of which serve to undermine the underground working system. According to my interviews with the women, these are strategic choices and performances, chosen deliberately to advance their collective and individual interests, even though not always explicitly done to *resist* or necessarily target and disturb power relations.

WARS, MYTHS AND WOMEN'S EXCLUSION

The dominant and most recent mining history has exclusively focused on men, with women on the fringes of that narrative – mainly as the outside 'other' and their bodies seen as incompatible with mine work. A longer scoping of history, however, shows that women have been in mining, doing all kinds of work, since the early 1400s in different parts of the world, and certainly in southern Africa.

In countries such as Japan, Philippines, Bolivia, China, Papua New Guinea and India, women were involved as part of family labour doing the same jobs as men. In fact, there is evidence that sometimes women did the heavier work while men supervised (Sone 2006; Lahiri-Dutt and Macintyre 2006; Crispin 2006; Alexander 2007; Burke 2006; Smith 2006; Sinha 2006). In most of these countries, mines were close to communities and mining was mainly done on a small scale, informally, with hardly any inspections; hence families, including young children, could be involved (Chaloping-March 2006; Alexander 2007; Caballero 2006). In these communal and cooperative mining arrangements mining was mainly done by hand, and women were stereotyped as better and gentler than men (Nash 1979), as a result of which some mining activities, such as panning, were reserved strictly for women (Caballero 2006; Chaloping-March 2006). In Brazil we see contrasting patterns, where on the one hand, mines are worked by families but on the other, they are worked by runaway slaves and offending citizens (Godfrey 1992; Graulau 2006).

While women were involved in mining, their participation was halted at certain historical moments, such as during the World Wars or during the Chaco War in Bolivia in the early 1930s, and more so with the spread of Victorian attitudes in parts of the world that were colonised (Hoecke 2006; Bocangel 2001; Nash 1979; Milkman 1987; Game and Pringle 1984; Cockburn 1985). All of these socio-historical events, with their changing patterns and legal shifts, had an impact on how mining and the role of women was conceived at particular historical moments.

When women were excluded, mines were considered 'a man's world' to a point where the relationship between men and mines was naturalised. As already stated, women's exclusion in South Africa and other parts of the world was largely informed by colonial Victorian, religious and cultural ideas about women's bodies. There were also superstitions and myths about women's bodies which normalised their exclusion, as well as cultural beliefs, some of which continue to prevail, associated with the presence of women in mining, and specifically underground. Locally, Peter Alexander (2007) argues that the colonial and apartheid history of South Africa restricted the movement and residency of Africans, especially women. Mechanisation, the geographical location of mines – often far from the bantustans and 'ghettos' where Africans were confined – single-sex hostels and the migrant labour system guaranteed the exclusion of women from mines.

There were exceptions, however, mainly on asbestos mines, where women were almost half of the workforce from the 1890s until the 1980s (McCulloch 2010). Despite evidence of women working in mines, cobbing and sorting ore, the myth of their bodies as weak and thus unsuitable for mine work persisted. Some scholars have drawn direct links between such taboos and modes of production (Newton 2012). The myths and beliefs in some areas were that women's bodies, due to menstruation, were seen as 'leaky', 'polluted' and also believed to have powers to influence seismic events underground, leading to rock falls and mineral disappearance. In these discourses, menstruation was conceived as an energy-draining and body-weakening process that negatively affected women's capacities to labour (Phipps 2012; Johnston-Robledo and Chrisler 2013; Das 2008). In fact, some argued that menstruation weakened the immune system, thus making women highly susceptible to infections.

While the protectionist and policing discourses ensured that women remained on the outside, were stigmatised and their bodies delegitimised in mining, they conversely fostered the development of a discourse that naturalised men's bodies in mining. The argument thus went, ideal bodies were male and 'contained', as opposed to female and leaky or unruly and polluted (McDowell 1999; Riley 1988), or bodies which are 'governed by their menses' (Shilling 2005: 40). This evocation of myths about women's bodies as weak and inferior or unsuitable, some scholars have argued, was a way of safeguarding men's jobs and cementing the exclusion of women (Heemskerk 2000; Phipps 2012).

DESIRABLE 'TRIBAL' AND RACIALISED BODIES

While women were othered, men on the other hand, were viewed as the desirable bodies, naturally suitable for underground work, especially black men. Dunbar Moodie and Vivienne Ndatshe (1994) and Paul Stewart (2012) mention how machine technology on the mines has hardly changed. What has changed, though, is line management underground; white miners have been replaced by mainly black miners, some of whom used to be 'baas-boys'.[2] With regard to technology, the scraper winch that was introduced in the 1930s, for example, was marginally developed by the late 1990s. Some mines were, in fact, against the introduction of new technology, arguing that there were 'enough natives' who knew how to handle and were more precise with the hand hammer, which minimised waste. Drilling machines were viewed as less precise, and also emitted vibrations that could loosen the hanging walls underground. The 'natives' were preferred not only because they were 'precise' in drilling with hammers, but also because they – or their bodies – were seen as easier and 'cheaper' to maintain, compared to new technology. All managers had to do when a 'native' slowed down was give them a good hiding and that turned them into their best 'boys'. Machinery, on the other hand, was expensive to buy and maintain, required better-paid (white unionised) supervisors to operate it, and unlike 'native men', could not be given a hiding to improve performance.

The objectification and subjection of black men was cemented daily through racialised and gendered violence both at work and outside work. Sometimes mines evoked tribal stereotypes to get workers to be productive. While '"there was moral outrage at grievous assaults leading to serious injury" ... individuals had to stand up for themselves most of the time' (Moodie and Ndatshe 1994: 57). Through disciplinary power, violent methods and techniques deployed by the mines, the colonial and apartheid state, the mines constructed black miners as the natural labouring bodies.

To do this, mines delinked whiteness from the labouring class. Through job allocations and the reconfiguration of teams as mentioned above, mines (with mining unions) actively distanced white bodies from the 'degrading' and strenuous work underground, and bequeathed the honour of master upon them, the virtuoso in the underground mining world. They became, formally, the individuals who possessed outstanding technical ability and they were also charged with the vocation of maintaining white respectability and superiority. This distancing of white miners from underground and dirty, physically exhausting underground work was already evident in 1919. Moodie and Ndatshe (1994) argue that, from 1919, black baasboys were already being used to circumvent the mining regulation that necessitated the presence of a white miner underground. White respectability underground was further entrenched by the presence of 'pikininis' (a shift supervisor assistant) who cleaned and picked up after and before white miners. Moodie and Ndatshe (1994: 69) argue that pikininis were not a formal position, but by 1976 every white miner had one and they worked as personal servants underground and at the supervisor's home. Later, as more white miners were moved farther away from direct supervision underground to higher positions on the surface, pikininis took over, first as team leaders and later as miners.

As these changes were taking place on the work front and in politics, discourses about bodies and suitability were also morphing to reflect these changes. Whether advertently or inadvertently, there was insistent linking of particular traits with black bodies and black masculinities; these included risk-taking, physical work, working hard and the ability to tolerate dangerously hot and humid underground working conditions and deplorable hostel living conditions. They then encouraged, rewarded and valorised these traits underground, where rocks were constantly threatening to fall and thus threatening production or the bottom line profits of the mine. What became lost in this 'production machine' was how mines were not only producing platinum or gold, but were also producing the mining bodies they wanted in order to produce the minerals and metals they 'needed'.

For decades, black men's bodies were targeted, trained, managed – essentially 'disciplined' to enable mining companies to 'extract' not only minerals, but labour power by mobilising masculinity. I am deliberately emphasising bodies because in mining these men were hardly seen or treated as deserving of recognition as full humans, but rather as efficient hammers, handlers, cleaners and thorough lashers.

The production of these masculine mining bodies that are seen as expendable and easily exploitable has become more prominent with the inclusion of women in mining. Hence, mining masculinity, which facilitated the exploitation of black men's bodies and their objectification, became closely guarded as it was synonymous with productivity, the production of surplus value and ultimately profits. The exclusion of women was thus necessary, and of white men, desirable in the context of a racist apartheid workplace order. The marginality that women perform then is a negotiation of multiple historical and contemporary workplace politics at play in the underground workplaces they inhabit.

STRATEGIC REFUSALS

The inclusion of women in mining illuminates how mining bodies are produced, how men's bodies have for a long time been targeted, scrutinised and 'disciplined' in order to help mines 'extract' not only minerals, but labour power by mobilising black masculinities. The insistence on excluding women, therefore, seems to have had as much to do with protecting men's jobs, as it had with protecting profits that depend on the mobilisation of mining masculinity and the reproduction of its logics and practices.

While women have been included in mining in recent years, they remain on the margins or excluded in reality and in daily experiences of work. As I argue elsewhere, their exclusion happens through alienation from their day-to-day work and spatial separation and isolation from their teams – using the argument of their bodies as incongruous with mine work, 'leaky' and out of place underground.

What has been given little attention in discourse when making sense of women's marginality in mining is perhaps the fact that it is this marginality that has allowed women some autonomy. This is a productive marginality with emancipatory possibilities. We have not paid much attention to how some women are also using self-exclusion as a strategy to escape the daunting and dangerous mine work, how they are using their alienation and isolation as a means of 'independence' at and from work. They are free from expectations to be productive at all costs, even to their demise – an expectation that is at the core of mining masculinity.

When using a feminist lens to make sense of how women negotiate underground, self-exclusion becomes a strategic refusal, a refusal to be turned into an efficient and methodical machine, exploited underground and discarded once wounded or sick, like the half a million men disabled by mine accidents, or sick and dying with tuberculosis and silicosis, throughout southern Africa. How then do these refusals manifest at work, and how do women perform them?

QUIET REBELS: LEAVING STOPES AND NEGOTIATING WORK

The refusal by some women takes the form of 'quietly' refusing to be permanently located inside the stopes, where drilling and blasting are the epitome of masculinity, or quietly refusing to do the work. What I observed during the time that I worked and lived with women miners was that those who did not want to be inside the hot and humid stopes could choose to dilly-dally or quietly refuse to be permanently located inside the stopes. The strategy employed would involve doing either important auxiliary work outside the stope and far from the gangs despite being officially allocated work, or an occupation inside the stope. They made themselves indispensable outside the stope, sometimes fixing telephone cables that are important when operating a winch, or painting direction lines that facilitate movement underground, or pumping out water accumulated in the gully, or fetching timber used to support the hanging wall. These women chose differently. They chose invisibility and separation as a way of releasing themselves from the expectations put on workers inside stopes, the expectations to be productive no matter what the conditions, even when the stope is not properly ventilated and there are looming dangers. The choosing of daily tasks concerned with *assisting* the gang but outside the stopes was thus a deliberate one, even though some of these tasks reinforced domesticity and femininity, exactly what other women tried very hard to dissociate themselves from. While the 'quiet rebels' deliberately chose to avoid being inside the stope, others adopted different strategies that took them closer and inside the stopes. Both actions were refusals but were pulling in different directions. The former resisted the strenuous and dangerous work underground while reinforcing stope norms, the latter transgressed the stope norms by wanting to be inside the stopes and doing what is deemed men's work.

These actions by women mineworkers were sometimes read as disobedience by their colleagues; indeed, women's presence as permanent 'fixtures' underground was seen as a refusal, a demonstration of courage, a deliberate choosing, a form of defiance of feminine tropes that are unable to accommodate 'disobedient' femininities (Gasa 2007; Motsemme 2004: 910). These were avowedly organic emancipatory feminist practices. Unlike men whose scripts of obedience and control were clear and thus tightly regulated, for women it was not so. As a result, women consistently chose differently and negotiated multiple and varying positions.

Other refusals involved not only avoiding the stope, but avoiding work altogether, especially if deemed difficult. Some women argued that to 'quietly' refuse to do work sometimes comprised working slowly, what workers called to *swaya-swaya*. To *swaya-swaya* has an impact on productivity and ultimately profits. One woman gave an example, explaining what to *swaya-swaya* means:

> If they send you to the stores to get material and you are tired of going up and down the stairs, you just swaya-swaya … so you take maybe an hour or two hours just to go to the stores instead of twenty minutes. Then they come to look for you and when they find you in the stores, they shout and shout and you just keep quiet and don't look at them … they carry the things you didn't want to carry in the first place … at that time you are smiling … they don't even know that they are helping you, they are thinking they are making things move fast and you are delaying them … you don't say no I won't do it, you just swaya-swaya … (Maria, interview, April 2012)[3]

To *swaya-swaya* also includes agreeing to do work, but doing it your own way, not in the mine's way or men's way, that is, refusing to do masculinity in order to do the work.[4] For Tee, another woman mineworker, this involved refusing to work after *shayile* (knock-off) time; at other times it was about the techniques she adopted when doing work or making a plan for work. To appreciate the significance of these actions one must appreciate that underground there are tacit rules which accompany every action or inaction. These rules implicitly dictate your movements, your still moments, your sitting and your working. These range from how you dress for a specific task, whether you put on the full PPE (personal protective equipment) gear or not and what you leave out and when; how you move your hands in relation to your body; your breathing; and how you use your fingers when doing particular tasks. Everything has its place and time, dictated to all by the covert scripts of underground rationalities. To refuse carrying out or performing tasks as dictated by these covert scripts of underground rationalities was to risk failure, or risk stigma as yet another inexperienced 'foreigner' underground.

REJECTING FANAKALO AND REFUSING 'HONORARY CITIZENSHIP'

Alongside refusing to be in the stope underground and do mine work, there was also a refusal to use the spatially corresponding language underground, Fanakalo. Fanakalo is the underground mining language, one that legitimises your position and gives you the status of being a 'real' mineworker. When a woman speaks Fanakalo she is given 'honorary citizenship', and this citizenship comes with work and productivity expectations. Some refused that citizenship and chose to be outsiders. The refusal to speak Fanakalo was their way of distancing themselves from the mineworker identity, the underground world, its culture and logics, and of symbolically distancing the self from the masculinity both associated with the language and seen as key when mobilising productivity underground.

Mama Mavis, for instance, explained to me that she does not speak Fanakalo at all because it is for men, not women. In her words: 'It's not our language as women, it's for men … not us' (Mama Mavis, interview, October 2012). Some women associated Fanakalo with men who work on the mines. Women who were heard speaking Fanakalo were sometimes told, '*Haye o tswaneli*' (It does not suit you), as a way of discouraging them from speaking Fanakalo. The women's refusal to speak Fanakalo was also a refusal to give an impression that one identified as a mineworker, which was read as identifying closely with men, with the mines, their demands and culture. I read the attempts to discourage other women from speaking Fanakalo as attempts to sanitise those within one's feminine radius, lest their 'discolouration' with masculinity or 'ways of the mines' be read as contamination. This refusal to use a spatially corresponding language then was more a refusal of proximity, a containment, an attempt to protect one's femininity and refuse that 'other' stigmatised world that could not be mapped perfectly on their bodies.

PIKININIS AND UNIONS: CONTESTING NAMING
AND CHOOSING DIFFERENTLY

Women working as a helper to a shiftboss supervisor refused to be called 'pikininis', insisting on being called 'shiftboss assistants'. Others refused to be referred to as mineworkers, insisting instead that they be called 'women who work in mining'.

During an interview with Babalwa, who had worked as an equipment helper under-ground but had been transferred to the surface to work as a pikinini, she said: 'The shiftboss asked me to help him on surface … I'm his assistant now [pikinini], I help him with plans and measurements underground … As a shiftboss assistant I give instructions – [what's a shiftboss assistant?] – they call it a pikinini, but I don't like that, I'm an assistant. I do all the work that a chibass [shiftboss/shift supervisor] does …' (Babalwa, interview, July 2012).

These were ways of contesting and rejecting the naming, which for the women symbolised objectification and turning workers into machines or servants. Babalwa's refusal to be called a pikinini, insisting on being called a 'shiftboss assistant' instead, was not only a contestation of naming but of a particular status as a *malayisha* (lasher) and expectations that you would give your all to work – including doing all overtime work – and would work in particular prescribed ways.

Sometimes the women refused to interact with the union or to join the same unions which the majority of underground male workers joined. Instead, some chose to join unions associated with above-ground workers, unions that they argued 'take women's demands seriously'. One such preferred union was the United Association of South Africa (UASA), a union that historically organised white and coloured workers. Those who preferred UASA claimed that they got benefits such as access to lawyers in addition to union representatives as well as maternity benefits directly from the union, discounts for bus fares and funeral benefits. The women who refused to join traditional unions argued that unions were discon-nected from the ground and did not serve workers, let alone women workers. While some refused to join traditional unions, others joined them but refused to partic-ipate in their activities, arguing that they were male-oriented, sidelined women's issues and sometimes even threatened women in meetings if they expressed unpop-ular views. These women found refuge in women's structures which organised to prioritise women's issues, including pregnancy issues and sexual harassment and gender-based violence, both inside and outside the mines (Benya, forthcoming).

CONCLUSION

These women's refusals thus 'got in the way' (Ahmed 2014) of workplace order and conditions necessary for the exploitation of workers by disrupting, while also rein-forcing, gender stereotypes and gender expectations to their individual and collective benefit. In some cases, they refused their objectification and actively chose to deviate from the underground orders and norms. It was these organic emancipatory actions, the deviation or 'wandering' away from the official and unofficial but generally accepted masculine paths that enabled them to lay claim to some 'freedoms'. The wilful acts of these women were reinforced by their marginal status in mining, the status which comes with 'not being male', not performing or embodying mining masculinity.

Through their actions the women mineworkers were saying: 'We refuse to be what you want us to be, we are what we are, and that's the way it's going to be'; they were thus choosing 'that space of refusal, where one can say no' (hooks 1990: 150). They were refusing to assimilate, to mimic men, and were choosing instead to carve a space for themselves on the margins where they could be who they wanted to be; where they could live or work in alternative ways and refuse domination and co-optation into sustaining mining masculinity as the norm. These women's organic, active and strategic refusals allowed them to take certain subject positions that were not objectifiable, even though still exploited. Their refusals challenged the superficial (neo)liberal feminist notions of equality that narrowly focus on representation without asking critical questions, or that zealously pander to the rhetoric of 'equality with men' at all costs, even to the point of furthering one's own exploitation and demise.

I suggest that these refusals should be read as windows through which to reimagine resistance and male mineworkers should borrow from some of the strategies deployed by women in the construction of their social and political subjectivities and for the liberation of the working class.

Declaration: A shorter version of this chapter was published in the Global Labour Column. http://www.global-labour-university.org/fileadmin/GLU_Column/papers/No_330_Benya_mining_bodies.pdf.

NOTES

1   I conducted both formal and informal interviews with women. The formal interviews were with all the women I worked closely with during my fieldwork, women who were active in the union and women structures and those who were prominent in the different shafts I worked in. I also relied on informal interviews with other women. These informal interviews were mainly in the form of conversations which took place while going to our stopes, or while waiting for the cage, during nights out, while changing into our uniforms at the change house, and so on.

2   Assistants or personal 'servants' in the underground mining hierarchy, especially during apartheid.

3   All interviewee names used in this chapter are pseudonyms.

4.   Foot dragging by workers is not new. See Scott (1992).

REFERENCES

Ahmed, S. 2014. *Willful Subjects*. Durham, NC: Duke University Press.

Ahmed, S. 2016. *Living a Feminist Life*. Durham, NC: Duke University Press.

Alexander, P. 2007. 'Women and coal mining in India and South Africa, c1900–1940', *African Studies* 66 (2–3): 201–222.

Baaz, M., Lilja, M., Schulz, M. and Vinthagen, S. 2016. 'Defining and analyzing "resistance": Possible entrances to the study of subversive practices', *Alternatives* 41 (3): 137–153.

Benya, A.P. 2009. 'Women in mining: A challenge to occupational culture in mines', unpublished Masters dissertation, University of the Witwatersrand, Johannesburg.

Benya, A. Forthcoming. 'Patriarchal collusions and women's marginalisation'. In M. Tshoaedi, C. Bischoff and A. Bezuidenhout (eds), *The Future of Labour Movements in South Africa*. Johannesburg: Wits University Press.

Bocangel, D. 2001. *Small-scale mining in Bolivia: National study mining minerals and sustainable development*. Mining, Minerals and Sustainable Development (MMSD) Working Paper No. 71. International Institute for Environment and Development, London.

Burke, G. 2006. 'Women miners: Here and there, now and then'. In K. Lahiri-Dutt and M. Macintyre (eds), *Women Miners in Developing Countries: Pit Women and Others*. Farnham: Ashgate Publishing, pp. 25–50.

Caballero, E.J. 2006. 'Traditional small-scale miners: Women miners of the Philippines'. In K. Lahiri-Dutt and M. Macintyre (eds), *Women Miners in Developing Countries: Pit Women and Others*. Farnham: Ashgate Publishing, pp. 145–160.

Chaloping-March, M. 2006. 'The place of women in mining in the Cordillera region, Philippines'. In K. Lahiri-Dutt and M. Macintyre (eds), *Women Miners in Developing Countries: Pit Women and Others*. Farnham: Ashgate Publishing, pp. 183–206.

Cockburn, C. 1985. *Machinery of Dominance: Women, Men and Technical Know-how*. London: Pluto Press.

Connell, R.W. 2002. *Gender: Short Introductions*. Cambridge: Polity.

Crispin, G. 2006. 'Women in small-scale gold mining in Papua New Guinea'. In K. Lahiri-Dutt and M. Macintyre (eds), *Women Miners in Developing Countries: Pit Women and Others*. Farnham: Ashgate Publishing, pp. 253–262.

Czarniawska, B. 2013. 'Negotiating selves: Gender at work', *Tamara Journal of Critical Organisation Inquiry* 11 (1): 59.

Das, M. 2008. 'Menstruation as pollution: Taboos in Simlitola, Assam', *Indian Anthropologist* 38 (2): 29–42.

Game, A. and Pringle, R. 1984. *Gender at Work*. London: Pluto Press.

Gasa, N. 2007. 'Feminisms, motherisms, patriarchies and women's voices in the 1950s'. In N. Gasa (ed.), *Women in South African History: Basus' iimbokodo, bawel'imilambo/they remove boulders and cross rivers*. Cape Town: HSRC Press, pp. 207–229.

Godfrey, B.J. 1992. 'Migration to the gold-mining frontier in Brazilian Amazonia', *Geographical Review* 82 (4): 458–469.

Graulau, J. 2006. 'Gendered labour in peripheral tropical frontiers: Women, mining and capital accumulation in post-development Amazonia'. In K. Lahiri-Dutt and M. Macintyre (eds), *Women Miners in Developing Countries: Pit Women and Others*. Farnham: Ashgate Publishing, pp. 285–302.

Heemskerk, M. 2000. *Gender and gold mining: The case of the Maroons of Suriname*. Working Paper No. 269. Women in International Development, Michigan State University.

Hoecke, E.V. 2006. 'The invisible work of women in the small mines of Bolivia'. In K. Lahiri-Dutt and M. Macintyre (eds), *Women Miners in Developing Countries: Pit Women and Others*. Farnham: Ashgate Publishing, pp. 265–283.

Hollander, J.A. and Einwohner, R.L. 2004. 'Conceptualizing resistance', *Sociological Forum* 19 (4): 533–554.

hooks, B. 1990. *Yearnings: Race, Gender and Cultural Politics*. Boston, MA: South End Press.

Idahosa, G. and Vincent, L. 2014. 'Losing, using, refusing, cruising: First-generation South African women academics narrate the complexity of marginality', *Agenda* 28 (1): 59–71. http://dx.doi.org/10.1080/10130950.2014.874766.

Johnston-Robledo, I. and Chrisler, J.C. 2013. 'The menstrual mark: Menstruation as social stigma', *Sex Roles*, 68 (1–2): 9–18.

Jorgenson, J. 2002. 'Engineering selves: Negotiating gender and identity in technical work', *Management Communication Quarterly* 15 (3): 350–380.

Kvande, E. 1999. '"In the belly of the beast": Constructing femininities in engineering organizations', *European Journal of Women's Studies* 6 (3): 305–328.

Lahiri-Dutt, K. and Macintyre, M. (eds). 2006. *Women Miners in Developing Countries: Pit Women and Others*. Farnham: Ashgate Publishing.

Macintyre, M. 2006. 'Women working in the mining industry in Papua New Guinea: A case study from Lihir'. In K. Lahiri-Dutt and M. Macintyre (eds), *Women Miners in Developing Countries: Pit Women and Others*. Farnham: Ashgate Publishing, pp. 131–144.

McCulloch, J. 2003. 'Asbestos mining in Southern Africa, 1893–2002', *International Journal of Occupational and Environmental Health* 9 (3): 230–235.

McCulloch, J. 2010. 'Women mining asbestos in South Africa 1893–1980', *Journal of Southern African Studies* 29 (2): 413–432.

McDowell, L. 1999. *Gender, Identity and Place: Understanding Feminist Geographies*. Minneapolis, MN: University of Minnesota Press.

Mercier, L. and Gier, J. 2009. *Mining Women: Gender in the Development of a Global Industry, 1670 to the Present*. London: Macmillan Press.

Milkman, R. 1987. *Gender at Work: The Dynamics of Job Segregation by Sex during World War II*. Urbana, IL: University of Illinois Press.

Moodie, T.D. and Ndatshe, V. 1994. *Going for Gold: Men, Mines and Migration*. Johannesburg: Wits University Press.

Motsemme, N. 2004. 'The mute always speak: On women's silences at the Truth and Reconciliation Commission', *Current Sociology* 52 (5): 909–932.

Nash, J.C. 1979. *We Eat the Mines and the Mines Eat Us: Dependency and Exploitation in Bolivian Tin Mines*. New York: Columbia University Press.

Newton, V.L. 2012. 'Status passage, stigma and menstrual management: "Starting" and "being on"', *Social Theory & Health* 10 (4): 392–407.

Phipps, S. 2012. 'Comfortable with their bodies: Menstruation, culture and materialism in America', unpublished undergraduate dissertation, Georgia State University.

Pyke, K.D. and Johnson, D.L. 2003. 'Asian American women and racialized femininities: "Doing" gender across cultural worlds', *Gender & Society* 17 (1): 33–53.

Riley, D. 1988. *Am I that Name: Feminism and the Category of 'Women' in History*. London: Macmillan Press.

Sasson-Levy, O. 2003. 'Feminism and military gender practices: Israeli women soldiers in "masculine roles"', *Sociological Inquiry* 73 (3): 440–465.

Scott, J.C. 1985. *Weapons of the Weak: Everyday Forms of Peasant Resistance*. New Haven, CT: Yale University Press.

Scott, J.C. 1992. *Domination and the Arts of Resistance: Hidden Transcripts*. London: Yale University Press.

Shilling, C. 2005. *The Body and Social Theory*. London: Sage.

Sinha, S.S. 2006. 'Patriarchy, colonialism and capitalism: Unearthing the history of Adivasi women miners in Chotanagpur'. In K. Lahiri-Dutt and M. Macintyre (eds), *Women Miners in Developing Countries: Pit Women and Others*. Farnham: Ashgate Publishing, pp. 89–107.

Smith, D.W. 2006. 'Digging through layers of class, gender and ethnicity: Korean women miners in Prewar, Japan'. In K. Lahiri-Dutt and M. Macintyre (eds), *Women Miners in Developing Countries: Pit Women and Others*. Farnham: Ashgate Publishing, pp. 111–130.

Sone, S. 2006. 'Japanese coal mining: Women discovered'. In K. Lahiri-Dutt and M. Macintyre (eds), *Women Miners in Developing Countries: Pit Women and Others*. Farnham: Ashgate Publishing, pp. 51–72.

Stewart, P.F. 2012. 'Labour time in South African gold mines: 1886–2006', unpublished PhD dissertation, University of the Witwatersrand, Johannesburg.

INTERVIEWS

Babalwa, July 2012, Rustenburg

Mama Mavis, October 2012, Rustenburg

Maria, April 2012, Rustenburg

CLASS, SOCIAL MOBILITY AND AFRICAN WOMEN IN SOUTH AFRICA

Jane Mbithi-Dikgole

INTRODUCTION

Despite the post-apartheid government's quest for an inclusive economy to reduce structural inequalities, African women continue to be marginalised in the labour market, where unemployment remains high. Notwithstanding the introduction of various policies[1] aimed at redressing the inequalities of the past by supporting the assimilation of previously disadvantaged groups into the labour market, unequal access to jobs and labour discrimination remain evident, with unemployment rates being significantly higher for women and particularly African women (Van Klaveren et al. 2009; Bhorat and Goga 2013; Shepherd 2008; Ranchhod 2010). However, in South Africa participation in the labour market remains largely influenced by race, class and gender. African females are not a homogeneous group as their experiences of race, class and gender depend largely upon their location in these social structures, where socio-demographic factors such as financial resources, economic opportunity and quality of education affect individuals differently (Department of Women 2015; Meiring et al. 2018). The prospects of upward social mobility amongst African women are further determined by factors including an individual's family background, parental education and household economic status as well as their own educational status (Louw et al. 2006; Tonheim and Matose 2013).

This chapter aims to show that participation in paid work and the division of unpaid labour within households is a gendered struggle as well as a class-based struggle. Gender inequality in unpaid care work results in labour outcome gaps and influences how women experience productive work. Social reproduction theorists argue that the continuation of capitalism is dependent on the human labour that produces life itself (Luxton 2006: 36). The chapter highlights the myriad ways in which social reproduction is unevenly differentiated and distributed by race, class and gender, resulting in poor women largely bearing the burden of income inequality. Most importantly, the availability of work opportunities for women is not sufficient to gauge the progress in gender equality in the workforce and the home, nor does it signify that women are automatically emancipated by participating in the workforce. The chapter highlights the importance of disaggregating the category 'women' by class in order to prioritise the needs of women, to ensure actual emancipation rather than mere formal equality. I show that intersectionality as a framework is key to understanding African women's conditions in South Africa and further illustrate African women's social mobility through a class perspective. The empirical findings from a study that I conducted to ascertain the effects of social class on African women's future work choices and the process through which these expectations develop and shape their prospects regarding paid work, will be employed to support and enrich some of the arguments made in this chapter. Through in-depth interviews, I explored middle-class and working-class African women entrepreneurs' career aspirations and labour market choices and how these limit their social mobility.[2]

CHALLENGES FACING AFRICAN WOMEN BEFORE AND DURING COVID-19

A Statistics South Africa (StatsSA 2017) vulnerability report revealed that women are the most vulnerable to poverty due to social inequalities and rising unemployment. While gender equality and the empowerment of women has been central to South Africa's democracy, unemployment and poverty remain widespread amongst African women. The highly stratified society and labour market prevalent during apartheid forced African women to occupy the lowest positions in both arenas due to restrictions on education, training, housing, work and pay (Lalthapersad 2002). Despite the progress made since 1994, from a socio-economic viewpoint, South Africa still remains one of the most unequal countries in the world. According to Murray Leibbrandt et al. (2012), 85 per cent of income inequality is caused by labour market income, with unemployment being the driver of inequality. The StatsSA

Quarterly Labour Force Survey (2018) reported that the unemployment rate was higher amongst African women (33.2 per cent) than amongst coloured (22.9 per cent), Indian/Asian (12.2 per cent) and white women (7.4 per cent). However, class position is a determining factor in terms of how women experience their levels of material wellbeing and life opportunities. The findings from my study exemplified that class influences women's expectations about future work and affects their occupational choices. Both middle-class and working-class women's perceptions of future work opportunities were formed mainly by the availability or absence of educational opportunities as well as the race and gender dynamics in the South African workforce. For instance, educational equality does not guarantee equality in the workplace for middle-class women as the 'glass ceiling' effect continues to hinder their progress in the workplace. More so, working-class women without specialised skills due to lack of educational opportunities anticipate working in menial jobs. The relationship between education and workforce participation is not straightforward in South Africa, as systematic discrimination in the labour market affects African women's access to opportunities, regardless of their class and education.

In South Africa, African women make up a large percentage of the poor, mainly in rural areas where they live in dire poverty. Thus, poverty patterns continue to be gendered and female-headed households are more likely to have low incomes, to be dependent on social grants, and less likely to have employed members (StatsSA 2010). Due to poverty and unemployment, women are at more risk of contracting HIV/AIDS than are men. HIV/AIDS infections are highest among African females (Drimie 2002; Shisana et al. 2014; Harrison et al. 2015; Zuma et al. 2014; Gilbert and Selikow 2011; Williams et al.2017). Since most of those affected by HIV are poor adults and women, the human capital of these adults will also be lost, which can lead to a chain reaction, including a negative impact on socio-economic status by constraining the individual's ability to work and earn income, hence affecting future generations and intergenerational mobility.

The vulnerability of poor women was further exposed during the Covid-19 pandemic.[3] A report commissioned by the United Nations Development Programme (UNDP) South Africa revealed that women in the informal sector were more impacted by the consequences of the Covid-19 outbreak than those employed in the formal sector (UNDP 2020). African women are overrepresented in the informal sector and are susceptible to higher poverty risk across the spectrum of informal employment types; they hold less secure jobs and have less capacity to absorb economic shocks, which aggravates existing inequalities (Rogan and Alfers 2019; International Labour Organization 2020; United Nations 2020; Jain et al. 2020). Recent surveys conducted by the National Income Dynamics Study (NIDS) and the Coronavirus Rapid Mobile Survey (CRAM)[4] during the national lockdown showed that the restrictions on individual mobility and business activities have a direct impact on people's employment prospects (Ranchhod and Daniels 2020). Daniela Casale and Dorrit Posel (2020), who utilised the NIDS-CRAM survey to study the early effects of Covid-19 in the paid and unpaid economies in South Africa, found that the lockdown measures destabilised work in the unpaid care arena, with the childcare burden increasing rapidly for many women who were already bearing this responsibility pre-lockdown. Additionally, the increasing tensions and distress caused by Covid-19 resulted in an increase in intimate partner violence (IPV). African working women are particularly at risk of experiencing IPV because of their 'poor living conditions with already burdened access to health, safety, policing and socioeconomic needs' (Parry and Gordon 2020; Blouws 2020). Without a doubt, the existing systemic instabilities of capitalism were exposed by the crisis of work caused by the Covid-19 pandemic. The feminisation of unpaid labour, violence and the reproduction of patriarchy, as argued by Nigam (2020), have exposed the unequal power relations which predominantly affect women. Consequently, the devaluation of work typically performed by women is central to processes of capital accumulation and gender plays a key role in the dynamics of social reproduction but not one that operates in isolation from relations of class and race (Stevano et al. 2021; Bannerji 2011). At the same time it can equally be argued that while the class location of women is considered in intersectional feminism, the cause and endurance of class positions are not straightforward and may not be adequately explained. Bell hooks (2014: 40) quotes an American feminist writer, Rita Mae Brown, to emphasise that class is much more than an issue of money. According to Brown, 'class involve[s] your behavior, your basic assumptions, how you are taught to behave, what you expect from yourself and from others, your concept of a future … how you think, feel, act'. Thus, while the presence or absence of social mobility for African women can be attributed to these dimensions, the neoliberal economy persistently increases social inequalities across racial, gendered and class lines. The incorporation of women into the labour market is far from turning out to be always positive, especially given that the majority of women are concentrated in undervalued and poorly protected sectors where neoliberal reforms have pushed them into even greater precarity and vulnerability (Falquet 2016; Talahite 2010). This is why a gender-based analysis cannot proceed without a simultaneous analysis in terms of class and race.

Shulamith Firestone (1972), as cited in Cock and Luxton (2013: 128), argues that '"the economy" and "the family" are distinct sites generating class and gender hierarchies and that the subordination of women was a necessary precondition for the development of class inequalities'. In South Africa, the radically changing forms of employment pose a far-reaching threat to economically vulnerable groups that are mostly African women who lack options to assemble a livelihood (Mabilo 2018). This results in the feminisation of labour, which signifies low-wage, itinerant jobs and a lowering of employment conditions for women.

CONCEPTUALISING SOCIAL REPRODUCTION AND SOCIAL MOBILITY

The gendered nature of social reproduction is not atypical in South Africa and class inequalities lead to a disparity in care work, with women taking on a far greater share of unpaid and paid care work under difficult working conditions, particularly for those living in poverty. In short, women bear the burden of care work and work in the home; reproductive work is informally cast as not 'real work' and mostly performed by women even as they increase the time they allocate to paid work (Delaney and Macdonald 2018; Budlender 2008). This may result in some women leaving their paid positions in the labour market or opting for the more flexible hours offered by temporary employment, as they juggle household responsibilities and unpaid caring for family members (Parry and Gordon 2020). In order to create an equilibrium between paid work, caring for children and other unpaid care-work activities, women living in poverty may seek out more precarious forms of employment which may restrict their choices about work location. Nancy Folbre (2006: 185) argues that 'as women juggle productive and reproductive work, time becomes a limited resource as the time they use to fulfil care responsibilities could be spent developing their educational skills in market-related activities'. Frene Ginwala, Maureen Mackintosh and Doreen Massey (1992) note that this pressure on women's time can hinder the networks of relations among women which are so important to community strength and survival.

Consequently, the obligation of unpaid care work confines African women's progress and opportunities to various spheres such as education, skills development and employment. Citing the feminist movement, Jacklyn Cock and Meg Luxton (2013: 131) posit that in order to thrive, capitalist economies depend on the unpaid care work of women, which acts as a significant subsidy for the private profit making essential to capitalism, and that the divisions of labour that make this care work central in women's lives are key to the maintenance of women's oppression and subordination. Based on this analysis, the integration of relations of production and reproduction 'as part of the same socio-economic process' has been echoed by social reproduction theorists (Bezanson and Luxton 2006: 37).

As discussed in the previous section, neoliberalism is one of the causes of gender inequality globally. In South Africa, the post-apartheid neoliberal policies have not benefited previously disadvantaged groups and have intensified African women's economic vulnerability. The inability of the post-apartheid state to transform the position of women, particularly black women, has confined women in a poverty trap, leaving many with limited choices. The formation of the Women's National Coalition by the African National Congress (ANC) Women's League mobilised women from all walks of life with the aim of putting gender at the centre of the agenda, but lacked an integrated approach to promote women's interests. The ANC Women's League has not challenged the neoliberal project of the ANC state which causes the crises of social reproduction faced by African women.

Jacklyn Cock (2018) argues that the feminist analysis of the relation between a gendered division of labour and women's oppression is often affirmed, but seldom questioned. This unconscious liberal feminism is not changing power relations and class dynamics and advances a particular form of social mobility which is truly exclusionary. Precariousness should thus be studied and recognised beyond employment and should include the 'precarization of social reproduction' (Candeias 2004: 1), as these spheres interact with and condition each other.

Allison Pugh (2015) addresses the relation between precarious work and gender inequality by emphasising that there is class and gender difference in how people respond to the culture of insecurity. According to her, middle-class persons seem able to maintain a moral wall between market and home as they derive a sense of confidence and privilege from their immersion in market transactions. On the other hand, working-class members adopt a more detached or independent stance within both paid employment and family life, as they have too few resources to support such boundary work (Pugh 2015). This was confirmed in my study, which revealed that African women, irrespective of their class location, struggle to create an equilibrium between paid work and family responsibilities. However, socio-economic privileges influence the strategies that women employ to overcome role conflict. As pointed out by Shireen Hassim and Shahra Razavi (cited in Fakier and Cock 2009), increasing poverty and the commodification of the economy are changing the coping strategies of households, causing disruptions in gender and generational configurations of work and responsibility. The findings from my study showed that economic privileges compelled middle-class African women to consider hiring domestic workers and/or nannies or enrolling their younger children in childcare centres in order to reduce household demands on their time, while increasing available time to grow their businesses. On the other hand, working-class women relied heavily on family members, especially older children and relatives, as well as communal support such as neighbours and friends, to overcome the role conflict. The reliance on marginalised women to do domestic work allows middle-class women to engage in paid work, which accentuates that class location affects how women assume social reproduction, or not. The desperation for better opportunities leads to the 'feminization of survival', a term used by Saskia Sassen (cited in Fakier and Cock 2009) to describe a process where economically desperate women leave the responsibilities of social reproduction in their households in the hands of other women in search for opportunities or to engage in economic activities outside the home. This is exemplified in this woman's account: 'My extended family and neighbours have always been support and make my life easier since I explore business opportunities outside my community. I never worry as I know my children are in good hands. Without their help, I am not sure I would have achieved much' (Mathabo, interview, July 2014).[5]

Clearly, the desperation for better opportunities results in women, especially working-class women, participating in a 'care chain', as noted by Khayaat Fakier and Jacklyn Cock (2009), which results in African working-class households becoming sites of a 'crisis of social reproduction' and indeed the shock absorbers of this crisis. This crisis is further explained by Jacklyn Cock and Meg Luxton (2013: 132) in their analysis of domestic labour amongst working class women. They argue that

> from a social and structural perspective, in raising their children, parents are ensuring the generational reproduction of the working class. This analysis theorised households, families, kinship systems as crucial relations in any social formation and exposed the material basis of working-class women's subordination and its links to the political economy of the capitalist society. It demonstrated housework's contribution in maintaining the capitalist system and showed the important link between working-class housewives and capitalist economies.

The National Gender Machinery (NGM), which stemmed from the national Policy Framework for Women Empowerment and Gender Equality, meant that the state came to be viewed as the site through which equality for women would be created. The NGM was to provide the channels through which women would exercise policy influence with regard to women's interests and serve as structural nodes through which gender equality would be effected (Gouws 2005). The NGM rarely functioned as an instrument to reduce gender inequalities and has been described as insensitive to women's demands and often perceived as being co-opted by the state (Hassim 2005; Meer 2005). The creation of laws does not necessarily translate into the elimination of gender discrimination and, as Nomthandazo Ntlama (2020) argues, the effectiveness of the law depends on the understanding of the dynamics which are the subject of gender equality. Consequently, to ensure women participate and shape the implementation of policies, policy 'production' should

151

assume a bottom-up approach. How women in these structures engage the dialogues in the state contributes to the influence of such structures or machineries. There is a need for policies that seek to improve the conditions of women in paid and unpaid work and that expand women's options in the paid economy. It is not about women enjoying equal status with men, as this does not guarantee equality in jobs and opportunities. Rather, policies ought to take the specific needs of women into account if holistic transformation is to occur (Hassim 1991).

For the above to be realised, the state remains an important vehicle for advancing just and equitable conditions for women through diverse resources that will enable differently positioned women to actualise freedom and equity (Bailey 2016). In South Africa, the state envisioned the adoption of measures to redress social imbalances, such as affirmative action and employment equity, as fundamental to promoting the upward mobility of women in the labour market and to breaking the glass ceiling (Van Zyl and Roodt 2003). However, affirmative strategies have failed to address and transform the underlying causes of the inequalities that women face, in both productive and reproductive spheres. Although it is important that the necessary legislative frameworks are in place to ensure gender equality and the equal employment of women, having these frameworks in place will not in itself change women's positions; it is only effective implementation that will do so. For affirmative action to be effective, it must extend to the advancement and promotion of women in all spheres, which includes social mobilisation and policy actions to overcome the crisis of reproduction and in order to redress the unpaid work that perpetuates neoliberal capitalism (Ginwala 1991; Randriamaro 2013). For Erin Nel (2011), in order to thwart the systematic racism and classism that is prevalent in society, class-based affirmative action would be a more transformative strategy as it is directly concerned with material deprivation and could have the effect of transforming, rather than affirming, reified racial identities.

One of the limitations of liberal feminism is exemplified in the assertion that society in general would benefit from educated women, without paying adequate attention to the conditions of working-class women. The working-class women interviewed in my research acknowledged that their lack of education and skills forced them into precarious employment at an early age in order to support their families. From that point forward, many remained in low-paying jobs with poor working conditions, thus restricting their access to the resources and opportunities that allow people to work towards (or not work towards) fulfilling their potential and experiencing social mobility (Potgieter 2016). Thus, inadequate education and lack of skills limit the employment prospects of poor women in the labour market, leading to poor access to salaried income and limits to social mobility (Lekezwa 2011).

CLASS ANALYSIS AND INTERSECTIONALITY

The various forms of exploitation that women have endured are largely explained through an intersectional framework of class, race and gender that has perpetuated inequality. Intersectionality is understood in a wide variety of ways, as both a theoretical and an analytic tool (Sigle-Rushton and Lindstrom 2013). As Elizabeth Cole (2009: 170) asserts, the concept of intersectionality was offered 'to describe the analytic approaches that simultaneously consider the meaning and consequences of multiple categories of identity, difference and disadvantage that affect a person's beliefs about their capabilities and define their opportunities'. Kimberlé Crenshaw (1989) states that intersectionality symbolises how black people (and more particularly black women) continue to exist at the crossroads of oppression.[6]

The theoretical debates about women, class and work can be situated at the intersection of Marxism and feminism. Socialist feminists reformulated the 'women question' by rethinking key categories of Marxist logic, including production, reproduction, class, consciousness and labour (Hennessy and Ingraham 1997: 6). Although Karl Marx's work did not specifically address the oppression of women, Martha Gimenez (2005: 15) is of the view that his theoretical insights are necessary to contend with 'the oppression of women under capitalism, and with the limitations capitalism poses to feminist politics'. However, for some, the contribution of Marxism to feminism is not straightforward. Heidi Hartmann's (1979) work on the 'unhappy marriage of Marxism and feminism'[7] strongly stressed that the merging of feminism and capitalism was unsustainable and would result in an unhappy marriage as it was marked by extreme inequality, since it subsumed the feminist struggle into the 'larger' struggle against capital (Hartmann 1979: 1). From a South African standpoint, Belinda Bozzoli (1983) noted that the collapsing of female oppression into the capitalist mode of production is the central tendency in analyses of women in South Africa. Thus Hartmann proposed that 'either we need a healthier marriage or we need a divorce' (Hartmann 1979: 1). Wendy Brown (2014) proposes that Marx's work can be used to understand the historical development of women's nature, while Silvia Federici (2018: 19) emphasises that Marx's methodology has given feminists tools to weave together 'gender and class, feminism and anti-capitalism'. Writing from the South African context, Puleng Segalo (2015) proclaims that these dimensions can be used to appreciate the multifaceted levels at which social injustices and inequalities occur to generate a system of oppression. Frene Ginwala (1991) echoed this sentiment by positing that the fundamental issue we have to confront is the interface of race, class and gender that has shaped our society.

The transition to democracy brought gender into the spotlight yet it is obvious that South African society is structured in terms of social groups and it is within the class system that social divisions and inequality occur (Lushaba 2005; Seekings 2003). To fully capture African women's social mobility trend in post-apartheid South Africa, which can be described as the individual's trajectory within a social structure over their lifespan, the social class perspective will help us dissect the many ways inequality is produced and sustained amongst African women from different class groups. The hierarchical structure of society in South Africa, which largely defines access to wealth, prestige and power, was constructed on the basis of race, placing restrictions on where people could live, and the type of education and work occupations they had access to (Taylor and Yu 2009).

To effectively theorise class, Joan Acker (2006) asserts that we need to think of class as constituted by race and gender. Miriam Glucksmann (2009) expanded on the debate on class and gender by arguing that the manner in which labour is divided up in a particular society is highly differentiated by gender and includes productive and reproductive work, paid and unpaid. I argue that incorporating class is essential in order to fully understand the struggles faced by African women in both paid and unpaid work, as women's class location shapes their beliefs and decisions about work and unpaid work. In addition, reproductive work in some cases determines the type of work that women engage in and is experienced differently, given one's class location. My research showed that the women's perceptions of future work opportunities were formed mainly by the availability or absence of educational opportunities, as well as the race and gender dynamics in the South African workforce. Therefore, class influences women's expectations about their future work opportunities and affects their occupational choices. The class factor cannot be ignored as family background and status play a role in women's preparation for and decisions related to paid employment (O'Reilly et al. 2013). Luxton (2006: 37) expounds on the need to consider class analysis in order to understand how production and reproduction are linked. According to her, 'by developing a class analysis that shows how production and reproduction of goods and services and the production of life are part of the integrated process, social reproduction does more than identify the activities involved in the daily generational reproduction of daily life. It allows for an explanation of the structures, relationships and dynamics that reproduce these activities'.

The data from my research revealed that family expectations, which are linked to the family's class location, play a significant role in shaping an individual's career choice and aspirations for the future. As a result, socio-economic standing is distributed along racial lines in South Africa and a family's background has significant consequences for an individual's future and social mobility prospects. A family's socio-economic background shapes the type of support that an individual receives and ultimately the choices they make regarding a future career. The working-class women, who were predominantly raised in working-class homes, highlighted that their parents expected them to work, as expressed by this participant:

> My mum did her best to raise me in times where she had limited choices and resources. She worked as a domestic worker as she never had the opportunity to go to school; hence there were no other jobs for people like her. She was constantly frustrated and would often stress that I should ensure that I find a better job than hers so that my life could be better. As a result, I started working at a young age to help her as we were struggling financially. (Ulwazi, interview, October 2014)

On the other hand, some middle-class women who grew up in middle-class homes explained that their parents encouraged them to seek high-paying jobs as this would guarantee them a financial safety net and reduce the possibility of future financial strain: 'I was constantly told that a job was not enough unless it paid well. My parents believed that a high-paying job acted as a safety net but also kept one motivated. They expected me not to settle for less when I started working' (Kensani, interview, September 2014).

From the above accounts, it is evident that based on their current social class, parents from different classes develop their own social and cultural values, which impact on their children's career choices and decisions. Class thus affects occupational choices by imposing the values and expectations of that social strata on their children's career choices. A class-centred approach to intersectionality can thus be useful to understand the condition of African women in post-apartheid South Africa and to show that their experiences are not homogeneous. Considering only gender is insufficient to fully explain the multidimensional and diverse paths that women across classes follow with respect to career aspirations and work choices (Mbithi 2020). The integration of class into the gender debate should therefore be explored to understand the factors that shape the career aspirations of African women and the process through which workforce expectations are established. Despite the drastic increase of African women in the workforce, many continue to experience what Michelle Fine calls 'the presence of an absence' (2002: 26). This signifies that their 'presence' may remain somewhat of a façade as many continue to face challenges that are directly linked to their class position, race and the fact that they are women. This is demonstrated further below.

AFRICAN WOMEN'S SOCIAL MOBILITY THROUGH CLASS

The Natives Land Act No. 27 of 1913 created socio-economic injustice in terms of poverty and dispossession of land from black South Africans. According to Ben Scully (2017), centuries of colonialism and racialised restrictions elicited a crisis in the traditional agrarian economy, which the majority still relied on as a main source of livelihood. Prior to the Natives Land Act, black South Africans owned and utilised land effectively for their welfare as well as for their economic stability (Modise and Mtshiwelwa 2013). Land dispossession thus led to many families finding alternative work to survive, which meant that they became dependent on employment for survival, thus creating a pool of cheap labour for the white-owned farms and mines (Rugege 2004). The destruction of peasant agriculture and restrictions on the informal economy under apartheid created a society that was overwhelmingly reliant on waged work (Seekings and Nattrass 2005). The migrant system that resulted from the need of black males to migrate to the cities and white farms in order to earn a living and provide for their families, in many cases resulted in the break-up of families and the dislocation of social life (Rugege 2004). Debbie Budlender and Francie Lund (2011: 926) describe the deliberate destruction of the family in apartheid South Africa as 'state-orchestrated destruction of family life'. This is because families were undermined by deliberate strategies implemented through the pass laws, forced removals, urban housing policy and the creation of the homelands (Hall 2017; Hall and Posel 2019).

Sarah Mosoetsa (2004) adds that family and kinship networks in South Africa were historically divided between town and homelands by the migrant labour system. As a result, many men migrated to the city but a range of restrictions prevented them from migrating with their families or settling permanently in urban areas (Budlender and Lund 2011 Posel 2010). Consequently, restrictions on settlement and employment divided families across space (Posel 2010). Rates of marriage and union formation, which were already low, continued to fall, remittances declined and unemployment rates remained persistently high (Hunter 2007; Posel 2010; Posel and Rudwick 2013). Katharine Hall and Dorrit Posel (2012) posit that the majority of African children in South Africa do not grow up in two-parent households, and where children do live with a parent, this is far more likely to be their mother than their father. The restrictions on settlement, commonly referred to as the pass laws, were paramount in ensuring that only employed blacks were allowed within designated white areas, while those who were unemployed and the families of labour migrants were forced to remain in the homelands and townships (Blalock 2014). As a result of male-dominated patterns of labour migration and the institutional constraints of the apartheid period, fathers are more likely than mothers to live separately from their children (Hatch and Posel 2018). This limited African women's economic participation by restricting their mobility and many became economically dependent, focusing on care duties. In the context of low and falling marriage rates in South Africa, women typically bear both economic and caregiving responsibilities for children (Hatch and Posel 2018).

Apartheid further limited black Africans' workplace advancement by denying them educational opportunities (Terreblanche 2002). In the post-apartheid context, unskilled employment within the formal sector has declined while employment within the informal sector has increased, further distorting labour mobility in South Africa and widening unemployment, inequality and poverty (Blalock 2014; Schiel 2014). Given the lack of formal or regular employment amongst African women, many employ livelihood strategies in response to vulnerability, deprivation and insecurity (Beall et al. 2000). One of the strategies that was introduced in South Africa is the social protection system of social grants, which includes, amongst others, old-age pensions, disability grants and a child support grant which currently (in 2020) stands at R740 (US$48.85) per child per month. These interventions are premised to guarantee a minimum livelihood to those who cannot reliably access sufficient income through labour (Dawson and Fouksman 2020).

For many poor women, as revealed in studies conducted by Michelle Williams (2018) and Granlund and Hochfeld (2019) in Cutwini and Keiskammahoek in the Eastern Cape respectively, grants are the only consistent and reliable source of income to meet basic needs and provide a measure of security, survival and increased dignity. This is, however, challenged in my research as most working-class women acknowledged that the child support grant was a temporary solution and insufficient to meet their basic needs. One woman described her situation as 'just getting by': 'This money is not enough given that there is no one else working in my family. We buy, but the money has not done much for us as we struggle every day. I end up borrowing money from relatives, but they are now tired of me because I do not have a job to pay back' (Mary, interview, October 2014).

A cash transfer alone does not alter the economic and political roots of poverty, which are largely structurally determined. As Leila Patel (2016) argues, social assistance has stepped in where the labour market has failed to provide the poor with a reliable means of income. Social grants have thus become a de facto safety net for the long-term unemployed and underemployed (Scully 2017), with female household members bearing the burden of caregiving and unable to compensate for the inadequacies of the labour market and basic service provision (Fakier and Cock 2009).

The increased number of black women in the labour market was followed by the development of the black middle class in South Africa. The middle class can

157

be described as those people who occupy either the middle strata of income distribution in a given country or a middle position between a lower class and an upper class with unique occupations and skills (Seekings and Nattrass 2005; Mattes 2015). Occupation and skills further determine an individual's life chances and are instrumental in class mobility. Roger Southall (2016) stresses the importance of family background, shaped by class, in determining children's life chances and class mobility. As noted, the family, as the primary and most important agent of socialisation, plays an important role in the vocational development and decision-making process of an individual – a process that starts in childhood. Consequently, a family's racial background and class location influence this process. Middle-class women participating in my research shared that parental support and education encouraged them to remodel the middle-class life: 'My parents were both teachers and worked hard to ensure that I went to the best schools and universities and that I had everything that I needed to perform well. They were also emotionally supportive and constantly stressed that I should work hard at school. This was the turning point for me as it highlighted the importance of education in shaping my future' (Lerato, interview, August 2014).

For other middle-class women, especially those who grew up in working-class homes, the lack of parental education as well as challenging circumstances within a household can also be motivating factors for one to aim for a better future and find work. In my research, the accounts of such women illustrate 'class escape', as their parents wanted them to have a better future: 'I felt as though my parents spoke to me through their daily struggles about valuing the opportunities I had. While they had very little, they worked hard and sacrificed financially so that I could attain a degree. It is evident that they wanted me to have a better life than the one they had which meant that I had to have a qualification and a better job' (Priscilla, interview, August 2014).

At the same time, huge numbers of African women are confined to an 'underclass' of unemployment, poverty and social exclusion. The 'underclass' refers to people who live in extreme poverty, and those involved in ad hoc or informal sector survival activities as they lack the basic education and skills needed for stable employment (Schlemmer 2005: 3; Wright 2015: 4). This was evident from the accounts of the working-class women in my research, who grew up in extreme poverty, as described by this woman:

> Growing up in a small town in rural Limpopo, my three siblings and I had a
> difficult childhood. My parents were unemployed, and poverty was rife. As
> the eldest of the three siblings, it was difficult to think about the future amid

the uncertainty that confronted me. I dropped out of school, a situation I had predicted, given my parents' inability to pay school fees. But that was not it; I felt that it was my responsibility to do something about the financial crisis at home. The pressure that my parents put on my shoulders to find work was the final stamp to the realisation that I had missed the most important phase of my life, which was getting an education. It was a gone dream, and I had to think about life without skills and qualifications. (Thulani, interview, July 2014)

As Sarah Damaske (2011) argues, women of different classes face uneven structural limitations and form different expectations about work and family that shape how their work trajectories and family trajectories are interrelated over the course of life. These expectations are further influenced by gender stereotypes and cultural expectations based on a family's class location. Traditional gender messages influence middle-class women with respect to, for example, their career choices and their role as caregivers in the home. As this woman puts it: 'Growing up, my dad would tell me that irrespective of how educated I am, I should always put my family first and take care of my husband. He kept emphasising that men leave when women are too occupied in their careers, and I should always think about this when I look for work one day. These comments affected my career choices' (Kopano, interview, August 2014).

On the other hand, working-class women are gendered in their desperation for work or marriage at an early age. The socio-economic challenges experienced by working-class women result in future work uncertainties: 'I was not surprised when my parents announced I was to get married, as it was the norm. The fact that I had not attended school gave me no other life choices. They also had to survive, and they viewed my marriage as a reward for the family from a monetary point of view. As a result, I never saw the possibility of having a career one day' (Thembeka, interview, October 2014).

According to Magda Rukhadze (2018), early marriage, especially for women, has socio-economic risks, among them reduced access to education and employment opportunities. Jeanette Bayisenge (2010) adds that the potential rewards for educating daughters are too far off; hence, many poor families do not recognise their education as an investment. The participant's account outlined above suggests that gender roles delineate what women and men are expected to do, which affects the talents they cultivate and the opportunities and constraints they encounter, and this correlates with the career paths they pursue.

CONCLUSION

This chapter has emphasised how social reproduction is differentiated by race, class and gender. African women continue to experience unequal access to jobs and labour market discrimination due to their position in a highly stratified society. African women also continue to experience high rates of poverty and unemployment and are overrepresented in the informal sector, where they hold less secure jobs with low pay and precarious working conditions. This aggravates their vulnerability and existing inequalities. Their dire situation is further exacerbated by unforeseen shocks such as Covid-19, which has threatened work in both paid and unpaid arenas. Unpaid care work further confines African women to the domestic sphere and restricts their participation in the public sphere. As highlighted in the chapter, any analysis of unpaid work and care work must be aware of how gender and class impact the economic lives of women differently. Women's disproportionate share of unpaid work shapes their home experience, limits their participation in and gains from the labour market and contributes to their vulnerability, particularly where labour outcomes such as wages and job quality are concerned. Integrating class into gender debates is crucial to an understanding of women's work choices and prospects, especially the multifaceted and diverse paths that women follow to remodel their work–family options across classes. However, it is worth emphasising an important dimension of social reproduction in capitalism, which is the work of 'making workers' – this includes not only the physical work but also affective labour and cultural transmission to children. In this regard, the way parents shape expectations for future employment is a direct part of social reproduction – not just equipping people for the labour market in terms of skills, education and so on, but also to accept their classed place in the labour market. This demonstrates the role of the family in the reproduction of social class and class inequalities (Crompton 2006). As exemplified in the excerpts from my study, the occupational position of parents has an effect on the intergenerational transmission of occupational types and social mobility for adults. Helen Hester and Nick Srnicek (2017) argue that care work is work (regardless of whether it is privatised, public or personal) and it plays a crucial role within the complex and systematic challenges of contemporary society. As illustrated by Cock and Luxton's (2013: 137) argument, 'both public and private forms operate within a capitalist framework and neither provides secure conditions of social reproduction for the majority, although the former modified somewhat the vulnerabilities produced by the market economies while the latter has undermined the capacities of a growing population to ensure its own social reproduction'.

Shamim Meer (2005) points out that the state continues to reinforce existing race, class and gender disparities. This can be attributed to institutions' failure to address the ways in which the state continues to reinforce these dimensions of oppression. While legislative frameworks are necessary to ensure gender equality and the equal employment of women, many have not been transformative and emancipatory, hence policies need to consider the particular needs of African women. The participation of women in the South African labour market is influenced by gender, race and class; the experiences of African women are profoundly shaped by their class location. Therefore, a class perspective to intersectionality will help us dissect the many ways in which inequality is produced and sustained amongst African women from different class groups, as class location has enduring effects on the future work expectations and social mobility of African women. Family background, shaped by class, is a leading factor in determining an individual's life chances and class mobility. According to Cock and Luxton (2013: 130), 'both the production of the means of life and the production of life itself are distinct but interrelated necessary social processes'. Moreover, the 'needs' of workers are not natural or constant but are themselves relative and determined socially, such that the standard of necessity at which workers are reproduced is 'enforced by class struggle' (Lebowitz, cited in Bhattacharya 2017: 79).

NOTES

1   Structural transformation to address poverty and inequality was pertinent after apartheid as South Africa entered a new era. Key policies included the Reconstruction and Development Programme (RDP), a Growth, Employment and Redistribution (GEAR) approach, the New Growth Path and the National Development Plan, which favoured a market system, as well as the affirmative action policies regarding employment, such as Broad-Based Black Economic Empowerment (BBBEE) for businesses (see Breakfast and Phago 2019: 46).

2   The purpose of the study was to gain a deeper understanding of the effects of class and gender on middle-class and working-class African women entrepreneurs and their perceptions of work and opportunities available to them. How do they perceive these experiences? How have these experiences affected them and how have they responded to these experiences? The research was conducted in Johannesburg and Pretoria, where the middle-class women operated their businesses, and in White River and Tzaneen, where working-class women operated survivalist businesses. The study employed a qualitative research method and utilised snowballing and purposive sampling techniques to select participants. In total, a sample of 103 women was selected and interviewed. Out of the 103, 41 were middle-class women and 62 were working-class women. Given my inability to speak the local languages, the recruitment of interpreters to assist in the research process was necessary, particularly with respect to the working-class

women, since most could not speak English. In-depth, face-to-face interviews were predominantly used to collect data and in some cases observations were paramount to understand the gender dynamics in the household and business, and how the women reconciled the trade-off between childcare and paid work. Data analysis software known as NVIVO was used to analyse the data.

3   The unprecedented economic impact of Covid-19 has resulted in many workers experiencing shocks related to earnings and employment. Simone Schotte and Rocco Zizzamia (2021) detail that the consequences of Covid-19 appear especially severe and long-lasting for those in informal work, whether in wage labour or self-employment.

4   The CRAM survey provides monthly nationally representative data on key outcomes such as unemployment, household income, child hunger and access to government grants (https://cramsurvey.org/about/).

5   All interviewee names used in this chapter are pseudonyms.

6   The theory of intersectionality was birthed from debates on critical theory. See Kimberlé Crenshaw's (1989) work.

7   Also see Cock and Luxton's (2013) engaging piece in which they debate whether Marxism and feminism is an 'unhappy marriage or creative partnership'.

REFERENCES

Acker, J. 2006. 'Inequality regimes: Gender, class, and race in organizations', *Gender & Society* 20 (4): 441–464.

Bailey, L. 2016. 'Feminism, liberal'. In N.A. Naples (ed.), *The Wiley Blackwell Encyclopedia of Gender and Sexuality Studies*. New Jersey: Wiley Blackwell, pp. 1–3.

Bannerji, H. 2011. 'Building from Marx: Reflections on "race", gender, and class'. In S. Mojab and S. Carpenter (eds), *Educating from Marx*. New York: Palgrave Macmillan, pp. 41–60.

Bayisenge, J. 2010. 'Early marriage as a barrier to girl's education: A developmental challenge in Africa'. In C. Ikekeonwu (ed.), *Girl-Child Education in Africa*. Nigeria: Catholic Institute for Development, Justice & Peace (CIDJAP), pp. 43–66.

Beall, J., Crankshaw, O. and Parnell, S. 2000. 'The causes of unemployment in post-apartheid Johannesburg and the livelihood strategies of the poor', *Tijdschrift voor Economische en Sociale Geografie* 91 (4): 379–396.

Bezanson, K. and Luxton, M. 2006. 'Introduction: Social reproduction and feminist political economy'. In K. Bezanson and M. Luxton (eds), *Social Reproduction: Feminist Political Economy Challenges Neo-Liberalism*. Montreal and Kingston: McGill-Queens University Press, pp. 3–10.

Bhattacharya, T. 2017. 'How not to skip class: Social reproduction of labour and the global working class'. In T. Bhattacharya (ed.), *Social Reproduction Theory: Remapping Class, Recentering Oppression*. London: Pluto, pp. 68–93.

Bhorat, H. and Goga, S. 2013. 'The gender wage gap in post-apartheid South Africa: A re-examination', *Journal of African Economies* 22 (5): 827–848.

Blalock, C. 2014. 'Labour migration and employment in post-apartheid rural South Africa', unpublished PhD thesis, University of Memphis.

Blouws, C. 2020. 'Covid-19: Womxn in South Africa more vulnerable than most', *Daily Maverick*, 24 March. Accessed 3 July 2020, https://www.dailymaverick.co.za/article/2020-03-24-covid-19-womxn-in-south-africa-more-vulnerable-than-most/.

Bozzoli, B. 1983. 'Marxism, feminism and South African studies', *Journal of Southern African Studies* 9 (2): 139–171.

Breakfast, N. and Phago, K. 2019. 'Post-development approach in the post-apartheid governance of South Africa', *Journal of Gender, Information and Development in Africa*, SI (2): 45–62.

Brown, W. 2014. Is Marx (Capital) Secular?', *Qui Parle* 23 (1): 109–124.

Budlender, D. 2008. 'The statistical evidence on care and non-care work across six countries'. Geneva: United Nations Research Institute for Social Development (UNRISD). Acce ssed 19 October 2020, https://www.unrisd.org/80256B3C005BCCF9/(httpAuxPages)/ F9FEC4EA774573E7C1257560003A96B2/%24file/BudlenderREV.pdf.

Budlender, D. and Lund, F. 2011. 'South Africa: A legacy of family disruption', *Development and Change* 42 (4): 925–946.

Candeias, M. 2004. *Double precarization of labour and reproduction: Perspectives of expanded (re) appropriation*. Berlin: Rosa Luxemburg Stiftung.

Casale, D. and Posel, D. 2020. *Gender and the early effects of the COVID-19 crisis in the paid and unpaid economies in South Africa*. Wave 1: NIDS-CRAM Working Paper No. 4. Accessed 12 July 2021, https://cramsurvey.org/wp-content/uploads/2020/07/Casale-Gender-the-early-effects-of-the-COVID-19-crisis-in-the-paid-unpaid-economies-in-South-Africa.pdf.

Cock, J. 2018. 'The climate crisis and a "just transition" in South Africa: An eco-feminist-socialist perspective'. In V. Satgar (ed.), *The Climate Crisis: South African and Global Democratic Eco-Socialist Alternatives*. Johannesburg: Wits University Press, pp. 210–230.

Cock, J. and Luxton, M. 2013. 'Marxism and feminism: "Unhappy marriage" or creative partnership'. In M. Williams and V. Satgar (eds), *Marxisms in the 21st Century: Crisis, Critique & Struggle*. Johannesburg: Wits University Press, pp. 116–142.

Cole, E. 2009. 'Intersectionality and research in psychology', *American Psychologist* 64 (3): 170–180.

Crenshaw, K. 1989. 'Demarginalizing the intersection of race and sex: A black feminist critique of antidiscrimination doctrine, feminist theory and antiracist politics', *University of Chicago Legal Forum* 1 (8): 139–167.

Crompton, R. 2006. 'Class and family', *The Sociological Review* 54 (4): 658–677. https://doi. org/10.1111/j.1467-954X.2006.00665.

Damaske, S. 2011. *For the Family? How Class and Gender Shape Women's Work*. New York: Oxford University Press.

Dawson, H. and Fouksman, E. 2020. 'Labour, laziness and distribution: Work imaginaries among the South African unemployed', *Africa* 90 (2): 229–251. https://doi.org:10.1017/ S0001972019001037.

Delaney, A. and Macdonald, F. 2018. 'Thinking about informality: Gender (in)equality (in) decent work across geographic and economic boundaries', *Labour & Industry: A Journal of the Social and Economic Relations of Work* 28 (2): 99–114.

Department of Women. 2015. *The Status of Women in the South African Economy*. Pretoria: Department of Women. Accessed 25 September 2020, https://www.gov.za/sites/default/ files/gcis_document/201508/statusofwomeninsaeconomy.pdf.

Drimie, S. 2002. 'The impact of HIV/AIDS on rural households and land issues in Southern and Eastern Africa'. Background paper prepared for the Food and Agricultural Organization, Human Sciences Research Council, Pretoria. Accessed 18 November 2020, http://www.fao.org/3/a-ad696e.pdf.

Fakier, K. and Cock, J. 2009. 'A gendered analysis of the crisis of social reproduction in contemporary South Africa', *International Feminist Journal of Politics* 11 (3): 353–371.

Falquet, J. 2016. 'A gender perspective on neoliberal globalization: "Global women" in the shadow of military- industrial systems'. *Contemporary Marxism Review* 13, Center for Contemporary Marxism Abroad, Fudan University, Shanghai.

Federici, S. 2018. 'Notes on gender in Marx's *Capital*', *Continental Thought & Theory: A Journal of Intellectual Freedom* 1 (4): 19–37.

Fine, M. 2002. '2001 Carolyn Sherif Award Address: The presence of an absence', *Psychology of Women Quarterly* 26 (1): 25–35. https://doi.org: 10.1111/1471-6402.00039.

Folbre, N. 2006. 'Measuring care: Gender, empowerment, and the care economy', *Journal of Human Development* 7 (2): 183–199.

Gilbert, L. and Selikow, T. 2011. 'The epidemic in this country has the face of a woman: Gender and HIV/AIDS in South Africa', *African Journal of AIDS Research* 10 (1): 325–334.

Giménez, M. 2005. 'Capitalism and the oppression of women: Marx revisited', *Science & Society* 69 (1): 11–32.

Ginwala, F. 1991. 'Women and the elephant: The need to redress gender oppression'. In S. Bazilli (ed.), *Putting Women on the Agenda*. Johannesburg: Ravan Press, pp. 62–74.

Ginwala, F., Mackintosh, M. and Massey, D. 1992. *Gender and economic policy in a democratic South Africa*. Collected seminar papers, Institute of Commonwealth Studies (44): 146–171.

Glucksmann, M. 2009. 'Formations, connections and divisions of labour', *Sociology* 43 (5): 878–895.

Gouws, A. 2005. 'Shaping women's citizenship: Contesting the boundaries of the state and discourse'. In A. Gouws (ed.), *(Un)Thinking Citizenship: Feminists Debates in Contemporary South Africa*. Cape Town: UCT Press, pp. 71–90.

Granlund, S. and Hochfeld, T. 2019. '"That child support grant gives me powers" – Exploring social and relational aspects of cash transfers in South Africa in times of livelihood change', *The Journal of Development Studies* 56 (6): 1230–1244.

Hall, K. 2017. 'Children's spatial mobility and household transitions: A study of child mobility and care arrangements in the context of maternal migration', unpublished PhD thesis, University of the Witwatersrand, Johannesburg.

Hall, K. and Posel, D. 2012. 'Inequalities in children's household contexts: Place, parental presence and migration'. In K. Hall, I. Woolard, L. Lake and C. Smith (eds), *South African Child Gauge 2012*. Cape Town: Children's Institute, University of Cape Town, pp. 43–47.

Hall, K. and Posel, D. 2019. 'Fragmenting the family? The complexity of household migration strategies in post-apartheid South Africa', *IZA Journal of Development and Migration* 10 (2): 1–20.

Harrison, A., Colvin, C., Kuo, C., Swartz, A. and Lurie, M. 2015. 'Sustained high HIV incidence in young women in southern Africa: Social, behavioral, and structural factors and emerging intervention approaches', *Current HIV/AIDS Reports* 12 (2): 207–215.

Hartmann, H. 1979. 'The unhappy marriage of marxism and feminism: Towards a more progressive union', *Capital & Class* 3 (2): 1–33.

Hassim, S. 1991. 'Gender, social location and feminist politics in South Africa', *Transformation* 15: 65–82.

Hassim, S. 2005. 'The gender pact and democratic consolidation: Institutionalising gender equality in the South African state', *Feminist Studies* 29 (3): 505–528.

Hatch, M. and Posel, D. 2018. 'Who cares for children? A quantitative study of childcare in South Africa', *Development Southern Africa* 35 (2): 267–282.

Hennessy, R. and Ingraham, C. (eds). 1997. *Materialist feminism: A reader in class, difference, and women's lives*. New York and London: Routledge.

Hester, H. and Srnicek, N. 2017. 'The crisis of social reproduction and the end of work'. In F. Gonzalez (ed.), *The Age of Perplexity: Rethinking the World We Knew*, pp. 372–389. Fundacion BBVA Open Mind Books, e-pub. Accessed 10 February 2023, https://www.bbvaopenmind.com/en/books/the-age-of-perplexity/.

hooks, b. 2014. *Feminism is for Everybody: Passionate Politics* (second edition). E-book. New York: Routledge.

Hunter, M. 2007. 'The changing political economy of sex in South Africa: The significance of unemployment and inequalities to the scale of the AIDS pandemic', *Social Science & Medicine* 64 (3): 689–700. https://doi.org: 10.1016/j.socscimed.2006.09.015.

International Labour Organization. 2020. *COVID-19 crisis and the informal economy: Immediate responses and policy challenges*. Geneva: ILO. Accessed 2 October 2020, https://www.ilo.org/wcmsp5/groups/public/@ed_protect/@protrav/@travail/documents/briefingnote/wcms_743623.pdf.

Jain, R., Budlender, J., Zizzamia, R. and Bassier, I. 2020. *The labour market and poverty impacts of Covid-19 in South Africa*. CSAE Working Paper WPS/2020-14. Centre for the Study of African Economies, University of Oxford.

Lalthapersad, P. 2002. 'Occupational segregation of work and income disparities among South African women', *South African Journal of Economic and Management Sciences* 5 (1): 111–122.

Leibbrandt, M., Finn, A. and Woolard, I. 2012. 'Describing and decomposing post-apartheid income inequality in South Africa', *Development Southern Africa* 29 (1): 19–34.

Lekezwa, B. 2011. 'The impact of social grants as anti-poverty policy instruments in South Africa: An analysis using household theory to determine intra-household allocation of unearned income', Master's dissertation, University of Stellenbosch.

Louw, M., Van der Berg, S. and Yu, D. 2006. *Educational attainment and intergenerational social mobility in South Africa*. Stellenbosch Economics Working Papers 09/06. Department of Economics and Bureau for Economic Research, Stellenbosch University. Accessed 9 November 2020, https://ideas.repec.org/p/sza/wpaper/wpapers23.html.

Lushaba, L. 2005. 'From apartheid social stratification to democratic social divisions: Examining the contradictory notions of social transformation between Indian and black South Africans'. In C. Hendricks and L. Lushaba (eds), *From National Liberation to Democratic Renaissance in Southern Africa*. Senegal: Codesria, pp. 111–139.

Luxton, M. 2006. 'Feminist political economy in Canada and the politics of social reproduction'. In K. Bezanson and M. Luxton (eds), *Social Reproduction: Feminist Political Economy Challenges Neo-Liberalism*. Montreal and Kingston: McGill-Queens University Press, pp. 11–44.

Mabilo, M. 2018. 'Women in the informal economy: Precarious labour in South Africa', unpublished Master's thesis, University of Stellenbosch.

Mattes, R. 2015. 'South Africa's emerging black middle class: A harbinger of political change?', *Journal of International Development* 27 (5): 665–692.

Mbithi, J. 2020. 'Class, gender and women's work: A case study of women entrepreneurs in South Africa', unpublished PhD thesis, University of the Witwatersrand, Johannesburg.

Meer, S. 2005. 'Freedom for women: Mainstreaming gender in the South African liberation struggle and beyond', *Gender and Development* 13 (2): 36–45.

Meiring, T., Kannemeyer, C. and Potgieter, E. 2018. *The gap between rich and poor: South African society's biggest divide depends on where you think you fit in*. Working Paper No. 220. Southern Africa Labour and Development Research Unit, University of Cape Town. Accessed 11 October 2020, http://www.opensaldru.uct.ac.za/bitstream/handle/1 1090/901/2018220Saldruwp.pdf?sequence=1.

Modise, L. and Mtshiwelwa, N. 2013. 'The Natives Land Act of 1913 engineered the poverty of black South Africans: A historico-ecclesiastical perspective', *Studia Historiae Ecclesiasticae* 39 (2): 359–378.

Mosoetsa, S. 2004. *The legacies of apartheid and implications of economic liberalisation: A post-apartheid township*. Working Paper No. 49. Development Research Centre, London. Accessed 7 October 2020, http://eprints.lse.ac.uk/28211/1/wp49.pdf.

Nel, E. 2011. 'The justifications and limits of affirmative action: A jurisprudential and legal critique', unpublished PhD thesis, University of Stellenbosch.

Nigam, S. 2020. 'COVID-19: India's response to domestic violence needs rethinking', *SSRN Electronic Journal*. https://doi.org/10.2139/ssrn.3598999.

Ntlama, N. 2020. 'Impediments in the promotion of the right to gender equality in post-apartheid South Africa', unpublished PhD thesis, University of South Africa, Pretoria.

O'Reilly, J., Nazio, T. and Roche, J. 2013. 'Compromising conventions: Attitudes of dissonance and indifference towards full-time maternal employment in Denmark, Spain, Poland and the UK', *Work, Employment and Society* 28 (2): 168–188.

Parry, B.R. and Gordon, E. 2020. 'The shadow pandemic: Inequitable gendered impacts of COVID-19 in South Africa', *Gender, Work & Organization* 28 (2): 795–806.

Patel, L. 2016. *Social Welfare and Social Development*. Cape Town: Oxford University Press.

Posel, D. 2010. 'Households and labour migration in post-apartheid South Africa', *Studies in Economics and Econometrics* 34 (3): 129–141.

Posel, D. and Rudwick, S. 2013. 'Changing patterns of marriage and cohabitation in South Africa', *Acta Jurdica* 13: 169–180.

Potgieter, E. 2016. *Social mobility in an unequal society: Exploring access and advantage in South Africa*. South African Reconciliation Barometer, Briefing Paper No. 4. Institute for Justice and Reconciliation, Cape Town.

Pugh, A. 2015. *The Tumbleweed Society: Working and Caring in an Age of Insecurity*. New York: Oxford University Press.

Ranchhod, V. 2010. 'Labour force participation and employment in South Africa: Evidence from Wave 1 of the National Income Dynamics Study', *Studies in Economics and Econometrics* 34 (3): 111–128.

Ranchhod, V. and Daniels, R. 2020. *Labour market dynamics in South Africa in the time of COVID-19: Evidence from wave 1 of the NIDS-CRAM survey*. Working Paper No. 265. Southern Africa Labour and Development Research Unit, University of Cape Town.

Randriamaro, Z. 2013. 'The hidden crisis: Women, social reproduction and the political economy of care in Africa', *Pambazuka News*, 6 March. Available at: https://www.pambazuka.org/gender-minorities/hidden-crisis-women-social-reproduction-and-political-economy-care-africa.

Rogan, M. and Alfers, L. 2019. 'Gendered inequalities in the South African informal economy', *Agenda* 33 (4): 91–102.

Rugege, S. 2004. 'Land reform in South Africa: An overview', *International Journal of Legal Information* 32 (2): 283–312.

Rukhadze, M. 2018. 'Early marriage as a barrier to the career and educational opportunity for the youth in Georgia', *Journal of Advanced Research in Social Sciences* 1 (1): 28–32.

Schiel, R. 2014. 'Migrant labour in contemporary South Africa', unpublished Master's thesis, University of Cape Town.

Schlemmer, L. 2005. *Lost in transformation? South Africa's emerging African middle class.* CDE Focus Occasional Paper No. 8. Centre for Development Enterprise, Johannesburg.

Schotte, S. and Zizzamia, R. 2021. *The livelihood impacts of Covid-19 in urban South Africa: A view from below.* SA-TIED Working Paper No. 168. Accessed 23 July 2021, https://sa-tied.wider.unu.edu/sites/default/files/SA-TIED-WP168.pdf.

Scully, B. 2017. 'The social question in South Africa from settler colonialism to neoliberal-era democracy'. In E. Webster and K. Pampallis (eds), *The Unresolved National Question in South Africa: Left Thought under Apartheid.* Johannesburg: Wits University Press, pp. 170–187.

Seekings, J. 2003. *Social stratification and inequality in South Africa at the end of apartheid.* CSSR Working Paper No. 31. Centre for Social Science Research, University of Cape Town. Accessed 26 September 2020, http://www.cssr.uct.ac.za/sites/default/files/image-tool/images/256/files/pubs/wp31.pdf.

Seekings, J. and Nattrass, N. 2005. *Class, Race, and Inequality in South Africa.* New Haven, CT: Yale University Press.

Segalo, P. 2015. 'Gender, social cohesion and everyday struggles in South Africa', *Psychology in Society* 49: 70–82.

Shepherd, D. 2008. *Post-apartheid trends in gender discrimination in South Africa: Analysis through decomposition techniques.* Stellenbosch Economic Working Papers 06/08. Department of Economics and the Bureau for Economic Research, University of Stellenbosch. Accessed 6 October 2020, https://resep.sun.ac.za/wp-content/uploads/2017/10/wp-06-2008.pdf.

Shisana, O., Rehle, T., Simbayi, L. and Zuma, K. 2014. *South African National HIV Prevalence, Incidence and Behaviour Survey, 2012.* Cape Town: HSRC Press.

Sigle-Rushton, W. and Lindstrom, E. 2013. 'Intersectionality'. In M. Evans and C. Williams (eds), *Gender: Key Concepts.* London: Routledge, pp. 129–135.

Southall, R. 2016. *The New Black Middle Class in South Africa.* Johannesburg: Jacana.

StatsSA (Statistics South Africa). 2010. *Social Profile of South Africa, 2002–2009.* Pretoria: Statistics South Africa.

StatsSA. 2017. *Vulnerable Groups Indicator Report.* Pretoria: Statistics South Africa.

StatsSA. 2018. *Quarterly Labour Force Survey Q2:2018.* Pretoria: Statistics South Africa.

Stevano, S., Ali, R. and Jamieson, M. 2021. 'Essential for what? A global social reproduction view on the re-organisation of work during the COVID-19 pandemic', *Canadian Journal of Development Studies / Revue canadienne d'études du développement* 42: 1–2: 178–199. DOI:10.1080/02255189.2020.1834362.

Talahite, F. 2010. *Genre, marché du travail et mondialisation.* Accessed 10 May 2023, https://ideas.repec.org/p/hal/journl/halshs-00606959.html.

Taylor, S. and Yu, D. 2009. *The importance of socio-economic status in determining educational achievement in South Africa.* Stellenbosch Economic Working Papers 01/09. Department of Economics and the Bureau for Economic Research, Stellenbosch University.

Terreblanche, S. 2002. *A History of Inequality in South Africa, 1652–2002.* Pietermaritzburg: University of Natal Press.

Tonheim, M. and Matose, F. 2013. 'South Africa: Social mobility for a few?' NOREF Report, October. Norwegian Peace Building Resource Centre, Stavanger. Accessed 3 November 2020, https://www.files.ethz.ch/isn/172098/c4bf541cc6e80e801a3efa4f5dab4bc4.pdf.

UNDP (United Nations Development Programme). 2020. *COVID-19 Rapid Emergency Needs Assessment for the Most Vulnerable Groups.* Pretoria: UNDP South Africa. Accessed 6

December 2020, https://www.za.undp.org/content/southafrica/en/home/library/rapid-emergency-needs-assessment.html.

United Nations. 2020. 'The impact of COVID-19 on women'. United Nations Policy Brief. Accessed 8 October 2020, https://www.un.org/sexualviolenceinconflict/wp-content/uploads/2020/06/report/policy-brief-the-impact-of-covid-19-on-women/policy-brief-the-impact-of-covid-19-on-women-en-1.pdf.

Van Klaveren, M., Tijdens, K., Hughie-Williams, M. and Martin, N. 2009. *An Overview of Women's Work and Employment in South Africa*. Decisions for Life MDG3 Project Country Report No. 3. Amsterdam Institute for Advanced Labour Studies (AIAS), Netherlands. Accessed 14 November 2020, https://www.ituc-csi.org/IMG/pdf/Country_Report_No3-South_Africa_EN.pdf.

Van Zyl, B. and Roodt, G. 2003. 'Female perceptions on employment equity: Is the glass ceiling cracking?', *SA Journal of Human Resource Management* 1 (2): 13–20.

Williams, B., Gupta, S., Wollmers, M. and Granich, R. 2017. 'Progress and prospects for the control of HIV and tuberculosis in South Africa: A dynamical modelling study', *The Lancet Public Health* 2 (5): e223–e230.

Williams, M. 2018. 'Women in rural South Africa: A post-wage existence and the role of the state', *Equality, Diversity and Inclusion: An International Journal* 37 (4): 392–410.

Wright, E.O. 2015. *Understanding Class*. London: Verso.

Zuma, K., Manzini, K. and Mohlabane, N. 2014. 'HIV epidemic in South Africa: A comparison of HIV epidemic patterns of two extreme provinces in South Africa', *Health SA Gesondheid* 19 (1): 1–5.

INTERVIEWS

Kensani, September 2014, Johannesburg
Kopano, August 2014, Johannesburg
Lerato, August 2014, Pretoria
Mary, October 2014, White River, Mpumalanga
Mathabo, July 2014, Tzaneen, Limpopo
Priscilla, August 2014, Johannesburg
Thembeka, October 2014, Tzaneen, Limpopo
Thulani, July 2014, White River, Mpumalanga
Ulwazi, October 2014, White River, Mpumalanga

8

GOVERNMENT'S COVID-19 FISCAL RESPONSES AND THE CRISIS OF SOCIAL REPRODUCTION

Sonia Phalatse and Busi Sibeko

INTRODUCTION

The South African government's fiscal response to the Covid-19-induced crisis has failed to take into account how economic production and social reproduction intersect. On 23 March 2020, President Cyril Ramaphosa declared a National State of Disaster, announcing a 21-day national lockdown that saw large parts of the economy come to a standstill, exacerbating the already existing crisis of social reproduction for working-class women. We define the crisis of reproduction broadly as 'the inability of people to adequately reproduce their livelihoods' (Dowling 2016: 5).

Despite looming destitution and hunger there was a lack of immediate socio-economic relief within a context where even before the crisis at least 55 per cent of South Africa's population (30 million people) were living below the Statistics South Africa (StatsSA) poverty line of R1 267 per person per month (StatsSA 2017). Early warnings of the lack of consideration given to social reproduction included school closures, which impacted over nine million school-going children reliant on school-feeding schemes, prior to the closure of businesses, and the lack of measures to support essential workers in their social provisioning, amongst others.

The crisis called for economic and social relief measures, which government heeded as a pragmatic neoliberal actor, and with some pressure from progressive forces. These measures were announced on 21 April 2020, almost a month after the commencement of the lockdown, and took even longer to come into effect. They centred on a R500 billion package (approximately ten per cent of GDP). While the theme of the package was saving lives and livelihoods, livelihoods were largely defined by proximity to formal sector production, with the majority of the response going to businesses and formal employment. Two months later, when the Supplementary Budget was tabled, it became evident that the allocations for the 2020/21 budget year did not reflect the president's 21 April announcement. The Medium Term Budget Policy Statement (MTBPS), tabled in October 2020, as well as Budget 2021, failed to address the inadequacy of the announced emergency response and further doubled down on fiscal consolidation with budget cuts of more than R300 billion over three years.

This should be viewed within the context of a fiscal framework, within a deeply neoliberal state, that systematically fails to account for social and, in particular, gender inequities. Although South Africa was one of the few countries globally to consider gender-responsive budgeting (GRB) – a framework advanced by feminist economic advocates – the state has continued to systematically ignore social reproduction, which is largely undertaken by women. Since 1998/99, the government has reneged on its commitment to GRB despite women and children, particularly those who are black and rural, being the most vulnerable to poverty and shouldering the cost and burden of social provisioning in the South African economy.

The purpose of this chapter is to unpack the relationship between social reproduction and fiscal policy in the context of a worsening economic crisis and post-crisis recovery, beginning with the historical underpinnings of the context. We argue that government's Covid-19 fiscal response was inadequate, punitive to women, and is likely to exacerbate existing structural inequalities. Furthermore, the Supplementary Budget and Budget 2021 proposed austerity measures[1] which would disproportionately affect women who, for the most part, carry the burden of social reproduction and therefore require more access to public services – which austerity takes away. These austerity measures undermine government's constitutional obligations as outlined by the Constitution of South Africa and rescind on government's commitment, stated in the National Development Plan 2030, to build a capable and caring state.

We discuss the trajectory of neoliberalism and the social reproduction crisis in South Africa. Demonstrating how capital accumulation has shaped this crisis, which has been exacerbated by Covid-19, we discuss the role of fiscal policy in addressing it.

NEOLIBERALISM AND THE SOCIAL REPRODUCTION
CRISIS IN SOUTH AFRICA

The social reproduction of black labour played an early and deliberate role in shaping the industrialisation process – and the trajectory of capitalist accumulation more generally – in South Africa (Cousins et al. 2018). The advent of this accumulation process was prompted by the discovery of gold, diamonds and coal, characterised by violent colonial expansion. This process has been built upon, and intersects with, the exploitation and oppression of the black working class, and specifically the social reproduction of undervalued labour. Under apartheid, this found expression in serving the interests of white capital.

The apartheid state played an active role in enforcing spatial and socio-economic separations between production and social reproduction. As articulated by Ben Cousins et al. (2018: 1081), the system of labour migration established to supply underpaid labour to the South African mining industry marginalised the land-based livelihoods of the rural population, 'with few compensating employment opportunities'. This dispossession of land from the black majority has also meant that they have been deprived of natural resources, such as water. This has made social reproduction, in the absence of wages and adequate state support, even more difficult – for instance, in the fight against disease and in securing adequate sustenance. These processes were compounded by labour relations that set black men apart from their families and contributed to men's detachment from childcare and the long-term fragmentation of families (Budlender and Lund 2011; Hull 2014). The result was the perverse, unequal distribution of caring labour, income, wealth, and economic and social outcomes across race, class, gender and geographical lines.

These inequalities have fundamentally framed the post-1994 economic policy. The economy is characterised by conservative economic policies, despite various inadequate efforts to implement state-led social provisioning such as nationwide social grant schemes. These policies have reinforced the concentration of wealth in historically dominant sectors underpinned by a system of accumulation based on heavy industries such as mining, and an increasingly sophisticated financial sector. South Africa has a Gini coefficient – a measure of income and wealth inequality – at 0.67,[2] the highest in the world; the richest ten per cent hold 71 per cent of the wealth, while the poorest 60 per cent hold a mere seven per cent (StatsSA 2020; Stent 2020). In addition, the lack of effective redistributive land reform meant that huge swathes of social reproduction in rural areas essentially subsidised the expansion of economic activity in the urban areas surrounding industrial activity.

Social reproduction in South Africa also gains particular salience under neo-liberalism because of premature deindustrialisation. Fiona Tregenna (2016) shows how the massive attrition of industrial and manufacturing jobs, particularly over the past two decades, resulted in a surplus population that does not have resources from wages or other income and depends on reproductive labour performed in the household (mainly) by women, for its survival. The consequence of a lack of structural transformation of the economy has contributed to a high unemploy-ment rate of over 30 per cent (StatsSA 2021). As a result of the Covid-19 crisis, unemployment in the first quarter of 2021 increased to a record high of 32.6% (expanded definition: 43.2%). Black African women and youth (defined as those between the ages of 15 and 24 years) are the most vulnerable in the current struc-ture of the economy. The unemployment rate for black African women is at a stag-gering 38.5% (over six million women out of the 11 million total unemployed) (StatsSA 2021).

While strides have been made in provisioning basic goods and services such as greater access to water and sanitation through redistributive fiscal policy, the remaining needs are still substantial, particularly for women residing in rural areas. Their inability to access these goods and services has made it difficult to secure social reproduction. The mainstreaming of gender into the neoliberal structure, which is characterised by the privatisation of social reproductive work and the par-ticipation of women in the market through employment, has been at the core of the government's strategy. Our critique is that this strategy reinforces neoliberal economic policies that limit state intervention and relegate care to the private sector while making reproductive work done in the household invisible. Government's approach has fallen into the dismal presumptions of economic policy 'neutrality', which fails to take into account that macroeconomic policies are predicated on distributive relations across different social groups that entail distributive choices across these groups, and within and across households (Floro and Hoppe 2005). Thus, despite government's interventions (or lack thereof), gender inequities have continued to be reproduced.

COVID-19 AS A CRISIS OF SOCIAL REPRODUCTION

A number of feminist scholars, such as Tithi Bhattacharya (2020) and Alessandro Mezzadri (2020), have characterised the pandemic as a crisis of social reproduc-tion. For Bhattacharya (2020), the pandemic has made clearer the centrality of life-giving activities and social reproductive work in any society. Gross domestic product (GDP) measures from this period do not sufficiently capture the contribution of reproductive activities to employment, production and inflation, as well as the stabilisation of economies, nor do they provide a clear indication of how domestic demands were met and the diverse income sources that have contributed to aggregate demand during this period. For example, the lockdown measures that closed schools for an extended period of time shifted childcare and learning to the household. The closure of schools was coupled with the termination of the National Schools Nutrition Programme, which also meant that more than nine million children who relied on the programme were not getting fed over the lockdown period (Damons 2020). Despite the reopening of schools in the second half of 2020, and since school reopening in January 2021, by May 2021 school feeding remained at a lower level than prior to the pandemic. The pandemic has also made abundantly clear that capitalism is incapable of preserving and nurturing life. Financialised capitalism has led to disinvestment in public goods, the privatisation of social services and welfare, and the deregulation of labour and financial markets alongside the stagnation of real wages. The current debilitated state of many public health-care systems, primarily because of the gradual hollowing out of state institutions and capacity through neoliberalism, has resulted in the inability of states to effectively care for their citizens (see Bischoff: chapter 9 of this volume). Asha Herten-Crabb and Sara Davies (2020) extend the intersectional understanding of health care in this context, by arguing that health outcomes and the economy are not separate, but intrinsically linked, because of the social determinants of health. The social determinants of health are not finite, but refer to 'the conditions which people are born, live, work and age in, and the systems put in place to deal with illness' (World Health Organization 2008: 1). Risk factors for diseases, in short, depend not merely on biological factors, but also on behavioural, societal and structural determinants. Social distancing measures are impossible to abide by for many households that reside in overcrowded informal settlements, and with limited or no access to adequate water, sanitation and electricity – let alone access to sanitisers – disease prevention measures are all but impossible (Hemson 2020).

The economic crisis induced by Covid-19 has deepened the crisis of social reproduction, particularly for working-class women. Women comprised the majority of those who experienced job losses (over two-thirds) during the first three months of the imposed lockdown. This trend continued because women are disproportionately concentrated in low-paying, low-skilled and semi-skilled occupations, making them more vulnerable. The majority of job losses were from grant-receiving households (Spaull et al. 2020), where the recipients are predominantly women. This directly threatens livelihoods and jeopardises the lives of many women; research by Chandré

Gould and Sello Hatang (2020), for example, found that food insecurity almost doubles the risk of men's perpetration of intimate-partner violence in South Africa.

Existing severe levels of social deprivation have been exacerbated by factors beyond the loss of income. Food insecurity has also been worsened by price increases. Despite measures to regulate pricing during the first part (March to April 2020) of the Covid-19 crisis, data from the Pietermaritzburg Economic Justice and Dignity Group (PMBEJD) indicates that between September 2020 and April 2021, the cost of the average food basket across South Africa increased by 8.8 per cent and by September 2021 sat at R4 198.93. This is expected to be further exacerbated by fuel and electricity price increases (PMBEJD 2021; see also Morgan and Cherry: chapter 5 of this volume).

At the same time, as schools and other childcare facilities were closed, the added burden of unpaid care and domestic work multiplied. Casale and Posel (2020) show that approximately 80 per cent of women were spending four more hours per day on day care, compared to 65 per cent of surveyed men. Even in households where domestic care work is paid, the absence of the workers due to lockdown meant that households had to internalise that work, including care of the elderly, children, the sick and others within the household through activities such as washing, cooking and cleaning (Sibeko et al. 2021). In addition, many working-class women – essential workers such as grocery tellers and health-care workers, for example – were faced with the alarming choice of engaging in often underpaid waged work, thus being exposed to the virus, or risk not receiving a salary. In contrast, the middle class not only made use of the services provided by these workers, but were also able to work from home.

As the crisis unfolded, it became clearer that not only was the proposed rescue package inadequate, but its implementation was also failing.

FISCAL POLICY'S ROLE IN ADDRESSING THE CRISIS OF SOCIAL REPRODUCTION

Orthodox economics perpetuates a binary between the public sphere of the market and the private sphere of the household or family. This narrow conceptualisation of the economy, advanced by mainstream economics, as merely a site of production and market-based activities has obscured the extensive social relations that are also essential for the reproduction of capital and the labour force. As a result, economic policies, including fiscal policies, have largely been biased towards the 'productive economy'. Rich literature from feminist scholars has advanced both theoretical and empirical arguments that production under capitalist conditions is underpinned by a number of intersecting social relations that are needed to reproduce the labour force, but are often undervalued and unrecognised.[3] There are a number of competing definitions of social reproduction. For Marx, social reproduction was considered the formation and the reproduction of the 'totality of the capitalist mode of production' (Harnecker 1980: 23). This definition distinguishes between production in the 'public' organisation of the market and activities that occur in the 'private' household. While social reproduction in Marx's analysis is understood to be an indispensable prerequisite for production in the public sphere, some social reproduction theorists have provided a more nuanced definition that eradicates the binary of the public sphere of the market and the private sphere of the household or family. Johanna Brenner and Barbara Laslett (1986: 383), for example, argue that Marx's definition is best understood as 'societal' reproduction, whereas 'social' reproduction refers to a range of activities, including

> the attitudes, behaviours and emotions and responsibilities directly involved in maintaining life, on a daily basis and generationally. It involves various kinds of socially necessary work – mental, physical and emotional – aimed at providing the historically and socially, as well as biologically, defined means for maintaining and reproducing the population. Among other things, social reproduction includes how food, clothing and shelter are made available for immediate consumption, how the maintenance and socialisation of children is accomplished, how care of the elderly and infirm is provided, and how sexuality is socially constructed.

By this definition, social reproduction is not only concerned with reproducing the labour force, but includes the work of reproducing, caring for and maintaining life. Nancy Fraser (2016) posits that in capitalist societies the vast majority of social reproductive activities occur mostly outside of what is deemed the market; however, any work produced within the market is impossible without it.

The separation between social reproduction and economic production, therefore, is an artificial distinction that, according to Fraser (2016), has been prevalent from at least the industrial era. In the context of unprecedented economic expansion in the late twentieth century, Silvia Federici (2019) argues that social reproductive activities were relegated to the private, domestic domain of the household, associated strongly as 'women's work', while economic production was seen as productive and thus compensated in the form of a wage. Alienating unpaid social reproduction from other human activities entrenched a 'newly institutionalised domestic sphere where its social importance was obscured or diminished' (Fraser 2016: n.p.).

Despite the critiques from feminist economists, including Isabella Bakker (2007), who explains how all profit-making economic activities carried out by both the state and the market depend on socially reproductive labour, governments – particularly in the global South – have continued on the path of limited state service provisioning with the expectation that the private sector will provide. The dominant approaches to macroeconomic policy over the last four decades – and prevalent in Africa since the International Monetary Fund's and World Bank's structural adjustment programmes of the 1980s – emphasise the 'supply side' of the economy. This has resulted in an emphasis on macroeconomic policy creating a 'conducive environment' for market mechanisms to expand production and grow the economy. Within this paradigm, the role of the state as a public provider of goods and services is minimised.

Today, under these neoliberal policies, the contradictions between capital accumulation and social reproduction have deepened (Cousins et al. 2018). The increasing commodification and privatisation of basic services, for example, has made social reproductive activities such as health care difficult to access, for working-class women in particular. Their pay conditions have also deteriorated, which in itself is informed by class, gender, race, location and other social standings (Bakker and Silvey 2008). These contradictions, explained by Adrienne Roberts (2012), were markedly exacerbated with the onset of the 2007/08 financial crisis in which the rush to maintain the existing socio-economic order via bank bailouts and austerity policies, shifted many of the costs associated with social reproduction onto families or the private sector.

Stephanie Seguino (2019) shows how gender inequalities perpetuated by the crisis of social reproduction – such as in health, education and unpaid labour – have substantial economy-wide detrimental effects. The inequalities 'threaten … to destabilise the very reproductive processes and capacities that capital – and the rest of us – need' (Fraser 2016: n.p.). For example, gender inequalities in education have been shown to have dampening effects on labour productivity (Seguino 2019; Elson 1996). Similarly, macroeconomic policies also have gendered effects. Austerity policies, for example, have hollowed out social welfare, resulting in the need for women's labour and time to fill the care gaps. Expansionary fiscal policies that target the care economy and social provisioning, therefore, have redistributive effects that lessen the burden of care work on women. This tension, or contradiction, forms the basis of the crisis of care, and the social reproduction crisis more broadly, and creates inherent instability throughout the socio-economic system.

It is clear that neoliberalism will not – indeed cannot – deliver a new economy and that a fundamental rethink of macroeconomics from an emancipatory feminist perspective is required. What feminist economists and activists agree on is that the radical redistribution of care work, and the expansion of the state's role in supporting social reproduction, is urgently needed. This is where we have focused our economic research, policy and advocacy – on attempting to influence contemporary discussions on economics in the face of an orthodox hegemony. The pandemic became a salient moment for the state to deliver on its constitutional obligations and ultimately highlighted the ways in which neoliberal economic policy in South Africa has failed to make South Africa a viable society for the majority. Our advocacy during this period focused on monitoring and influencing government's fiscal policy approaches to the pandemic. The next section highlights some of the critical areas of concern that emerged from our work during the Covid-19 pandemic.

SOUTH AFRICA'S FISCAL POLICY RESPONSE TO COVID-19

Three months after the initial enactment of the State of National Disaster and two months after the president's announcement on 24 June 2020, the Minister of Finance tabled a Supplementary Budget to give effect to the emergency Covid-19 expenditure. Progressive economists, budget analysts and activists, including ourselves, noted that not only was the package late and inadequate, it also reneged on President Ramaphosa's promised R500 billion rescue package announced on 21 April 2020 (Budget Justice Coalition 2020; Gqubule 2020; Lehohla 2020). They noted that the failure to implement the rescue package, as a result of capacity issues and corruption, would further undermine the protection of lives and livelihoods, particularly for women, children and foreign nationals. Despite the government announcing the largest emergency stimulus response on the continent (ten per cent of GDP), the Supplementary Budget presented a net increase to non-interest[4] spending in the 2021 fiscal year of just R36 billion, equating to less than one per cent of GDP. This was because, of the R145 billion targeted at Covid-19-related expenditure, R109 billion was funded through the suspension of baseline allocations and through reprioritisations, which all threaten long-term socio-economic development and social provisioning. Table 8.1 gives an overview of the Covid-19 relief areas and announced amounts.

Forty per cent of the pandemic response was biased towards business rescue, through monetary stimulus, as opposed to the ten per cent allocated to social security (for those not in employment). The response to businesses highlights the

177

Table 8.1: South Africa's R500 billion Covid-19 relief package

Relief area	Item
Social security	R50 billion (US$3.4 billion) towards new and existing grants (cut to R41 billion in the Supplementary Budget).
Job creation and protection	R100 billion (US$6.8 billion) to job protection and creation schemes.
Wage relief	R40 billion (US$2.7 billion) to pay wages and avoid job and income losses. Financed from Unemployment Insurance Fund (UIF) surpluses.
Credit guarantee scheme	R200 billion (US$34 billion) to provide loans to businesses, substantially guaranteed by government through the South African Reserve Bank and facilitated by the banks.
Tax relief	R70 billion (US$13.6 billion) in tax deferments.
Municipalities	R20 billion (US$1.4 billion) to support municipalities in providing proper water and sanitation, sanitary public transport, food, and accommodation for the homeless.
Health	R20 billion (US$1.4 billion) to support municipalities in the provision of health care.

Source: Institute for Economic Justice (2021)

contradictory approach to the role of the state under neoliberalism – limiting its 'interference' in the market on the one hand but rescuing businesses during crises on the other (Clarke and Newman 2012). Kevin Farnsworth and Zoe Irving (2018) argue that 'while a range of discretionary social provisions and services, from public spaces to social care, are erased from the social citizenship balance sheet, the post-financial crisis years have seen increased demand for state support for private business'. This demonstrates the bias towards what is considered to be 'productive' expenditure versus 'consumption' – an approach that fails to take into account the regenerative interaction between public investment, social reproduction, labour productivity, socio-economic development, rights and equity.

The Covid-19 crisis has laid bare the flaws of the current social protection system, including the lack of gender sensitivity in policy design. The system has failed to sufficiently target those who are in the non-waged economy, including caregivers and those who are unemployed and of working age, in particular black and coloured women and youth who are particularly vulnerable in the economy. Government has rescinded its constitutional commitment to ensuring minimum social protection – below which no one should fall – over the entire life cycle (SA Government 2012). This includes minimum income and access to basic services (e.g. health, education, housing, food, water and sanitation) which are critical for social reproduction.

Social protection

As provided by the Constitution, relief during crises must be made available through state provisioning (SA Department of Justice 1996). The president announced that R50 billion (ten per cent of the total package) would be allocated to social relief as follows:

- Child support grant (CSG) beneficiaries would receive an extra R300 in May and from June to October they would receive an additional R500 each month;
- All other grant beneficiaries would receive an extra R250 per month for the next six months;
- Between 23 April and 7 May, 250 000 food parcels would be distributed across the country; and
- For the next 6 months, a special Covid-19 Social Relief of Distress (SRD) grant of R350 a month would be paid to individuals aged 18 to 59 who, at the time, were unemployed and did not receive any other form of social grant or UIF payment.

The initial exclusion of caregivers from the Covid-19 SRD grant brought to the fore gender bias in its design. Subsequent briefings by the South African Social Security Agency (SASSA) indicated that the extra CSG payments would be a single increase for the caregiver (the recipient of the money) rather than the child (the beneficiary for whom the money is intended). This was despite the fact that 'the child support grant of R440 is set below the food poverty line of R561, and further below the average cost of R638.40 to secure a basic nutritious diet for a child in July 2020' (PMBEJD 2020).

The R50 billion social grant allocation was revised down to R41 billion in the Supplementary Budget, citing low uptake as a reason (Parliament of South Africa 2020). Meanwhile, there has been a systematic exclusion of unemployed applicants for the Covid-19 SRD grant. The criteria targeted people who are unemployed and who do not receive any other social grant from government or payments from the UIF, the South African Revenue Service and the National Student Financial Aid Scheme. These criteria have been particularly punitive to women who are registered caregivers within the system, excluding the 7.1 million caregivers, largely black women, who receive CSGs on behalf of children from accessing the supplementary R350 Covid-19 SRD grant. The majority of these caregivers (around six million) were unemployed or working in the informal sector prior to lockdown. According to Ina Conradie et al. (2020), the CSG attached to caregivers, combined with the closure of school feeding programmes and restrictions on caregivers' eligibility for the Covid-19 grant and food parcels, would plunge families with children into destitution. This would leave two million more people below the food poverty line than would otherwise have been the case, if the increases had been attached to every child. In addition, as a result of an outdated UIF database, 85 per cent of the UIF cases which had been rejected were found to qualify for the grant. The rejection left many unsupported between March and June 2020 (Mgwili 2020). Capacity constraints have contributed to the inadequate response to Covid-19.

The introduction of a caregiver allowance provides an interesting case for remunerating care work, which feminist economists have long been interested in. Feminists have argued that caregiver grants could be a way to compensate and value women's work in the economy. Some feminists hold that an unconditional income, independent of paid work, would enhance women's agency in families, households, the workplace and the community, with particular benefit for those facing multiple and intersecting forms of discrimination (Williams 2021). The existing evidence on grants in South Africa points to the same benefits.[5] The provision of a caregiver grant by government was not only an outcome of the government's ostensible desire to support households, it was also provided in such a way as to spend as little as possible. The assumption made was that caregivers would be better off because they would receive R500 instead of the R350 SRD grant per grantee. If the R500 was meant to provide additional support to children – as is the case – then the caregivers themselves were not receiving any benefit and were essentially unfairly excluded from the SRD grant. The exclusion of caregivers from the SRD grant undermines government's pro-women rhetoric, as policy considerations did not sufficiently take into account their intersecting oppressions and exploitations.

In the president's presentation of the Economic Recovery and Reconstruction Plan – which the 2021 MTBPS reinforced – it was revealed that the R350 Covid-19 SRD grant would remain in place until January 2020. In February 2021, the grant was further extended by another three months and terminated in April 2021. The R500 caregiver's allowance, as well as increases to the other grants, were not extended despite research that in the absence of extensions three million people would face hunger. Government did not heed the continuous calls from civil society that both the Covid-19 SRD grant and the caregiver's allowance be extended and increased to R585 per month to match the food poverty line (Institute for Economic Justice 2020). In October 2020 the Black Sash Trust, represented by the Centre for Applied Legal Studies, launched a Constitutional Court application against SASSA to protect social grants (Black Sash 2020). The Court did not rule in favour of the Black Sash Trust. This example is one of many advocacy initiatives by civil society to extend and increase the grants.

Austerity partly explains why the social protection measures have been approached in a stop-start manner, with civil society constantly having to advocate and fight for continued and expanded social protection measures. The stop-start manner highlights the supranational and Constitution-defying power of financial markets, international financial institutions and the business press, as well as the private sector's neoliberal influence on public policy. Government's response continuously sought to appease the market, advancing fiscal austerity to address debt concerns. This is compounded by neoliberal concerns of dependency and anti-poor arguments about laziness that are devoid of understandings of social reproduction.

Health

In South Africa, the public health-care system remains severely overstretched and underfunded. This sector demonstrates the intersecting effects of women's paid, unpaid and underpaid labour – particularly their role in providing care – during the Covid-19 pandemic.

Prior to the pandemic, the implementation of austerity had led to vacant posts and declining standards in many parts of the public health system (see Bischoff: chapter 9 of this volume). In May 2018, the Treatment Action Campaign reported that 38 217 posts were not filled. Despite being central to the implementation of primary health care, an estimated 60 000 community health-care workers, the majority of whom are women, were informally employed, with poor equipment and training, and reliant on a paltry stipend (Daviaud et al. 2018). Reducing the public sector wage bill has been a central tenet of austerity in South Africa, without serious consideration of how these measures impact on social reproduction – the macro–micro linkages.

Paid and underpaid working-class women in the health sector were tasked with being on the frontline of the pandemic, risking their own lives. Herten-Crabb and Davies (2020) argue that as Covid-19 placed strain on the economies of middle- and low-income countries, these countries faced the risk of women health-care workers contracting the virus during their provision of care, thereby leaving a gap in the health-care system that needed to be addressed through resource allocation from an already overstretched health-care system. Despite the systematic underfunding of health – between 2015 and 2020, the rate of growth of health expenditure per uninsured person slowed and, in 2016/17, was actually reduced – the net increase to the health vote was only 2.9 per cent in the Supplementary Budget. Budget 2021 simultaneously 'reduced planned spending on public health by an unprecedented R50.3 billion over the next three years' (Budget Justice Coalition 2021).

National Treasury has always chosen 'fiscal balance' above wellbeing and the consequences of the lack of adequate health-care provisioning have always been pushed onto households. Even during the height of the HIV/AIDs crisis, early intervention by government was thwarted by affordability arguments. Care was privatised into the household, with women and girls having to undertake the unpaid work of caring for the sick. Working-class women were forced to leave formal employment to buffer the shocks of the crisis. The aftermath of the HIV/AIDS pandemic 'resulted in great suffering in terms of loss of income, poor quality of life, morbidity and mortality, with children being destitute and orphaned at an alarming rapid rate' (Mogotlane et al. 2010). Even when large-scale provisioning for the HIV/AIDs pandemic was implemented, it was working women, for example, who undertook the underpaid work as community health workers to support the health system. The trajectory of neoliberal policy has always been to externalise care and social reproduction more broadly to the household.

Public goods and social infrastructure

While government took proactive and aggressive steps to 'flatten the curve' to reduce the impacts of the Covid-19 pandemic, the gains made by the public health response have been severely constrained by decades of neocolonial, neoliberal and increasingly financialised forces and structures. Basic services have continued to be a concern for feminists, particularly in the global South. In South Africa, our concern includes the use of neoliberal user-fee models in the provisioning of public basic services. The financialisation of everyday life has meant that people have had to, and continue to, borrow in order to consume, and the public provision of health, education and housing has been replaced by private provisioning of these public goods. The pandemic has highlighted the centrality of natural resources such as water and land in the fight against disease and the sustenance of social reproductive functions. These are the two areas we focus on here.

This includes the ability to socially distance in the context of numerous densely populated areas, particularly informal settlements. Cousins et al. (2018) argue that policies for land reform, accumulation and social reproduction should take into account land and property rights, fragmented classes of labour, communal areas, customary norms and values and customary and social institutions. Policies for land reform should be coupled with use of the fiscus to finance the radical redistribution of land and the public provisioning of basic services that will counter the spatial apartheid that continues to reproduce unequal access to basic services.

Local government, which is responsible for the provisioning of basic services, was not sufficiently capacitated to deal with the Covid-19 crisis. In the Supplementary Budget, R20 billion was allocated to municipal Covid-19 spend; the net increase to local government, however, equates to only R11 billion. These amounts were expected to provide adequate water and sanitation, sanitary public transport, food and accommodation for the homeless. The government promised to roll out 20 000 tanks of water, which the South African Food Sovereignty Campaign argued was not adequate (Mphahlele 2020). By May 2021, government reported that about 17 000 tanks had been rolled out. However, many communities reported water distress. Women, children and people with disabilities disproportionately bear the brunt of lack of access to water for the more than 50 per cent of South Africans who go without access to piped water in their houses (StatsSA 2019). The South African Human Rights Commission has referred to women and girls as the 'bearers of water' (SAHRC 2014). According to the Socio-Economic Rights Institute of South Africa, women and girls in informal settlements fetching water face an increased risk of violence or sexual assault while doing so (SERI 2018). This also applies to women who live in rural and peri-urban areas.

Part of the reason local government is failing to provide basic services in an equitable manner is that the government revenue model was built on the assumption that local governments would be able to generate their own revenues through user-fee models of basic services provision. This model has failed because it has not taken seriously the spatial apartheid – and in particular, the historic inequality in revenue-generating abilities – that exists in South Africa in the absence of interventionist macroeconomic policies to tackle unemployment, poverty and inequality. National Treasury admitted that the poorer provinces and municipalities would be the most impacted by cuts in the MTBPS 2020 (National Treasury 2020a).

The failure to address the land issue and the lack of investment (as a result of austerity) in the provisioning of public goods mean that households, especially working-class women, will continue to be forced to subsidise the state's failures through their social reproductive work.

Job creation and protection

As already indicated, the majority of the business support was off-budget initiatives. Small and informal businesses are particularly vulnerable to failure because they usually lack emergency savings. We posit that government should have considered using the fiscus during the Covid-19 crisis period to rescue such businesses. For example, Jane Battersby et al. (2016) have argued that almost 70 per cent of households in South Africa's poorer neighbourhoods get some of their food from informal businesses. There are also an estimated three million people (mostly women) work-ing in the informal sector and these funds and other support in the form of direct bailouts could have provided much needed support to their businesses, which are critical for food security (see Benya: chapter 6 of this volume).

Government has continuously promised to pay attention to the creation of jobs. As a response to Covid-19, R100 billion was promised for job creation and protec-tion. However, only R12.6 billion of the promised R100 billion was allocated as of July 2021. The allocation was made to the Presidential Employment Stimulus (PES), which is intended to provide 700 000 job opportunities. Our primary critique of this initiative is that as part of a larger initiative for driving employment creation in South Africa, it is incongruent. While the PES allocates short-term teacher's assistants to schools, the public sector wage bill cuts have entailed, for example, retrenchments of 4 000 teachers in KwaZulu-Natal (Khan 2021). Education is one of the main factors for the social reproduction of society and persistent cuts to the sector will have longstanding effects on it. In addition, not only is government contributing to persistent unemployment in the country through its mass retrench-ments, but job creation policy provides short-term employment to thousands with-out real plans to secure their future, ongoing employment. Government has missed the opportunity to invest in the care economy, for example, to generate employ-ment and redistribute unpaid care. Research by the International Trade Union Confederation (ITUC) on South Africa shows that multipliers are high in the care economy. ITUC shows that if two per cent of GDP were invested in the care sector, it would generate increases in overall employment of over 400 000 (ITUC 2017). However, because of the neoliberal inclinations, government will continue to wait for the private sector investment instead.

DEEPENED AUSTERITY AND THE CRISIS OF SOCIAL REPRODUCTION

While the government promised an emergency relief package immediately after the onset of the pandemic, and has called for a 'new economy', neither appears to have been enacted in practice; both the short-term emergency and medium-term responses threaten to deepen an already acute crisis. In the 2021 Budget, National Treasury noted that 'consolidated non-interest spending will contract at an annual real average rate of 5.2 per cent' (National Treasury 2021). This entails a fall in real per capita expenditure on public services, which will negatively impact on social reproduction. In October 2020, the National Treasury tabled the 2020 MTBPS with proposals to decrease expenditure by R300 billion over the next three years. The

2020 MTBPS failed to address the inadequacy of the emergency response package and the crises that have been exacerbated as a result, including that of social reproduction. The 2021 Budget reinforced National Treasury's extreme approach to fiscal consolidation. Diane Elson (2002) explains how this is contrary to expansionary feminist fiscal policy that prioritises substantial investments in the infrastructure that caters for social reproduction and other social security measures that directly target and benefit women within and outside the household.

The Budget Expenditure Monitoring Forum and the Alternative Information and Development Centre first raised concern over austerity in 2014 (Section27 2014). The Budget Justice Coalition has argued that since at least 2014/15, National Treasury has been systematically implementing fiscal austerity and the public has been made to believe that it is the only viable solution to our economic problems. The implementation of austerity has been presented as 'fiscal consolidation', 'rebalancing', 'cost containment' and 'stabilising the public finances' (Budget Justice Coalition 2019; National Treasury 2020a). The dominant narrative has been that cutting national budget expenditure will help to address South Africa's 'runaway' debt. Between 2016/17 and 2018/19, the increase in average non-interest expenditure was 0.9 per cent versus a 1.6 per cent increase in population growth, which indicates falling per person spending. Despite government's commitment to a counter-cyclical stance – which involves saving in periods of strong economic growth while sustaining spending in downturns – expenditure trends from 2014/15 have been procyclical, meaning cutbacks during periods of weak growth. The 2018 increase in the VAT rate from 14 to 15 per cent represents a clearly retrogressive measure, which, when combined with spending cuts, imposes a greater burden on the poor, particularly women. This logic has seeped into the economic and social relief measures to mitigate against the impacts of Covid-19. In the Supplementary Budget, expenditure was reduced by R230 billion (in nominal terms) for two years, with further cuts proposed for the medium term.

Prior to the Supplementary Budget, then finance minister Tito Mboweni stated that 'we're no longer as rich as we once were' (Felix 2020). The implicit message was that the Covid-19 response would be constrained by income in the same ways that households would be, and that future expenditure would need to pay back the increases. Thus, the Supplementary Budget, which was meant to give funding to the Covid-19 rescue package, was redefined as a moment to tackle our 'fiscal crisis'. The budget stated that 'the Supplementary Budget sets out a roadmap to stabilise debt, by improving our spending patterns, and creating a foundation for economic revival' (National Treasury 2020b: 5).

The general public is being moralised into providing 'disaffected consent' to austerity measures. Disaffected consent occurs when the public is made to believe that there is no alternative, so they give consent to the current status quo (Clarke and Newman 2012). Disaffected consent in South Africa has been strengthened by National Treasury's insistence that government spending has limited or no impact on the economy – it argues that the fiscal multipliers are zero or negative. This means, for every rand of government spend, there is no value created in the economy or that value is eroded. As activists we continue to ask how government spending can yield negative or no returns, when government, for example, spends on free education for low-income households. The responses always focus on total expenditure relative to debt, as opposed to what the expenditure is for.

The current moment is reminiscent of how austerity was moralised into the public consciousness across the world after the financial crisis of 2007/08, creating a 'new normal', allegedly in pursuit of economic recovery. This occurred in tandem with a concerted effort to redefine the global financial crisis as a supposed 'fiscal crisis'; a crisis due to government spending, not the systemic predatory behaviour of financialised capital. Governments made a moral appeal for shared sacrifice, suffering and collective obligation to correct the failures of the fiscal crisis – this was the moralisation of austerity.

International evidence has demonstrated that women bear the costs of austerity (Bras Gomes 2015; Himmelweit 2016). Austerity undermines the provisioning of goods and services, thus making social reproduction even more difficult than it already is. The Office of the United Nations High Commissioner for Human Rights *Report on Austerity Measures and Economic and Social Rights* concluded that austerity exacerbated the financial crisis of 2007/08 and, 'consequently, the ability of individuals to exercise their human rights, and that of States to fulfil their obligations to protect those rights, [was] diminished. This is particularly true for the most vulnerable and marginalised groups in society ... who suffer from decreasing access to work and social welfare programmes, and reduced affordability of food, housing, water, medical care and other basic necessities' (OHCHR 2014: 7).

With the probable onset of more budget cuts, government is likely to consider social reproductive work and sectors as the most expendable – this is already being observed. Budgets in sectors such as health and education have historically been the first to be cut.

CONCLUDING REFLECTIONS

Extensive research on social reproduction has uncovered the myth of the 'private' home as independent from the 'public' market. Rather, social reproduction is integral to the reproduction of both the labour force and capital and its neglect by policy makers and economic theorists more broadly perpetuates gendered inequalities that see reproductive work, predominantly performed by women, as limitless and freely given.

We argue that it is important to systematically address the crisis of social reproduction in a manner that reprioritises social reproduction and decentres profit. This means the South African economy will need to structurally transform to ensure that a number of intersecting inequalities are reversed. Constrictive fiscal policies, prioritising debt stabilisation in the form of budget cuts at the expense of developing a comprehensive social provisioning policy – which has only deepened since the onset of the global pandemic – have locked the economy into austerity policies that have worsened conditions for working-class women. What is needed is state-led expansionary fiscal policy that restores greater investments in social infrastructure, particularly care infrastructure (Sibeko and Isaacs 2020).

In our writing and advocacy, we have posited that there are a number of ways to reorient finances towards an expansionary fiscal policy of this kind (Sibeko and Isaacs 2020; Sibeko et al. 2021). As demonstrated by the United Nations Conference on Trade and Development (UNCTAD 2019), substantial financial resources in the current global financial architecture are either wasted (in inefficient bureaucratic systems), abused (for example, via corrupt state-capture processes), hidden (through illicit financial flows) or promised and not delivered (from Official Development Assistance resources that do not meet assistance targets). Reversing this will mean focusing on numerous potential revenue streams, such as clamping down on illicit financial flows, increasing tax revenue and increasing taxes on natural resource extraction. The point is that there are alternatives and sources of finances to support these alternatives.

Feminist approaches to fiscal policy which recognise the structural exclusions that are reproduced by the orthodox approach to economic policy making are urgently needed in South Africa. The reality is that without the strengthening class solidarities and coalition building in driving a 'radical politics of redistribution' as articulated by feminist scholars such as Ruth Castel-Branco (2020: 5), social reproductive work will continue to be pushed into the domain of the household, socialising the burden to working-class women. What is needed is the adoption of a fiscal framework that takes into account the regenerative interaction between public investment, labour productivity, socio-economic development, rights and equity: an economic framework that is concerned with challenging historical and ongoing intersectional, racialised and gendered inequalities in the economy. This would require the state to abandon neoliberalism. Without a fundamental rethinking of the economics in South Africa, the social organisation of labour (reproductive, productive and otherwise) will remain unviable for the majority.

Lastly, many have argued that we need political will to drive feminist alternatives. The pandemic has opened some space not only to contest previously held conservative assumptions about the role of the state and the economy, but to advance transformative alternatives to capitalism. These alternatives, articulated by feminists, are promoted through protest, coalition building, building power from below and making strategic alliances amongst progressive movements and labour.

NOTES

1   Budget cuts and/or regressive taxes (amongst other measures) implemented in order to reduce budget deficits.
2   A Gini coefficient of 1 indicates 100% inequality.
3   See for example Adrienne Roberts' 2012 paper on financing social reproduction.
4   Total government expenditure less debt servicing costs.
5   See Granlund and Hochfeld (2019).

REFERENCES

Bakker, I. 2007. 'Social reproduction and the constitution of a gendered political economy', *New Political Economy* 12 (4): 541–556.
Bakker, I. and Silvey, R. 2008. 'Introduction: Social reproduction and global transformations – from the everyday to the global'. In I. Bakker and R. Silvey (eds), *Beyond States and Markets: The Challenges of Social Reproduction*. London/New York: Routledge, pp. 1–15.
Battersby, J., Marshak, M. and Mngqibisa, N. 2016. 'Mapping the invisible: The informal food economy of Cape Town, South Africa'. In J. Crush (ed.), *Urban Food Security Series* (Vol. 24). Cape Town: African Food Security Urban Network.
Bhattacharya, T. 2020. 'Social reproduction theory and why we need it to make sense of the corona virus crisis'. *Tithi Bhattacharya* blog post, 2 April. Accessed 13 May 2021, http://www.tithibhattacharya.net/new-blog.
Black Sash. 2020. 'Media release: Black Sash takes SASSA to court over grants'. Accessed 13 May 2021, https://www.blacksash.org.za/index.php/media-and-publications/media-statements/67-media-release-black-sash-takes-sassa-to-court-over-grants.
Bras Gomes, V.B. 2015. 'The female face of austerity', *Human Rights Defender* 24 (3): 9–11.
Brenner, J. and Laslett, B. 1986. 'Gender and social reproduction: Historical perspectives', *Annual Review of Sociology* 15: 381–404.
Budget Justice Coalition. 2019. 'A Medium Term Budget Policy Statement that is blind to gender, inequality and ignores Constitutional duties on the state cannot take our country forward', 31 October. Accessed 13 May 2021, https://budgetjusticesa.org/media/medium-term-budget-policy-statement-is-blind-to-gender-inequality-and-ignores-constitutional-duties/.
Budget Justice Coalition. 2020. 'Government fails to live up to COVID-19 socio-economic relief promises', 28 October. Accessed 13 May 2021, https://budgetjusticesa.org/media/government-fails-to-live-up-to-covid-19-socio-economic-relief-promises/.
Budget Justice Coalition. 2021. 'Submission by the Budget Justice Coalition to the Select and Standing Committees on Finance on the 2021 Budget', 3 March. Accessed 13 May 2021,

https://www.iej.org.za/submission-by-the-budget-justice-coalition-to-the-select-and-standing-committees-on-finance-budget-2021/.

Budlender, D. and Lund, F. 2011. 'South Africa: A legacy of family disruption', *Development and Change* 42: 925–946.

Casale, D. and Posel, D. 2020. *Gender and the early effects of the Covid-19 crisis in the paid and unpaid economies in South Africa*. Wave 1: NIDS-CRAM Working Paper No. 4. Accessed 8 May 2021, https://cramsurvey.org/wp-content/uploads/2020/07/Casale-Gender-the-early-effects-of-the-COVID-19-crisis-in-the-paid-unpaid-economies-in-South-Africa.pdf.

Castel-Branco, R. 2020. *Universal basic income: A radical new idea for redistribution?* Southern Centre for Inequality Studies paper. Accessed 13 May 2021, https://www.wits.ac.za/scis/publications/opinion/universal-basic-income/.

Clarke, J. and Newman, J. 2012. 'The alchemy of austerity', *Critical Social Policy* 32 (3): 299–319.

Conradie, I., Hall, K. and Devereux, S. 2020. 'Transforming social protection to strengthen child nutrition security'. In J. May, C. Witten and L. Lake (eds), *South African Child Gauge 2020*. Cape Town: Children's Institute, University of Cape Town, pp. 125–134.

Cousins, B., Dubb, A., Hornby, D. and Mtero, F. 2018. 'Social reproduction of "classes of labour" in the rural areas of South Africa: Contradictions and contestations', *The Journal of Peasant Studies* 45 (5/6): 1060–1085.

Damons, M. 2020. 'Nearly two million learners still not receiving meals at school', *GroundUp*, 13 October. Accessed 13 May 2021, https://www.groundup.org.za/article/nearly-two-million-learners-still-not-receiving-meals-school/.

Daviaud, E., Besada, D., Budlender, D., Sanders, D. and Kerber, K. 2018. *Saving lives, saving costs: Investment case for community health workers in South Africa*. Cape Town: South African Medical Research Council. Accessed 13 May 2021, https://www.samrc.ac.za/sites/default/files/files/2017-10-30/SavingLivesSavingCosts.pdf.

Dowling, E. 2016. 'Valorised but not valued? Affective remuneration, social reproduction and feminist politics beyond the crisis', *British Politics* 11 (4): 452–468. Accessed 13 September 2021, https://eprints.mdx.ac.uk/20546/1/Dowling_Valorised%20But%20Not%20Valued_June%202016(1).pdf.

Elson, D. 1996. 'Appraising recent developments in the world market for nimble fingers'. In A. Chhachhi and R. Pittin (eds), *Confronting State, Capital and Patriarchy: Women Organizing in the Process of Industrialization*. Basingstoke: Macmillan, pp. 35–55.

Elson, D. 2002. 'Briefing paper for Commission on a Gender Equal Economy: Macroeconomic policy for a gender equal economy'. Macroeconomics and macroeconomic policy from a gender perspective, Public Hearing of Study Commission 'Globalisation of the World Economy-Challenges and Responses', Deutscher Bundestag, Monday 18 February. Accessed 13 May 2021, https://wbg.org.uk/wp-content/uploads/2020/06/Briefing-Paper-on-Macroeconomic-Policy.pdf.

Farnsworth, K. and Irving, Z. 2018. 'Austerity: Neoliberal dreams come true?', *Critical Social Policy* 38 (3): 461–481. https://doi.org/10.1177/0261018318762451.

Federici, S. 2019. 'Social reproduction theory', *Radical Philosophy* 2 (4): 55–57.

Felix, J. 2020. '"We're no longer as rich as we once were": Mboweni hints at zero-based budgeting', *News24*, 12 June. Accessed 13 May 2021, https://www.news24.com/news24/SouthAfrica/News/were-no-longer-as-rich-as-we-once-were-mboweni-hints-at-zero-based-budgeting-20200612.

Floro, M. and Hoppe, H. 2005. Engendering policy coherence for development. Dialogue on Globalization Working Paper No. 17. Friedrich Ebert Stiftung, Berlin. Accessed 22 August 2022, https://library.fes.de/pdf-files/iez/global/50085.pdf.

Fraser, N. 2016. 'Contradictions of capital and care', *New Left Review* 100. Accessed 13 May 2021, https://newleftreview.org/issues/ii100/articles/nancy-fraser-contradictions-of-capital-and-care.

Gould, C. and Hatang, S. 2020. 'Can we solve hunger in South Africa?', *Daily Maverick*, 10 June. Accessed 13 May 2021, https://www.dailymaverick.co.za/article/2020-06-10-can-we-solve-hunger-in-south-africa/.

Gqubule, D. 2020. 'Cyril Ramaphosa's dismal management of the economy must end', *Business LIVE*, 6 July. Accessed 13 May 2021, https://www.businesslive.co.za/bd/opinion/2020-07-06-duma-gqubule-cyril-ramaphosas-dismal-management-of-the-economy-must-end/.

Granlund, S. and Hochfeld, T. 2019. '"That child support grant gives me powers": Exploring social and relational aspects of cash transfers in South Africa in times of livelihood change', *The Journal of Development Studies* 56 (6): 1230–1244. DOI:10.1080/0022038 8.2019.1650170.

Harnecker, M. 1980. 'Mode of production, social formation and political conjuncture', *Theoretical Review* 17: 23–31.

Hemson, D. 2020. 'South Africa: The coming storm in health and state', *New Frame*, 6 April. Accessed 13 May 2021, https://www.newframe.com/south-africa-the-coming-storm-in-health-and-state/.

Herten-Crabb, A. and Davies, S. 2020. 'Why WHO needs a feminist economic agenda', *The Lancet* 395 (10229): 1018–1020.

Himmelweit, S. 2016. 'Conclusion: Explaining austerity and its gender impact'. In H. Bargawi, G. Cozzi and S. Himmelweit (eds), *Economics and Austerity in Europe: Gendered Impacts and Sustainable Alternatives*. London: Routledge, pp. 189–203.

Hull, E. 2014. 'The social dynamics of labor shortage in South African small-scale agriculture', *World Development* 59 (C): 451–460.

Institute for Economic Justice. 2020. *The case for extending the Covid-19 special grants*. Institute for Economic Justice Covid-19 Fact Sheet #5. Accessed 13 May 2021, https://iej.org.za/wp-content/uploads/2020/10/IEJ-COVID-19-factsheet-5-%E2%80%93-SRD-FINAL.pdf.

Institute for Economic Justice. 2021. *No recovery without rescue*. Institute for Economic Justice Covid-19 Rescue Package Scorecard Update, 11 February. Accessed 13 May 2021, https://www.iej.org.za/no-recovery-without-rescue-covid-19-scorecard-update/.

ITUC (International Trade Union Confederation). 2017. 'Investing in the care economy: Simulating employment effects by gender in countries in emerging economies'. Accessed 13 May 2021, https://www.ituc-csi.org/IMG/pdf/care_economy_2_en_web.pdf.

Khan, N. 2021. 'Unions concerned as 4000 teachers face retrenchment'. *Post*, 29 April. Accessed 15 May 2021, https://www.pressreader.com/south-africa/post-south-africa/20210929/page/4.

Lehohla, P. 2020. 'Opinion: Ben Turok's plea as Treasury reaches the point of no return', *Independent Online*, 8 July. Accessed 13 May 2021, https://www.iol.co.za/business-report/opinion/opinion-ben-turoks-plea-as-treasury-reaches-the-point-of-no-return-50538696.

Mezzadri, A. 2020. 'A crisis like no other: Social reproduction and the regeneration of capitalist life during the COVID-19 pandemic'. *Developing Economics* blog post, 20 April. Accessed 13 May 2021, https://developingeconomics.org/2020/04/20/a-crisis-like-no-other-social-reproduction-and-the-regeneration-of-capitalist-life-during-the-covid-19-pandemic.

Mgwili, Z. 2020. 'Sassa reviews rejected Covid-19 grant applications', *South Coast Herald*, 2 July. Accessed 9 September 2020, https://southcoastherald.co.za/408585/sassa-reviews-rejected-covid-19-grant-applications/.

Mogotlane, S.M., Chauk M.E., Van Rensburg, G.H., Human, S.P. and Kganakga, C.M. 2010. 'A situational analysis of child-headed households in South Africa', *Curationis* 33 (3): 24–32. Accessed 21 July 2022, www.scielo.org.za/scielo.php?script=sciarttext&pid=S2223-62792010000300004.

Mphahlele, D. 2020. 'Many communities still without access to clean water amid COVID-19: Campaigners', *East Coast Radio*, 27 May. Accessed 9 September 2020, https://www.ecr.co.za/news/news/many-communities-still-without-access-clean-water-amid-covid-19-campaigners/.

National Treasury. 2020a. 'Budget information'. Accessed 13 May 2021, http://www.treasury.gov.za/documents/national%20budget/2020/review/FullBR.pdf.

National Treasury. 2020b. *Supplementary Budget Review 2020*. Accessed 13 May 2021, http://www.treasury.gov.za/documents/national%20budget/2020S/review/FullSBR.pdf.

National Treasury. 2021. *Budget information*. Accessed 13 May 2021, http://www.treasury.gov.za/documents/national%20budget/2020/review/FullBR.pdf.

OHCHR (Office of the United Nations High Commissioner for Human Rights). 2014. *Report on austerity measures and economic and social rights*. Geneva: OHCHR. Accessed 13 May 2021, https://www.ohchr.org/Documents/Issues/Development/RightsCrisis/E-2013-82_en.pdf.

Parliament of South Africa. 2020. Standing and Select Committees on Finance: Post Supplementary Budget public hearing (webinar). Accessed 13 May 2021, https://www.youtube.com/watch?v=hj1MEtkj9Gw.

PMBEJD (Pietermaritzburg Economic Justice & Dignity Group). 2020. 'Food prices are rising as we approach the festive season'. Accessed 13 May 2021, https://pmbejd.org.za/index.php/2020/11/25/food-prices-are-rising-as-we-approach-the-festive-season/.

PMBEJD. 2021. 'Household affordability index, June 2021'. Accessed 14 May 2021, https://pmbejd.org.za/wp-content/uploads/2021/06/June-2021-Household-Affordability-Index-PMBEJD_30062021.pdf.

Roberts, A. 2012. 'Financing social reproduction: The gendered relations of debt and mortgage finance in twenty-first-century America', *New Political Economy* 18 (1): 21–42.

SA Department of Justice. 1996. The Constitution of the Republic of South Africa. Accessed 9 October 2021, https://www.justice.gov.za/legislation/constitution/saconstitution-web-eng.pdf.

SA Government. 2012. National Development Plan. Accessed 9 October 2021, https://www.gov.za/issues/national-development-plan-2030.

SAHRC (South African Human Rights Commission). 2014. 'Water is life. Sanitation is dignity: Accountability to people who are poor'. Accessed 13 May 2021, https://www.sahrc.org.za/home/21/files/FINAL%204th%20Proof%204%20March%20-%20Water%20%20Sanitation%20low%20res%20(2).pdf.

Section27. 2014. 'Civil society organisations: "The new finance minister is stuck with 'Plan A' and delivered an austerity mini-budget"'. *Budget Expenditure Monitoring Forum (BEMF) statement*. Accessed 30 July 2022, https://section27.org.za/bemf/.

Seguino, S. 2019. 'Gender inequality and economic growth: A cross-country analysis', *World Development* 28 (7): 1211–1230.

SERI (Socio-Economic Rights Institute of South Africa). 2018. 'Informal settlements and human rights in South Africa. Submission to the United Nations Special Rapporteur on adequate housing as a component of the right to an adequate standard of living'. Accessed 13 May 2021, https://www.ohchr.org/Documents/Issues/Housing/Informal Settlements/SERI.pdf.

Sibeko, B. and Isaacs, G. 2020. A *fiscal stimulus for South Africa*. Institute for Economic Justice Working Paper Series, No. 3. Accessed 12 January 2023, https://www.iej.org.za/a-fiscal-stimulus-for-south-africa/.

Sibeko, B., Phalatse, S. and Ossome, L. 2021. 'Feminist proposals on macroeconomic policies needed for a Covid-19 economic recovery'. Accessed 29 November 2021, https://www.iej.org.za/wp-content/uploads/2021/07/FeministMacroeconomicPolicies-Briefing.pdf.

Spaull, N., Ardington, C., Bassier, I., Bhorat, H., Bridgman, G., Brophy, T., Budlender, J. et al. 2020. 'NIDS-CRAM Wave 1 synthesis report: Overview and findings'. Accessed 13 May 2021, https://cramsurvey.org/wp-content/uploads/2020/07/Spaull-et-al.-NIDS-CRAM-Wave-1-Synthesis-Report-Overview-and-Findings-1.pdf.

StatsSA (Statistics South Africa). 2017. *Poverty trends in South Africa: An examination of absolute poverty between 2006 and 2015*. Statistics South Africa Report No. 03-10-06. Accessed 13 May 2021, http://www.statssa.gov.za/publications/Report-03-10-06/Report-03-10-062015.pdf.

StatsSA. 2019. *Inequality trends in South Africa: A multidimensional diagnostic of inequality*. Statistics South Africa Report No. 03-10-19. Accessed 12 January 2023, https://www.afd.fr/sites/afd/files/2019-11-10-11-57/report-inequality-trends-in-south-africa.pdf.

StatsSA. 2020. 'How unequal is South Africa?' Accessed 13 May 2021, http://www.statssa.gov.za/?p=12930.

StatsSA. 2021. 'Quarterly labour force survey Q1: 2021'. Statistical Release P0211. Accessed 13 May 2021, http://www.statssa.gov.za/publications/P0211/P02111stQuarter2021.pdf.

Stent, J. 2020. '15% of SA's wealth is in the hands of just 3,500 people, study finds', *GroundUp*, 10 March. Accessed 13 May 2021, https://www.groundup.org.za/article/15-sas-wealth-hands-just-3500-people-study-finds/.

Tregenna, F. 2016. 'Deindustrialisation and premature deindustrialisation'. In J. Ghosh, R. Kattel and E. Reinert (eds), *Handbook of Alternative Theories of Economic Development*. Cheltenham: Edward Elgar Publishing, pp. 710–728.

UNCTAD. 2019. *Trade and development report: 2019: Financing a global green new deal*. New York: United Nations Publications. Accessed 13 May 2021, https://unctad.org/en/PublicationsLibrary/tdr2019en.pdf.

Williams, L. 2021. *Universal basic income: Potential and limitations from a gender perspective*. UN Women Policy Brief No. 22. Accessed 9 October 2021, https://www.unwomen.org/en/digital-library/publications/2021/04/policy-brief-universal-basic-income.

World Health Organization. 2008. 'Social determinants of health: Backgrounder: Key concepts'. Accessed 13 May 2021, https://www.who.int/health-topics/social-determinants-of-health.

9

NURSING AND THE CRISIS OF SOCIAL REPRODUCTION BEFORE AND DURING COVID-19

Christine Bischoff

INTRODUCTION

South Africa's health-care workers play a critical role in many respects. They have had to struggle with the challenges of vast numbers of cases of HIV/AIDS and tuberculosis with inadequate resources to manage such diseases. The Covid-19 pandemic has again demonstrated the immense value produced by and society's reliance on paid health-care workers such as nurses (not forgetting doctors and other care workers such as teachers and domestic workers and essential workers in the retail and pharmacy stores) (Casale and Posel 2020). Paid health-care workers account for about a fifth (21 per cent) of all employed people in South Africa (Lund and Budlender 2009) and the nursing community, who are the majority in this employment sector, is indispensable to the nurse-based primary health-care system of delivery in South Africa (Conco et al. 2013). Nurses are on the frontlines and in carrying out their caring work, they look after the most vulnerable sections of our society (Rakovski and Price-Glynn 2009). If they are employed in the South African public sector, they play a critical part in the post-apartheid state's project to contribute to a fairer and more humane society and to unify a divided society (Chisholm 2004). Moreover, the nursing labour market is stratified by class, gender and race and in the nursing occupational hierarchy, the lower ranks are usually racialised.

In this chapter, attention is paid to the public health-care sector and the nursing profession as part of the care economy. The historical shifts in the South African nursing profession are briefly examined in order to provide a context for the ensuing critique of the crisis of social reproduction brought on by the Covid-19 pandemic. The chapter narrates the experiences of nurses who are members of the Democratic Nursing Organisation of South Africa (Denosa) and work in the public health-care system. As part of organised labour, these nurses also demand more support for the socially reproductive work of their profession and improved conditions of service, both of which are essential for them to be able to cope with their household responsibilities outside of the workplace. Thus the notion of social reproduction is a useful technique for appraising the working conditions of nurses in the public health-care sector and the state's support for this (Hashimoto and Henry 2017), as Covid-19 showed the value of health-care workers as a key resource in the response to the crisis.

SOCIAL REPRODUCTION AND NURSING AS CARE WORK

In addressing the gendered division of labour, feminist scholars employ the notion of social reproduction to describe the appropriate actions and outlooks, emotions, accountabilities and relationships that are required for the sustenance of daily life and intergenerationally. Social reproductive labour refers to the biological reproduction of human beings (sexual labour), support for individuals over their life cycle (that is, the physical and emotional part of caring for people) and the systemic reproduction (education and social bonds) that ensures the maintenance of the social system (Mezzadri 2019). Reproductive labour comprises a broad gamut of activities such as intimate health, social and sexual care services, to less intimate services like cooking, education, ironing, cleaning and general maintenance work that is obtainable on a waged and/or non-waged basis in domestic (household) and/ or institutional spheres. Reproductive labour produces labour power, not products or commodities. There are disparities in the allocation of social reproduction work across the market, family, community and state, as well as between women and men (Yeates 2006). Feminist economists draw attention to women's unpaid work in social reproduction.

While Marxist feminists argue that reproductive labour contributes to the accrual of surplus value and to the continued operation of capitalism (Fraser 2014), they extend this empirical field of inquiry in order to fully grasp how the reproduction of capitalist life as a social formation is produced by other labour and labourers (Andrucki et al. 2017).

Social reproduction is a necessary albeit secondary prerequisite for the prospect of capitalist production and for the continuation of modes of production. In capitalist societies, social reproduction takes place in households and neighbourhoods as well as in public institutions such as health-care facilities, schools and childcare centres. The state is critical to the persistent power of patriarchal relations in production and in social reproduction via social policy, laws and regulatory regimes (Rai et al. 2014).

Nurses perform care which is a form of social reproductive labour (Kofman 2012), comprising reproductive, or physical, life-preservation work as well as work that is planned, emotional, compassionate and interpersonal. The term 'care work' describes spheres of work that are usually feminised and involve the nurturing of others (Waldby and Cooper 2010). Care work is defined as a variety of relationships and activities that support the physical and emotional wellbeing of people 'who cannot or who are not inclined to perform these activities themselves' (Yeates 2004: 371). Importantly, paid forms of caring labour are integrated into non-market life when incorporated into the labour market as waged labour (Wichterich 2019). Paid care work involves emotional and physical caring in intimate, continuing and productive connections established with clients (Himmelweit 1999). Wolkowitz (2002) lists a broad variety of occupations that are located in the sphere of body work, which is an aspect of paid care work, such as nursing. Professions such as nursing are depicted by reference to women's abilities for nurturance and selflessness (Kofman 2012). Nursing involves the total physical, mental and emotional wellbeing of the patient and this comprises preventive, promotive and curative work. The higher up in the professional hierarchy a nurse is, the less likely she or he is to be occupied with the bodily care of a patient (Lund and Budlender 2009), whereas nurses lower in the hierarchy look after the curative needs of ill people and basic care tasks, including activities such as feeding people and cleaning bedpans. In the higher-status groups, tasks involving control, supervision and management are imperative while the responsibilities of the lower-status groups are constructed in terms of servicing or caring for other bodies. There are specialised fields of nursing health-care work that necessitate specific training and accreditation, such as psychiatric, orthopaedic and geriatric nursing and midwifery, which further the divisions amongst the nursing workforce along the lines of qualification, skill and income. Nursing assistants have very few years of training and are paid less than nursing managers, who hold postgraduate degrees and are paid far more. Professional nurses are paid more than associate professional nurses. Doctors and other health-care professionals are paid more than nurses.

Health-care work is a vital area of public service delivery and health-care workers provide skilled care to the most vulnerable sections of society. Even though

South Africa's human resources for health (HRH) provisioning exceeds the expectations set by the World Health Organization (WHO) and the country's HRH is well above those of most other African countries (Van Rensburg and Van Rensburg 2013), this masks the inequalities within the health system. South Africa's HRH is beset by the same problems and restrictions that most developing countries experience. The HRH challenges include staff shortages, a skewed skills mix, the unequal distribution of available staff and many health professionals. In contrast, the private sector has the bulk of total health-care resources in that many doctors, specialists, dentists and pharmacists work in this sector to the advantage of the well-off but minority part of the population. However, nurses in both sectors migrate to developed countries for better pay and working conditions.

The inequality in the provision of health care in post-apartheid South Africa exists along many intersecting lines, such as public/private, rural/urban, poor/ wealthy and state dependent/private and medically insured and the divisions have strong racial undertones (Van Rensburg 2014). The bulk of the population accesses health care at the overloaded, understaffed and ill-equipped public health facilities where there is a heavy patient load. A 2020 Oxfam report on health-care work in South Africa identified serious gaps in policies, workplace practices and social conditions for health-care workers. In the report, Basani Baloyi and Ruth Mhlanga (2020) maintain that there is a lack of 'decent' work in the health-care system, where work conditions are characterised by long working hours, low pay and social protection, gender-based violence and lack of safety, and the increasing casualisation of health-care work. In the dual health-care system, it is typically the black African female health-care workforce that bears the brunt of these conditions.

NURSES: THE HISTORY OF THE PROFESSION, TRAINING AND RESOURCING

Typically, the nursing sector in South Africa is female dominated, characterised by occupational segregation and segmented by race and class. South Africa's provision of health services, its health-care institutions as well as its health-care workforce were shaped by the racial policies of colonialism, apartheid and separate development. In South Africa, employment opportunities for educated Africans were always extremely limited because of racial segregationist policies and practices. For black African women in particular, the nursing profession was one of their best prospects and it was considered prestigious. The nursing profession in South Africa was closely linked to the work of missionaries.

Nurses generally experienced exploitative rates of pay and often had to work under terrible conditions. Until the 1940s, the nursing of black Africans was conducted in mission hospitals. Black Africans were nursing auxiliaries and orderlies that moved the patients. Black African nurses performed most of the rough work and nursed black African patients in racially segregated hospitals. Although there was no formal colour bar in nursing, the profession was nevertheless entrenched in segregationist practices in South African hospitals (Marks 1990), marked by a racial hierarchy with white nurses at the top and black African nurses below them.

Two statutory bodies, the South African Nursing Association (Sana) and the South African Nursing Council (Sanc) were established as a result of the Nursing Act No. 45 of 1944. Even though the legislation did not make distinctions amongst nurses along racial or other lines, the Sanc was white dominated and gave preferential treatment to the training of white nurses at better-equipped hospital schools and nursing colleges. By contrast, black African nurses were subjected to tougher conditions within badly resourced hospital settings, nursing homes and educational environments. It was mandatory for all registered nurses, student nurses and midwives to belong to Sana in order to practise in South Africa. In effect, both Sana and Sanc countered the need for a trade union for nurses.

The Nursing Amendment Act No. 69 of 1957 formally segregated the nursing profession. Black African nurses continued to work in congested hospitals reserved for black people and auxiliary nurses cared for the black African urban workforce. However, there were not enough white nurses in the health-care labour force and 15 years after the passage of the 1957 Act, more black African nurses were employed in white hospitals, in nursing homes and in the private sector. As a result, the status of nursing as a profession rose even further among the black African community (Marks 1994). Apartheid legislation passed in 1978 and 1982 created separate organisations for nurses in the bantustans, with their own departments of health and welfare. To align the nursing profession with these political developments, Sanc implemented the Nursing Act No. 50 of 1978 and made Sana a professional nursing association for nurses practising within the republic only, thus ruling out those in the homelands. The 1978 Act ruled that strikes were illegal. However, one of the most famous strikes by nurses took place in November 1985 at Baragwanath Hospital, where 2 000 nurses went on strike (Southall 2016) to protest against their appalling wages and working conditions. In 1993, South African nurses unified to align the profession with political developments taking place (that is, the homelands were suspended and Sana united with the other nursing organisations). The reunification was also informed by the new Constitution and democracy, which brought widespread political, social and legal transformations into the nursing profession. Post-1994, health reforms included the implementation of affirmative action policies, which improved race and gender representivity amongst staff in public health-care facilities and in the health professions (Van Rensburg and Van Rensburg 2013).

Whilst the apartheid state offered subsidised health care for poor white families and some black African families, a significant private sector in health care developed (Seekings and Nattrass 2005). South Africa's Constitution of 1996 endorses an egalitarian health-care system and an increase in government financing of public health care. From 1992 to 1997, the redistribution of health-care resources to poorer provinces, in line with the objective of addressing geographic disparities in health-care spending generated during apartheid, took place.

Another important change in the post-apartheid health-care landscape is that the focus of health care changed from hospital-centred care to a primary health-care approach. In order to provide reasonable, readily available and suitable basic health care to the bulk of the population, health services were decentralised to district and local levels, known as the district-based primary health-care system (Breier et al. 2009). Nurses form the backbone of the primary health-care system (Van Rensburg and Van Rensburg 2013).

The Nursing Act No. 33 of 2005 requires all nurses to register with Sanc and the body sets and maintains standards of the profession. There has been an intense focus on professionalising nursing, with the minimum entry qualification being a Bachelors' degree (President of Denosa, interview, April 2018). Indeed, growth in the production of nursing qualifications has taken place at the higher end of the educational spectrum in South Africa (Breier et al. 2009). Currently, nurses who complete four years of training (that is, in a university or a public nursing college, the outcome of which is a nursing degree or diploma, respectively) have to be registered with Sanc. Registration with Sanc permits one to be identified as a registered nurse (RN) or a professional nurse (PN). Often these terms are used interchangeably yet the term 'professional nurse' can be used only for those who have completed the four-year programme as it involves training in community nursing, midwifery and psychiatric nursing, as well as general nursing. A nurse who has been part of a bridging programme is competent to practise general nursing only and they are called 'registered nurses'. The bridging programme is a two-year course intended to improve the qualifications of nurses. In the clinical milieu, PNs and RNs are addressed as 'sisters'. Sanc has two further categories of nurses on its roll, collectively known as 'sub-professional' nurses: enrolled nurses (ENs) (also known as staff nurses), who have two years of training, and enrolled nursing auxiliaries (ENAs), who have 12 months of training. Nurses who obtain a degree and those higher up on the occupational ladder (such as specialists) are paid at higher rates, irrespective of whether they are employed in the private or the public health-care sector.

Sanc developed detailed accreditation measures for nursing education institutions. Nursing education in South Africa is carried out in markedly complex education and training spaces, comprising universities and universities of technology, nursing schools attached to public hospitals, public stand-alone nursing colleges, private colleges administered by hospital groups, private colleges linked to old-age homes and private colleges that train for profit. Nursing students at all levels have to acquire 1 000 hours of clinical experience per annum.

The number of nurses registered and who work in the public and private health-care sectors has increased over 11 years (1996 to 2017) (Sanc 2017). About 38 per cent of nurses are employed in the private health-care sector. Nurses occupy the bulk (81 per cent) of professional posts in the public health-care sector, that is, PNs, ENs, RNs, nursing assistants and student nurses (Valiani 2019). According to Sanc data, approximately 83 per cent of public sector nurses (of all categories) are black African (Breier et al. 2009). Regionally, Gauteng has the highest number of nurses, followed by KwaZulu-Natal and the Western Cape. There are also more nurses in urban areas than in rural areas (Becker 2016).

There is a shortage of PNs in the public health-care sector and it is estimated that only 13 per cent of undergraduate nursing students in South Africa graduate (Rispel and Moorman 2015). There is a shortage of nursing skills in the private sector too and this means that larger workloads and nursing staff dissatisfaction are factors that must also be taken into account (Thomas et al. 2010). Initially, to increase the number of PNs, the 'Strategic Plan for Nurse Education, Training and Practice 2012/13–2016/17' was developed. It was subsequently replaced by the 'National Strategic Direction for Nursing Education and Practice: A Roadmap for Strengthening Nursing and Midwifery in South Africa 2020/21–2025/26'. According to the Department of Health (2020), as of 2019, the first professional nursing qualifications were aligned with the Higher Education Qualification Framework and were registered in the National Qualifications Framework (NQF). Nursing education institutions that comply with the accreditation criteria and requirements may now offer nursing qualifications that lead to professional registration in categories prescribed in the Nursing Act No. 33 of 2005.

Nursing skills and staffing shortage crises are global phenomena. Despite this, low salaries are still paid to health-care workers, which is linked to the fact that they work in a female-dominated sector and their work is underfunded, undervalued and hence underpaid (Pillinger 2010).

THE HEALTH-CARE SYSTEM, NURSES' REMUNERATION
AND WORKING CONDITIONS

From 1994 onwards, to improve the health of the population and increase opportunities for accessing health-care services, universal access to health care, a
socio-economic right, has become a crucial public policy matter. The National
Health Insurance (NHI), the proposed national health system, aims to support
people's health and guard them against the risk of overwhelming financial burdens
related to illness by lowering or eradicating out-of-pocket spending. The objective
is to accomplish a type of universal health coverage through a single payer system (Shisana et al. 2006). The NHI Bill was tabled by the Department of Health in
2018 but parts of the bill, particularly governance and financing, need further work.
There are immense differences in real health-care spend per person between the
public and private health-care systems.

In the fiscal year 2018/19, health expenditure per uninsured person (that is,
in the public health-care system) was considerably less (R4 480) than that in the
private health-care system (R17 225) (Institute for Economic Justice 2019). What
accounts for these disparities is that spending on public health was curtailed with
the introduction of the Growth, Employment and Redistribution Strategy in 1996.
Government spending on public health care decreased in two ways: firstly, limits on the tax to GDP ratio came into effect, which meant that tax collection was
limited for the ways in which health and other social spending is financed, and
secondly, public spending could only grow at a rate lower than that of economic
growth (Valiani 2019). National and provincial spending on health care will be cut
in real terms in subsequent years, thereby increasing the disparity between the private health-care sector and the public health-care sector.

Salaries and working conditions of public health-care sector nurses are determined through a collective bargaining process at the national level. The Public
Health and Social Development Sectoral Bargaining Council was established for the
health and welfare sector and annual increments are negotiated between the trade
unions and the employer. There are many trade unions that nurses can belong to,
such as the Health and other Personnel Trade Union of South Africa, which is affiliated to the Federation of Unions of South Africa; the National Education, Health
and Allied Workers' Union, which is affiliated to the Congress of South African
Trade Unions (Cosatu); the Health and Allied Workers Indaba Trade Union,
which is affiliated to the South African Federation of Trade Unions (Saftu) and is a
women-led health-care workers' union; the National Union of Public Service
and Allied Workers, which is also a Saftu affiliate; and Denosa, which is a Cosatu

affiliate and the largest nurses' organisation in South Africa, priding itself on being 'a female-dominated organisation' (Denosa 2007). These trade unions represent a wide spread of nurse occupational groupings and they are heterogeneous in terms of gender and race, skills and professional occupational categories.

Inadequate salaries have long been acknowledged as the topmost reason for dissatisfaction amongst public health-care sector nurses. In September 2007, the state introduced the Occupation Specific Dispensation (OSD) to improve the pay and conditions of service, promotions, salary progressions and generally upgrade service delivery for skilled staff in the public sector. The OSD was first carried out in the nursing sector. It was hoped that the OSD would contribute to promoting the status of nursing as well as attract nurses back into the public sector from the private sector (Motsosi and Rispel 2012). This reform entailed a redefinition of, amongst other elements, salary scales, frequency of pay progressions, career pathing, recognition of experience, and required levels of performance for public sector workers. In many cases, the OSD earned by nurses covers their basic necessities such as food and medicine for their families. Netcare increased salaries for their nurses in line with the OSD when it came into effect.

However, comprehensive information about pay scales for nurses employed in the private health-care sector is not readily available (Kisting et al. 2017), and Baloyi and Mhlanga (2020) note that data for the workforce composition and pay scales for the public health-care sector are lacking.

In 2018, a public-service wage increase agreement was negotiated, tasking provincial governments with the responsibility of catering for salary increases in their compensation budgets. In 2019, National Treasury planned to cut the public sector wage bill in the Medium Term Expenditure Framework. Public sector health-care staff were given the option of taking early retirement packages, potentially exacerbating existing staff shortages. Currently (2023), there is a (growing) shortage of nurses in both the public and the private health-care sectors. According to Melanie Alperstein, steering committee member of the People's Health Movement, 'health budget cuts are one aspect outside of the profession and affect the number of all health-care workers needed for the country to be at an optimal level. Posts are frozen and qualified nurses are sitting at home without work' (quoted in Jeranji 2021).

Salaries remain the key source of income for most households (64.8 per cent) and for black African households (63.5 per cent) (StatsSA 2018). In most black African households, only one family member works and their wage supports an average of 4.6 persons (PMBEJD 2020). Just under half of black African households (48.6 per cent) are grant beneficiaries, with more female-headed black African households (59 per cent) than male-headed black African households (41 per cent) receiving grants (StatsSA 2018). Whether employed in the private sector or the public sector, nurses work very long shifts. At public sector urban tertiary hospitals, registered nurses work a condensed working week of 12-hour shifts and shifts are rostered to include weekends; nurses work for about 160 hours per month or 40 hours per week, with not much flexibility available in the working time arrangement. An extra overtime shift is offered by management to 12-hour shift workers, but nurses have the choice of whether or not to work this extra shift. Nurses who opt to work overtime receive their payment only months later. It is thought that the compressed working week and the possibility of a 12-hour overtime shift with a ceiling of 20 hours of overtime per week may turn out to be what works best for women with family responsibilities (Thomas et al. 2010).

Nurses care for more than 30 people in a ward, making their clinical workload high. Absenteeism among nursing staff is often connected to their personal circumstances as well as fatigue because of their work overload. Coping with staff shortages and having to work with dated or inadequate equipment is equally challenging for nurses (Kisting et al. 2017). Many nurses on 12-hour shifts also have to deal with extra administrative responsibilities and non-clinical tasks, such as the ordering and organising of medical stores. This should not occur, as the guidelines given in the 'Code of Good Practice on the Arrangement of Working Time' in the Basic Conditions of Employment Act No. 75 of 1997 state how the hours that nurses spend doing administrative work can be reduced, such as employing support staff to pick up on these tasks (Baloyi and Mhlanga 2020). Nurses in the private sector also work a main 12-hour shift but there is a contractual arrangement in place for each nurse of only 12 hours of overtime per week. Nevertheless, public sector nurses have a higher workload than their private sector counterparts, serving six times more patients than private sector nurses (Van Rensburg and Van Rensburg 2013).

Even with their long working hours, nurses employed in the public sector are allowed to take on other remunerative work, or 'moonlight', and do so to supplement their income. They take on work in the private sector and may do so as long as there is no conflict of interest,[1] as per section 30 of the Public Service Act No. 103 of 1994. Therefore, nurses who work in the public sector on a permanent basis can also be employed by commercial nursing agencies. The employment service providers are registered with Sanc and report to the national departments of Health, and Employment and Labour. They supply nurses on a part-time basis to both private and public sector hospitals. There is extensive use of temporary agency staff in the public health-care sector and a substantial amount of money is spent on temporary staff through nursing agencies. The reasons for using agency staff range from the fact that specialised nurses can be sourced via this route (there are chronic skilled nursing shortages in the specialty departments such as oncology, and in theatre and intensive care units as well as a dire shortage of PNs and ENs in the maternity and critical care units) to high levels of permanent nursing staff absenteeism. Whilst the agencies help alleviate shortages, nurses who work through the agencies are not entitled to any benefits and they work for very long hours. This sector is not as well regulated as it should be, in that a detailed database of all registered agencies does not exist (Rispel and Moorman 2015).

The rate of casualisation of the health-care workforce in both the private and public sectors is increasing. In 2015, some 3 784 nurses in 80 public and private sector hospitals were surveyed and the data revealed that almost a third moon-lighted and that this was 1.5 times higher for those who were mothers. Many nurses are single parents and due to their working schedule, they battle to fulfil their family responsibilities. For example, they do not spend time with their children on the days that they work, even at family mealtimes. They rely on their extended family members or pay for help to care for their families. It is clear from their working time arrangements that nurses (and community health-care workers) are not supported by their employers with regards to their familial duties (Baloyi and Mhlanga 2020). Only 5.8 per cent of nurses have access to childcare facilities, which are expensive, placing an extraordinary financial burden on them (StatsSA 2013).

NURSES' EXPERIENCES OF WORK IN THE PUBLIC HEALTH-CARE SECTOR AND TENSIONS IN SOCIAL REPRODUCTION

Qualitative data on female black African nurses working in the public health-care sector in the province of Gauteng, who were members of Denosa, were gathered in 2018 for my doctoral study (Bischoff 2020).[2] The health-care work performed by the African nurses in state hospitals was an important subject of the study.[3] Through interviews conducted in 2018, and two years later in 2020, I gathered information about their daily working experiences, their intense workload as health-care workers in a predominantly female labour force within the public sector and the people in their households who were dependent on them. The concept of social reproduc-tion helped to locate health-care work in a broad setting of activities and sites. The support nurses provide to people within their households was thus not considered separately, but rather as interconnected with their professional work (Kofman 2012).

At the time of the first interview in 2018, Annie[4] was 40 years of age, married and had a nursing diploma which she had completed at a nursing college. She was studying towards her nursing degree. She had been working as an RN in the neonatal intensive care unit (NICU) at a public sector hospital since 2004. Annie's family home was in Limpopo and there were nurses amongst her extended family members. She had joined Denosa in 1999 and at the time of the interview, she was a part-time shop steward in the union. Her husband worked in the entertainment industry and they lived together in a house owned by Annie with a bond from the bank. Annie earned R19 000 gross per month but she found it hard to cope financially.

Annie needed her salary in order to buy food and groceries for her household, to pay for electricity and water, petrol and school fees and she funded her own studies. She had recently bought a car, for which she had taken out a loan. She had a medical aid, a provident fund and she received a housing subsidy. With Annie included, there were three people in her household: two people worked and the third was a scholar. A child and one of her parents were her dependents and Annie received a child grant.

Annie considered herself as a professional first in that she put her work with her patients first, before her domestic responsibilities, but she felt demotivated. She always came home from work exhausted; she always had to do hard physical work; she always found her work stressful and she was completely dissatisfied with her job. This was further exacerbated by her dissatisfaction with what she earned and the other bread-and-butter issues that were very important to her, such as the non-payment of her performance bonus and her overtime pay. Annie's salary was the only support for her child and her parent and even the child grant she received was not helping her to make ends meet.

Annie noted the real decline in the standards of service delivery in the public health-care system, which undermined the government's commitment to patient-centred care. Annie did not blame the nurses who left the public sector health-care system to work in the private sector. Annie was of the view that nurses left the public sector for better payment or payment of their overtime, which was guaranteed in the private sector. In addition, they had better opportunities to fulfil their professional obligations in a well-resourced environment.

Zanele was 54 years old at the time of the interview in 2018, and she was single. She was a PN, had a Bachelor of Nursing degree and worked as an advanced general nurse and an advanced midwife in the maternity clinic of a public sector hospital. Zanele was the first nurse in her family. She was a member of Sana before it merged with Denosa.

Zanele started working at the hospital in 2008 and before that she had worked as a nurse in Saudi Arabia for 11 years. Zanele owned her house, where she lived with her daughter. Zanele earned R36 167 gross per month and used her salary to buy food and groceries for the household and for public transport. She managed to save money every month. She had a medical aid, a provident fund and she received a housing allowance. Including Zanele, two people lived in her household and Zanele was the only one who worked. Zanele supported her daughter, who had a degree but had been looking for a job since 2013. In total, Zanele had seven dependents and she found that she stressed over meeting her financial commitments. Zanele's work necessitated that she deal with other peoples' feelings and in the course of performing her work, she found herself making adjustments to her own emotional state so as to maintain her professionalism. Zanele felt that the emotional labour performed as a nurse was invisible and not remunerated. For example, the patients often followed Zanele to the bathroom, and they looked for her when she was on tea. Zanele always came home from work exhausted; she always had to do hard psychological work and she always found her work stressful. She felt that the then Minister of Health did not respect nurses and in her opinion, this was why nurses did not have a good reputation and were treated in the way that they were. Zanele found that her problems were compounded by the lack of resources for the work she was expected to do. For example, she noted that the lack of toilet paper and soap in the toilets in the maternal clinic led to poor hygiene standards, which increased the risk of infection. The lack of supplements for expectant and nursing mothers in a country like South Africa, which already had multiple burdens such as high maternal and child mortality, highlighted the heartbreaking inadequacy of services in public-health hospitals. In Zanele's view, not even the basic standards of maternal care were being met.

These nurses highlighted the deterioration of the public health-care sector in post-apartheid South Africa and how dire the working conditions for health-care workers are. Earning a fair salary as well as having a well-resourced work environment enables nurses to improve their living conditions and to fully engage in life. Yet nurses are struggling to support their dependents and household members due to limited financial as well as emotional and mental resources, and there is a perceived lack of support for their plight from the state. Annie's and Zanele's demands for better compensation and for the guarantee of better working conditions emphasises the empirical intersections between social reproduction and trade union membership (Hashimoto and Henry 2017). Performing a type of commodified socially reproductive work – care work in the public health-care sector – and as Denosa members, Annie and Zanele expected the state to ensure that there were better conditions of service in order to provide for their families. In stressing the fact that the work that they do is valuable, these nurses centred social reproduction in their expectations of improved salaries, bonuses and a safer environment for nurses and patients in the public health-care sector.

NURSES DURING THE COVID-19 PANDEMIC AND THE INTENSIFICATION OF SOCIAL REPRODUCTIVE WORK

When a state of disaster was declared in the middle of March 2020 and South Africa went into a lockdown for 35 days at alert level 5, many people worked from home whilst caring for their children, as schools and childcare facilities closed. Before the lockdown, an estimated 26.7 per cent or 4.5 million workers were employed in essential industries or occupations, and of these, 650 000 were health-care workers (Kerr and Thornton 2020), part of the essential occupation cohort. National Treasury relaxed normal tender regulations to hasten the provision of health supplies such as personal protective equipment (PPE) as part of the emergency response to Covid-19. Subsequently, there were several reports of PPE corruption scandals linked to this lapse in the tendering process across the country. The Special Investigating Unit looked into irregular PPE tenders worth R8 billion, involving 700 companies.

By October 2020, the WHO (African region) reported that the number of health worker infections continued to increase steadily, with 43 984 (3.6 per cent) infections reported in 43 countries since the start of the outbreak (WHO Africa 2020). South Africa was the most affected. In October 2020, the finance minister announced three years of budget cuts in the 2020 Medium Term Budget Policy Statement (MTBPS). The civil service wage bill (that is, the salaries of nurses, doctors, teachers and police officers) is the largest budgetary item and the largest proportion of cuts stem from wages. National Treasury reneged on the 2018 wage agreement for the civil service and there was no wage increase in 2020. The MTBPS catered for an additional three years of zero per cent increases, which after inflation represented a real cut in wages for the essential service workers in the public sector. Activist groups stated that this was far from decent wages for those employed in the public sector who work on the frontlines of the Covid-19 pandemic (AIDC 2020). Public sector unions across the spectrum declared a dispute at the Public Service Co-ordinating Bargaining Council against the government for not honouring the 2020/21 wage increase agreements.

When contacted in October 2020, Zanele said that the Covid-19 pandemic had been very difficult for her; her brother and sister had both been infected. Zanele's sister was a nurse who worked at the same public sector hospital as Zanele. Zanele's sister was experiencing the lingering effects of the virus – she was extremely tired and depressed and this worried Zanele. Her brother had to work every alternate week and was no longer receiving his full salary. Zanele's nephew had moved in with her and she was supporting him, along with three other people, on her salary.

Zanele was concerned that her salary had not been increased in April 2020, despite the fact that a contract had been signed. Her daughter had moved to the United States to work as a volunteer as she could not find work in South Africa. Zanele hoped that her daughter would manage to find employment afterwards, as 'it is scary – in four years' time I need to go on pension and at this stage my daughter has not settled yet' (Zanele, interview, October 2020).

Zanele noted that her cost of living had increased and that she was dipping into her savings, which was worrying as 'once you withdraw your money, you cannot put that money back' (Zanele, interview, October 2020). Zanele had received full PPE but she had to tailor it as it did not fit well, although she was grateful to have it. She was critical of the government's attitude towards the sacrifices that health-care workers were making:

> There is nothing from government, not even a R10 to help you. As health-care workers, we are on the frontline and we have looked Covid-19 in the eye and seen our colleagues get sick and die in front of us. The government does not care about the health workers. They say that at any time, they can get other people to replace us. Yet what can we do? We have to look after the sick people. When I use the taxi to get to work, I see people in the taxi who are not wearing masks. I ask them where their mask is. I tell them that I am a health worker and I work in a hospital. I ask them if I should buy a mask for them. It really frustrates me. It stresses me when I see this behaviour. Where I work, four nurses got Covid-19 and a cleaner died. (Zanele, interview, October 2020)

By August 2020, Annie remarked that she had been working in the public health-care sector for 15 years. In order to complete her degree, Annie had resigned in March 2020 from her position in the NICU at the public sector hospital and she had cashed in her provident fund to pay off the bond on her house. Being an employee in the entertainment industry, Annie's husband had lost his job when South Africa went into level 5 of the lockdown in March 2020. As a result, Annie had to support herself, her husband and her child on her provident fund and she said that 'I was just grateful to have a roof over my head' (Annie, interview, August 2020).

Annie was pleased that she had more time to complete the last two modules for her degree, which she managed to do online. She then decided to take up part-time work in the private health-care sector in July 2020, but she planned to return to work in the public health-care sector eventually. At the private hospital where she worked, Annie said that hand sanitisers had been installed and that temperatures were screened.

However, nurses were given one surgical mask only per shift, which bothered Annie immensely as it was an N95 mask. In addition, she found the quality of the aprons to be poor. In her opinion, the PPE issued to nurses was inadequate. Annie worked in the ICU surgery unit and there was a separate ward for the Covid-19 patients. Annie was concerned that patients in her ward were not tested for Covid-19. She was nursing a patient over a weekend, who was on a ventilator and coughing and whose temperature had increased to 39°C. Annie also observed that when nurses took blood samples, they did not wear gloves, nor did they put their masks on. Annie lectured these health-care workers on the risks that they were taking. She was concerned about infection control at the hospital and had reported this to the managers, who had given her no feedback. Annie also observed that nurses who tested positive for Covid-19 were not told to go into quarantine; instead, they could continue working as there were severe staff shortages at the hospital.

Annie was very concerned that she was the only RN in her ICU unit and the rest were staff nurses (lower status ENs) who were carrying out certain tasks, such as ventilating and resuscitating patients, which was not permitted as per the nursing scope of practice defined in the Nursing Act No. 33 of 2005. Annie said the reason why she was the only RN and the rest were staff nurses was that 'in the private sector, they only care about the costs. The staff nurses are paid lower salaries. Private hospitals are business-oriented so employing staff nurses keeps their costs low' (Annie, interview, August 2020).

In the ICU surgery unit, the correct ratio of nursing categories is one RN to two staff nurses, but this was not followed. Staff nurses assist RNs to perform their duties. They are guided by the scope of practice defined in the 2005 Nursing Act and they work under the supervision of the RN. Annie was appalled by the violation of the code of practice but she was even more concerned that patients in her unit could die if the staff nurses did something wrong.

As described in more detail earlier, there is a professional hierarchy among nurses (Breier et al. 2009) in that the core of highly qualified and better paid nurses (the PNs and the RNs), such as Annie, have pushed the lower paid and less qualified nurses, who carry out the more menial nursing tasks, further down the occupational ladder (Rakovski and Price-Glynn 2009). Annie decided to protect herself, as she could lose her certificate as an RN if she did not do so. She therefore refused to condone the violation of the nursing code of practice and spoke out against it: 'I am not delegating to somebody [a staff nurse] who is incompetent. I am a nurse. I do not know how to run a business. I am ready to meet [management] at the Sanc and in court. You [the private hospital] are cutting costs. Please remove me from your database. You will not discipline me. I am a shop steward and Cosatu does not approve of this' (Annie, interview, August 2020). More worrying for Annie was how many nurses worked without PPE, which further exposed them to the risk of becoming infected. One of Annie's closest friends contracted Covid-19 and almost died. Denosa had called for the payment of a Risk Allowance for Covid-19 for essential workers, but this was ignored. In facilities that were short-staffed and were admitting Covid-19 patients, no additional staff had been employed, although funds had been set aside for this.

Annie's and Zanele's experiences of Covid-19 and the precarity of life under-scores the fact that they perform paid social reproductive work that contributes to the reproduction of everyday life (Stevano et al. 2021). That is, the importance of their reproductive work intensified under Covid-19 as the demands for health care increased and engulfed hospitals, where health-care capacity was already con-strained, in both the private and the public health-care sectors. These nurses were subjected to immense psychological stress, physical fatigue and the unbearable agony of losing their colleagues and their patients due to Covid-19.

The Covid-19 pandemic revealed the immense gaps in the state's response capac-ity, especially the inadequate provision of human resources and protective equipment, which were critical to mitigating the risks of the virus. The nurses' prioritsation of their safety was evident in their activism around the quality of care in Covid-19 wards and workplace safety concerns related to the adequacy of the PPE provided. Without safe working conditions, the nurses and the patients they cared for faced the risk of being infected. Annie's and Zanele's concerns for the precariousness of life were also presented in their anxieties about how inadequate infection control in their work-place could affect their ability to continue supporting their family members without also subjecting them to the risk of infection. As social reproductive workers, these nurses stressed the necessity of the conditions for a healthy life for themselves, for their patients and for their own household members (Chersich et al. 2020).

Thus, the Covid-19 pandemic exposed many tensions related to the social repro-ductive work of nurses, one being that it is critical for reproducing life but that it is consistently undervalued by the state: the state reneged on its obligations to pay the nurses their performance bonuses and did not compensate the vital yet risky work undertaken by the nurses during the Covid-19 pandemic.

CONCLUSION

The non-honouring of payments owed to nurses, even during times of crises, despite the budgetary constraints that the government currently faces, is proof that there is a 'persistent devaluation of caring work' (Berdes and Eckert 2007: 341). The nursing practice environment is beset with resource, administrative and adequate-care challenges and these are most pronounced in the public health-care system. The public sector nurses pointed to the protracted lack of staff, and the shortage of equipment and medicine. These are chronic deficiencies and yet the government denies that there are major problems in the public health-care system. Nurses constitute the largest group of health service providers and their care work involves looking after people's health and delivering essential health services; as such, it is also a critical social reproduction function as it involves caregiving and collaboration, which helps create and sustain social bonds. The non-payment of performance bonuses, their overtime pay and then their non-existent salary increases posed serious challenges for the nurses engaged in already poorly remunerated work. It is no wonder that there is dwindling attraction to the profession and that nurses feel demoralised. The poorly remunerated care work performed by Annie and Zanele, coupled with their long working hours, placed an incredible burden on the fulfilment of social reproduction of their own households. The Covid-19 pandemic highlighted the links between inequalities in the health-care sector and the poor working conditions for health-care workers. Having to contend with shortages of health-care workers and the inadequate provision of PPE, the nurses laboured to reproduce life during the Covid-19 pandemic. With austerity budgeting by the state comes more chronic understaffing, a persistent underfunding of the health-care system, a deterioration of standards in working conditions and further salary cuts which present a crisis for the social reproduction of post-apartheid South African society.

NOTES

1   Technically, 'moonlighting' is a term used only when there is no permission given to a professional to take on private remunerative work.
2   This section is based on research undertaken for my doctoral thesis and involved interviews with several nurses employed in the public health-care sector.
3   My interest in nurses was inspired by the experiences of my aunt, a single woman and mother of one who is a nurse working in the public health-care sector, trying to manage the pressures of her long working hours and raising her child on her own.
4   All interviewee names used in this chapter are pseudonyms.

REFERENCES

AIDC (Alternative Information & Development Centre). 2020. 'The Cry of the Xcluded rejects potential budget cuts in the Medium-term Budget Policy Statement!' Press statement, 26 October. Accessed 29 October 2020, http://aidc.org.za/the-cry-of-the-xcluded-rejects-potential-budget-cuts-in-the-medium-term-budget-policy-statement/.

Andrucki, M., Henry, C., Mckeithen, W. and Stinard-kiel, S. 2017. 'Introduction to beyond binaries and boundaries in "social reproduction"', *Society and Space forum*. Accessed 10 July 2022, https://www.societyandspace.org/forums/beyond-binaries-and-boundaries-in-social-reproduction.

Baloyi, B. and Mhlanga, R. 2020. *The Right to Dignified Health-Care Work Is a Right to Dignified Health-Care for All*. Cape Town: Oxfam South Africa.

Becker, E. 2016. 'A cry for help from the nursing sector', *The Citizen*, 1 June. Accessed 19 August 2020, https://citizen.co.za/business/business-news/1530237/cry-help-nursing-sector/.

Berdes, C. and Eckert, J. 2007. 'The language of caring: Nurse aides' use of family metaphors conveys affective care', *The Gerontologist* 47: 340–349.

Bischoff, C. 2020. 'Class, contradictions and intersections: The emergence of organic workerism in South African public sector unions?', unpublished PhD thesis, University of Pretoria, South Africa.

Breier, M., Wildschut, A. and Mgqolozana, T. 2009. *Nursing in a New Era: The Profession and Education of Nurses in South Africa*. Cape Town: HSRC Press.

Casale, D. and Posel, C. 2020. *Gender and the early effects of the COVID-19 crisis in the paid and unpaid economies in South Africa*. Wave 1: NIDS-CRAM Working Paper No. 4. Accessed 30 January 2023, https://cramsurvey.org/wp-content/uploads/2020/07/Casale-Gender-the-early-effects-of-the-COVID-19-crisis-in-the-paid-unpaid-economies-in-South-Africa.pdf.

Chersich, M.F., Gray, G. and Fairlie, L. et al. 2020. 'COVID-19 in Africa: Care and protection for frontline health-care workers', *Globalization and Health* 16, article no. 46.

Chisholm, L. 2004. *Changing Class: Education and Social Change in Post-Apartheid South Africa*. Cape Town: HSRC Press.

Conco, D., Mulaudzi, F., Seekoe, E. and Netshikweta, L. 2013. 'Professional development and organisation', *Trends in Nursing* 2 (1): 1–13.

Denosa (Democratic Nursing Organisation of South Africa). 2007. *Denosa Strategic Plan 2007/11*. Accessed 20 August 2020, https://www.denosa.org.za/wp-content/uploads/2021/07/DENOSA-STRATEGIC-PLAN-2001-2011.pdf.

Department of Health. 2020. *National strategic direction for nursing and midwifery education and practice: A road map for strengthening nursing and midwifery in South Africa*. (2020/21-2025/26). Pretoria: Department of Health.

Fraser, N. 2014. 'Behind Marx's hidden abode for an expanded conception of capitalism', *New Left Review* 86 (Mar/Apr): 55–72.

Hashimoto, Y. and Henry, C. 2017. 'Unionizing for the necessity of social reproduction', *Society and Space* essay. Accessed 10 July 2022, https://www.societyandspace.org/articles/unionizing-for-the-necessity-of-social-reproduction.

Himmelweit, S. 1999. 'Caring labor', *The Annals of the American Academy of Political and Social Science* 561: 27–38.

Institute for Economic Justice. 2019. *Fact sheet: Funding the right to health*. Accessed 16 January 2023, http://section27.org.za/wp-content/uploads/2019/05/2019-IEJ-S27-Health-Fact-Sheet.pdf.

Jeranji, T. 2021.'South Africa take note: Employing more nurses can slash total health costs study suggests', *Daily Maverick*, 25 May. Accessed 8 February 2023, https://www.dailymaverick.co.za/article/2021-05-25-south-africa-take-note-employing-more-nurses-can-slash-total-health-costs-study-suggests/.

Kerr, A. and Thornton, A. 2020. *Essential workers, working from home and job loss vulnerability in South Africa*. DataFirst Technical Paper 41. University of Cape Town, South Africa.

211

Kisting, S., Dalvie, A. and Lewis, P. 2017. *South Africa: Case study on working time organization and its effects in the health services sector*. ILO Working Paper No. 311. International Labour Office, Geneva.

Kofman, E. 2012. 'Rethinking care through social reproduction: Articulating circuits of migration', *Social Politics* 19 (1): 142–162.

Lund, F. and Budlender, D. 2009. 'Paid care providers in South Africa: Nurses, domestic workers, and home-based care workers'. UNRISD Research Report No. 4. United Nations Research Institute for Social Development, Geneva.

Marks, S. 1990. 'The nursing profession and the making of apartheid'. Structure and experience in the making of apartheid series, History Workshop conference, University of the Witwatersrand, Johannesburg, 6–10 February. Accessed 16 January 2023, https://core.ac.uk/download/pdf/39666875.pdf.

Marks, S. 1994. *Divided Sisterhood: Race, Class and Gender in the South African Nursing Profession*. Johannesburg: Wits University Press.

Mezzadri, A. 2019. 'On the value of social reproduction: Informal labour, the majority world and the need for inclusive theories and politics', *Radical Philosophy* 2.04: 33–41.

Motsosi, K. and Rispel, L. 2012. 'Nurses' perceptions of the implementation of occupational specific dispensation at two district hospitals in the Gauteng province of South Africa', *Africa Journal of Nursing and Midwifery* 14 (2): 130–144.

Pillinger, J. 2010. 'Pay and the gender wage gap in health and social care. Report of EPSU Study on pay in the care sector in relation to overall pay levels and the gender pay gap in different countries in the European Union'. European Public Service Union, Brussels.

PMBEJD (Pietermaritzburg Economic Justice and Dignity Group). 2020. 'Pietermaritzburg household affordability index, September 2020'. Accessed 8 February 2023, https://pmbejd.org.za/wp-content/uploads/2020/09/PMB-September-2020-Household-Affordability-Index_30092020.pdf.

Rai, S., Hoskyns, C. and Thomas, D. 2014. 'Depletion', *International Feminist Journal of Politics* 16 (1): 86–105.

Rakovski, C. and Price-Glynn, K. 2009. 'Caring labour, intersectionality and worker satisfaction: An analysis of the National Nursing Assistant Study (NNAS)', *Sociology of Health & Illness* 32 (3): 400–414.

Rispel, L. and Moorman, J. 2015. 'The indirect costs of agency nurses in South Africa: A case study in two public sector hospitals', *Global Health Action* 8 (26494). DOI:10.3402/gha.v8.26494.

Sanc (South African Nursing Council). 2017. Sanc statistics, 1996 to 2017. Accessed 17 August 2020, http://www.sanc.co.za/stats/an.htm.

Seekings, J. and Nattrass, N. 2005. *Class, Race and Inequality in South Africa*. New Haven, CT: Yale University Press.

Shisana, O., Rehle, T., Louw, J., Zungu-Dirwayi, N., Dana, P. and Rispel, R. 2006. 'Public perceptions on national health insurance: Moving towards universal health coverage in South Africa', *South African Medical Journal* 96 (9): 814–818.

Southall, R. 2016. *The New Black Middle Class in South Africa*. Johannesburg: Jacana Media.

StatsSA (Statistics South Africa). 2013. 'A survey of time use 2010'. Pretoria: Statistics South Africa.

StatsSA. 2018. 'General household survey'. Statistical Release P0318. Accessed 20 January 2021, https://www.statssa.gov.za/publications/P0318/P03182018.pdf.

Stevano, S., Ali, R. and Jamieson, M. 2021. 'Essential for what? A global social reproduction view on the re-organisation of work during the Covid-19 pandemic', *Canadian Journal of Development Studies / Revue canadienne d'études du développement* 42 (1–2): 178–199.

Thomas, A., Venter, A. and Boninelli, I. 2010. 'Addressing the nursing shortage at Netcare: A new remedy or the same prescription?', *South African Journal of Labour Relations* 34 (1): 46–67.

Valiani, S. 2019. 'Public health care spending in South Africa and the impact on nurses: 25 years of democracy?', *Agenda* 33 (4): 67–78.

Van Rensburg, A. and Van Rensburg, D. 2013. 'Nurses, industrial action and ethics: Considerations from the 2010 South African public sector strike', *Nursing Ethics* 20 (7): 819–837.

Van Rensburg, H. 2014. 'South Africa's protracted struggle for equal distribution and equitable access – still not there', *Human Resources for Health* 12 (1): 1–16.

Waldby, C. and Cooper, M. 2010. 'From reproductive work to regenerative labour: The female body and the stem cell industries', *Feminist Theory* 11 (1): 3–22.

WHO (World Health Organization) Africa. 2020. *Over 10 000 health workers in Africa infected with COVID-19.* Accessed 11 July 2020, https://www.afro.who.int/news/over-10-000-health-workers-africa-infected-covid-19.

Wichterich, C. 2019. *Care extractivism and the reconfiguration of social reproduction in post-Fordist economies.* ICDD Working Paper No. 25. International Center for Development and Decent Work, University of Kassel, Germany.

Wolkowitz, C. 2002. 'The social relations of body work', *Work, Employment and Society* 16 (3): 497–510.

Yeates, N. 2004. 'Global care chains: Critical reflections and lines of enquiry', *International Feminist Journal of Politics* 6 (3): 369–391.

Yeates, N. 2006. 'Changing places: Ireland in the international division of reproductive labour', *Translocations* 1 (1): 5–21.

INTERVIEWS

Denosa president, April 2018, Johannesburg
Annie, Denosa member, June 2018, August 2020, Johannesburg
Zanele, Denosa member, June 2018, October 2020, Johannesburg

WHERE TO FOR EMANCIPATORY FEMINISM?

10

CRISES, SOCIO-ECOLOGICAL REPRODUCTION AND INTERSECTIONALITY: CHALLENGES FOR EMANCIPATORY FEMINISM

Vishwas Satgar

INTRODUCTION

Social reproduction theory (SRT) made its return in the early 2000s and is now part of a fourth wave of feminism. SRT no longer faces marketisation of life worlds, but after four decades, it faces the devastating and accentuated consequences of such a process. Despite stark gendered and racialised class inequalities, the economising of everything has continued unabated. Remaking the world in the image of the USA and transnationalising capital has been a process of disruptive and patriarchal social engineering, in the global North and South. China as a hub of cheap labour has also played its part in this process of deep globalisation and restructuring. Every scale and level of globalising accumulation has brought precariousness, new enclosures, ecosystem collapse, climate shocks, lumpen ruling-class formation and state contraction. Subaltern women have not been winners in this process, and even less so in the Covid-19 conjuncture. As peasants, urban and rural working classes and as the permanently poor unemployed, life has been tenuous. A patriarchal global division of labour has meant a global outside has been created where many of these women exist as unrecognised and disconnected from wage-earning circuits yet they carry the burden of social reproduction.

At the same time, capitalism is in the throes of a civilisational crisis. Despite its own internally constructed dynamics of overaccumulation, capitalism's ecocidal logic is destroying the ecological substratum of life (human and non-human) on earth. Turbo boosted by finance and the creation of a global economy, the ecologies of capital have reached their limits. Soils are seriously depleted; biodiversity loss is rapid; non-human species extinction is accelerating; the biochemistry of the planet is changing due to over-use of toxic chemicals (nitrogen and phosphates in globalised agriculture are a good example); oceans are polluted (including through micro-plastics); and sky-rocketing emissions (despite the Covid-19 pause) are reshaping the planetary geography, with zones of unliveability, for instance, becoming more pronounced. Eco-feminist analyses, strategic politics and movement building have been confronting these realities for a while. Yet mainstream feminism has not taken these issues on board. Instead, there has been a preoccupation in the mainstream with theorising and clarifying intersectional analysis, identity differences and the strategic implications of such modes of analysis.

This chapter seeks to engage sympathetically but critically with dominant Marxist approaches to SRT, to affirm strengths but to also explicate areas that need further development. It is argued that dominant Marxist approaches to SRT have the potential theoretically to also explain the contemporary crises of capitalism. In other words, SRT can also be applied to explain the general and historically specific crises of contemporary capitalism. Up to now, within its remit have been powerful theoretical arguments and analyses about how subaltern women's exploitation and oppression is structurally implicated in financialised capitalism and its reproductive regime. However, these perspectives do not grapple with the multidimensional crises of capitalism. Moreover, the ecological dimension of SRT has to be strengthened. Drawing on Marx's ecology and eco-feminism, SRT can provide an ecological approach to social reproduction but as socio-ecological reproduction theory (SERT). It needs to be 'greened'. In terms of resistance, sharp debates have emerged between Marxist/socialist feminists championing SRT and intersectional feminists. The position argued in this chapter is that SRT (and SERT) also can work with some currents within intersectional feminism while recognising its limits. The chapter concludes with the relationship between SERT and a rising emancipatory feminism, while highlighting the challenges such a feminism faces.

DOMINANT APPROACHES TO SOCIAL REPRODUCTION THEORY AND ANALYSIS

SRT began to make its appearance again in the early 2000s as financialised restructuring further intensified the remaking of the welfare state in the global North.

Several important contributions led by Marxist and socialist feminists highlighted precarity in the realm of production, the roll-back of social welfare, a new politics of the family and how class, race and gender articulate in the financialised reproductive regime. It also became clear that gains made by second-wave feminism in the 1960s–1980s were now in jeopardy. The space for transforming gender relations within capitalism was closing as inequalities widened and precariaty defined social life. In this context, the post-modern current within third-wave feminism with its emphasis on cultural identities and difference, as well as its disavowal of macro-social analysis and its vaunting of the 'end of meta-narratives', could not explain these new material realities. Married to liberal feminism, it became part of the problem and reached its limits. The neoliberal conjuncture required feminism to restore capitalism as central to its analysis to explain how a few women advanced at the expense of the many, as well as the emergence of a universal condition of precariaty in life-making. More nuanced readings of Marx's and Engels' work on gender and the family, as well as anti-racism, together with the republication of Lise Vogel's (2013) *Marxism and the Oppression of Women: Towards a Unitary Theory*, shed a whole new light on the relationship between Marx's Marxism and oppression, including women's oppression.[1] Simple caricatures, such as the subject of history in Marx's writings, the white male factory worker, proved to have been mere misrepresentation.

Today SRT is gaining ground in the academy and in everyday feminist struggles. There is a flourishing of SRT contributions.[2] For the purposes of this chapter, I will focus on just two leading theorists and the contributions they have made that are shaping the frontiers of SRT development. The point of departure in this regard is the contribution of Lise Vogel's text, first published in 1983. It emerged in a context in which second-wave socialist feminism was exhausted and she made an attempt to grapple with some of its limits. In particular, it made two important contributions that provide a bridge to contemporary SRT, which is being developed further. First, Vogel's intervention dispelled the idea of a singular cause for women's oppression. It displaced the white working-class household and unpaid labour at the centre of second-wave socialist feminist theory, thus challenging the dualistic emphases on patriarchy and capitalism, on the one hand, and on the other, class reductionism. Hence the sub-title of her book: 'Towards a Unitary Theory'. Second, her approach provided a structural and material conception of women's oppression. It was situated within the contradictory relationship between reproductive labour and processes of capital accumulation. Various oppressive sites, mechanisms and social relations where imbricated in this contradictory dynamic but required concrete historical and empirical study. Such studies were necessary to show how reproduction of the working class was necessary for capital while at the same time capital denigrated and devalued life-making.

Tithi Bhattacharya (2017b) builds on the framework and lineage of Vogel's work. Her contribution recentres the centrality of the working class and its formation utilising social reproduction theory. At an abstract level, her starting point is classical Marxism, affirming the working class, living human beings in all their variegated aspects, as the source of value. At the same time, beyond juridical equality, coercion and domination define the labour–capital social relation. From here, and following SRT theorists like Vogel, she shows how labour power or capacity to labour is a commodity within capitalism, but how it is reproduced is not adequately dealt with in Marx. While recognising that women carry a disproportionate burden under capitalism, including in the household, for the biological reproduction of the worker, which includes care labour, the kinship family is not the only site of reproduction in the broader circuits of reproduction. In these circuits public education, health care, leisure facilities, pensions, elderly support, slavery and immigration are ways in which the working class is reproduced. Mediating this would be race, nationality and gender relations.

At another level of abstraction, following Marx, Bhattacharya affirms that production and reproduction are part of a whole. The moment of value creation and the moment of creating the working class are part of a larger process of the social reproduction of capitalism. In this 'whole' of extended reproduction, however, the capital–labour relationship is predicated on: (i) the necessity for the worker to enter this relationship to meet needs due to separation from the means of production, and (ii) the fact that the worker enters the wage relation to meet subsistence needs. Drawing on the work of Michael Lebowitz, she demonstrates how the standard of necessity is not given but subject to class struggle. With increased productivity capitalists seek to drive down wages while workers seek to increase wages. Moreover, there are two moments of production: labour power is a means to satisfy the need for surplus value by capital while for workers this is about satisfying the goal of self-development. But this is a contradictory process with capital wanting greater surplus value, which prompts the creation of new needs for the working class and the production of new commodities. Ultimately, there is a second circuit for the reproduction of labour, while integral to capital's own circuit of reproduction, but this is not theorised by Marx. The production and reproduction of the labour power circuit is about a process of the worker's self-transformation as part of meeting social needs. This has implications for social reproduction as a framework for strategic working-class politics, including an expansive conception of the working class and broader struggles related to the social reproduction of labour power.

Nancy Fraser (2017) is one of the most original and innovative Marxist-feminist theorists today. Her contribution to social reproduction theory expands on Vogel's contribution in several pathbreaking ways. Her starting point is recognising that care labour is both material and affective but without it society cannot be reproduced: there can be no culture, economy or political organisation. The crisis of care is part of a larger crisis of social reproduction of society and a general crisis of capitalism. The social reproduction strand of the crisis is directly imbricated in the general crisis but has to be grasped together with the other structural contradictions. Theoretically, the social-reproductive contradiction of financialised capitalism exists because social reproduction is necessary for capitalist accumulation, but endless accumulation threatens to undermine the reproductive processes and capacities that capital and society need. This contradiction sits at the interconnection between production and reproduction; it is not 'intra-production' and neither is it 'intra-domestic'. As the logic of capitalism destabilises social reproduction, it also undermines long-term accumulation. Every capitalist society harbours a deep-seated systemic tendency towards a crisis of social reproduction. The background condition of social reproduction, together with nature and politics are crucial for capitalism to exist. This also means capitalism cannot be understood in a narrow economistic way but has to be understood in a broader sense as it relates also to its 'non-economic' background conditions.

Fraser provides a concrete and rich historicisation of how waged labour and unwaged care labour (in its expanded sense and not exclusively in the family), or reproduction-production regimes, span nineteenth-century liberal competitive capitalism, post-World War Two state-managed capitalism and, more recently, financialised capitalism. She explores the social reproduction contradiction (both in the centres and on the peripheries), its crisis tendencies and ruling-class responses to the making of the gender order. In this historical tracing, Fraser pinpoints how the realm of social reproduction was constituted and gender relations institutionalised: factory legislation and a bourgeoisie imaginary of domesticity shaped the liberal production-reproduction regime; public investments in social goods, mass consumption and a compromise between marketisation and social protection shaped the gender order of state-managed capitalism; and low-wage employment, corporate and state divestment from social welfare and privatised reproductive care (buttressing the mobility of professional middle-class women), and debt marked the financialised capitalist gender order. It is in this context that there has been an upsurge of boundary struggles, intertwined with class struggles, but related to production/social reproduction. Moreover, she argues, a triad of forces – marketisation, social protection and emancipation – are contending in these boundary struggles. Ultimately, she hopes social protection and emancipation triumph and determine how the boundaries between production/reproduction and capitalism/society are set.

Both Bhattacharya and Fraser provide important structural perspectives on gender and, more generally, oppression. Like Vogel, they do not treat social reproduction as an add-on or sideshow but demonstrate how it is central to the reproduction of the working class, gender orders, production and society. The social relations entwined in this include class, gender, race and imperialism. At the same time, within these theoretical apparatuses there is space for agential and strategic politics. Bhattacharya's call for a more expansive conception of the working class and the need for struggles related to the reproduction of the working class provide for a wider political field of struggle, ranging from food and water to a universal basic income, for instance. Fraser's conceptual approach to boundary struggles, linked to class struggles, is extremely novel and holds out potentials for a trans-feminist politics within this framework. These are crucial strengths for Marxist SRT. However, there are three areas that require systematic development and clarification to further enrich the role these approaches to SRT can play in relation to emancipatory feminism. The first relates to nuancing SRT understandings of the contemporary civilisational crisis of capitalism; the second relates to ecology and SRT; and the third is about SRT/SERT, intersectionality and the relationship to intersectional feminism. What follows are contributions to enrich and rethink certain areas of SRT.

THREE AREAS OF RETHINKING CONTEMPORARY SOCIAL REPRODUCTION THEORY AND ANALYSES

Everything in crisis

As part of the return of SRT, Isabel Bakker penned an essay on the critical questions that such a research agenda needs to ask. She prioritised three areas (Bakker 2007: 553–554): '(i) reproduction for what and for whom?; (ii) for what purposes and what consequences?; and (iii) what are the alternatives to dominant practices that are transforming social reproduction and what prospects do they hold for greater empowerment and democracy?' These research questions were penned before the financial crisis of 2007–2009; the worsening ecological crises, including the climate crisis with a 1°C overshoot of planetary temperature since prior to the Industrial Revolution in 2015 and its attendant climate shocks; alarming reports on biodiversity loss; at least four major food system crises since 2006/07; and the Covid-19 pandemic, as well as the crisis of liberal democracy due to the privileging of the sovereignty of capital over states and publics. These are interconnected, cascading and ramifying systemic contradictions through global capitalism. It is in this context that the neoliberal class project has entered a conjuncture of crisis marked by the rise of extreme right, neofascist and authoritarian forces in the largest democracies (India, Brazil and the USA) in the world[3] (Williams and Satgar 2021), Biden's neo-Keynesian push back against financialisation through massive spending bills, Putin's invasion of Ukraine and Xi's commitment to share the gains of globalisation through 'prosperity for all'.

Today SRT has to grapple with the manifold crises of capitalism and how these relate to social reproduction in the domestic realm and more generally at the level of society and global capitalism. Bhattacharya's contribution to SRT does not deal explicitly with the crises of capitalism. Although there is potential in her approach to connect these systemic and conjunctural crisis dynamics to thinking through the crisis of the reproduction of the working class, this requires a shift to a different level of analysis, closer to concrete history. Fraser, on the other hand, has a firm theoretical and analytical grasp of the social reproduction contradiction and how it operates as a systemic crisis tendency within financialised capitalism. However, there are two issues that require greater nuance and development. First, it is necessary to be a bit more historically specific about the general crisis of contemporary capitalism. Capitalism has been through three major crises: in the late nineteenth century, with the 'great depression' and during the early 1970s. We are now living the fourth major crisis of capitalism since circa 2007 to the present (Satgar 2015). Second, each crisis has its own systemic and conjunctural crisis tendencies that have to be explicated. In this regard Fraser's work on SRT has to be integrated with other work she has done on climate and the legitimacy crisis of financialised capitalism.[4] Put differently, the structural divides of production/reproduction, nature/society and economy/politics and the attendant background conditions she identifies have to be brought together into an analysis of the total systemic and conjunctural crises of financialised capitalism. More than any other Marxist-feminist theorist she has the conceptual and analytical resources to achieve this scale of analysis of the general crisis of social reproduction (or socio-ecological reproduction) of capitalist civilisation. More generally, SRT theorists also have to grapple with the crisis of everything; crisis as crises, in the plural.

Ecology and social reproduction

The rereading of Marx in the recent period to bring out his conception of natural relations has led to the development of a Marxist ecology understanding of Marx. While Marx is not vaunted as the founder of modern ecology, a post-productivist Marx has been discovered. This has brought to the fore both crucial ecological premises underpinning his thought and a revisiting of his conception of being human (Satgar 2022). Marx has four crucial ecological premises to his thought: (i) humans are dependent on nature and this is a starting point for historical materialist analysis; (ii) human beings are part of nature; (iii) nature is a source of wealth together with labour; and (iv) human impacts and the limits of nature are of concern. From this standpoint of Marx's ecology, humans are not merely social beings but are actually socio-ecological beings. This implies that SRT is actually about SERT.

Several eco-feminists, particularly eco-feminist socialists, have developed these aspects of Marx's thought and have also gone beyond. Eco-feminist political economy starts from the premise that the capitalist patriarchal system externalises the costs of gendered care labour and damage to nature. However, making the link between social reproduction (the exploitation of women) and natural relations has entailed various theoretical innovations, which in different ways affirm the existence of socio-ecological reproduction. Maria Mies and Vandana Shiva (2014: 70–90), in their classic *Ecofeminism*, show how development and growth impact negatively on women, children and nature and actually continue a colonial form of enclosure and extraction. More growth and development has meant crises of socio-ecological reproduction. Ariel Salleh (1994) explored how the nature–women–labour nexus is the primary contradiction of capitalism, while James O'Connor (1996) argued for the second contradiction of capitalism, which refers to the structural conditions within which the production process exists, i.e. reproduction and the natural environment. With the intensifying ecocidal (mass destruction of human and non-human life) logic of contemporary capitalism as part of the fourth crisis of capitalism, conceptualising the crisis of socio-ecological reproduction at different scales and in different locales has become absolutely essential. It provides a crucial theoretical and analytical resource, informed by Marxist ecology and eco-socialist feminism, as SERT for emancipatory feminism. SERT provides a direct challenge to Bhattacharya's approach to SRT through its appreciation of the deeper, embodied materiality of reproducing labour as part of natural relations. For Fraser, there is space to bring in an alternative historicising of 'socio-ecological reproduction regimes' under liberal, state monopoly and financialised capitalism.

Intersectionality and SRT/SERT

Intersectional feminism has come to the fore through black American feminism. It derives from a particular context but has travelled and gained ground in different parts of the world. For Marxist feminists such as Delia Aguilar (2015), intersectionality represents the deradicalisation of feminism and is complicit in the 'conservatism' of the historical period. 'Put more sharply, the reformulations of intersectionality by feminists today merely reflect the corporatization of the academy and its increasing subservience to a neoliberal global regime' (Aguilar 2015: 203). However, what Aguilar misses is that intersectional feminism is not homogeneous; it includes various currents, ranging from post-modern identity/difference intersectional feminists to liberal/neoliberal market pluralists to anti-capitalist intersectional feminists. A sharp debate has raged in the academy and in activist circuits about the differences between Marxist feminists and intersectional feminists (Bohrer 2022). On the one hand, Marxist feminists have been accused of class reductionism (thus occluding other relations of oppression such as sexism, racism and heteronormativity), attempting to universalise the experience of the white working-class/middle-class family (particularly Marxist-inspired second-wave socialist feminism) and utilising binary or dualistic structures such as patriarchy and capitalism. On the other hand, some Marxist feminists have hit back against, intersectional 'oppression gymnastics' and its own hierarchies, its 'ontological atomism', including individualising oppression and identities and a lack of appreciation for the distinctiveness of class.

This chapter approaches intersectional feminism, following David McNally (2017: 313 epub), in the spirit of a 'dialectically revitalised social reproduction theory – one that rises to the critical challenges posed by intersectional analysis'. At the same time, it means recognising that Marx himself, through his own revolutionary humanism, went beyond abstract and general conceptions of the working class and embraced class (including the peasantry), gender, race and an appreciation of the deleterious consequences of colonialism (Anderson 2020). Marx had his own intersectional approach to the capitalism of his time. At the same time, several intersectional feminists do not reject the relationship between oppressions and capitalism. The Combahee River Collective, Angela Davis and eco-socialist feminists such as Maria Mies, Vandana Shiva and Ariel Salleh are good examples. This is important common ground and has implications for where oppressions are located within SRT/SERT.

Both Bhattacharya and Fraser provide single-systems frameworks in which women are not homogenised or essentialised; class, race and gender relations of oppression all matter. Similarly, with SERT there is an additional emphasis on ecological relations of oppression. In a sense they have taken on board many of the criticisms of intersectional feminists. For Bhattacharya a host of relations of oppression inform and shape the reproduction of the working class, across a variegated set of mechanisms and sites. Moreover, in her expansive conception of the working class and strategic struggles for the reproduction of the working class, various intersectional possibilities exist. Similarly, for Fraser reproductive regimes have been shaped by various relations of oppression, including the role of colonialism, imperialism and financialised debt. In addition, in her conception of boundary struggles, intersectional possibilities abound. However, both Bhattacharya and Fraser work in a Marxist-feminist register and have not explicitly evoked 'intersectionality' but affirm the relationship between oppressions and capitalism. SERT certainly occupies the same ground, but embraces an intersectionality approach that recognises the link between capitalism and oppression. A dialectical embrace of intersectional feminism recognises its limits but converges on common ground.

THE CRISES OF SOCIO-ECOLOGICAL REPRODUCTION AND CHALLENGES FOR EMANCIPATORY FEMINISM

For struggles today, SERT theory is crucial in order to centre women's anti-oppression struggles – but as anti-capitalist struggles. In some parts of the world this is articulated as 'feminism of the 99%' or 'popular feminism' as part of a fourth wave of feminism. In this volume we refer to this feminism as emancipatory feminism. Emancipatory feminism (Marxist, socialist, eco-feminist and indigenous) has immense transformative potentials. Grounded in SERT and an analysis of the crises of global socio-ecological reproduction, it is strategically positioned at the frontlines of the civilisational and conjunctural flashpoints of contemporary capitalism. Moreover, harnessing SERT as a single-systems framework centring various relations of oppression – class, race, gender and ecological relations – brings intersectionality into resistance against an ecocidal capitalism. However, these potentials could be stymied if three important challenges are not dealt with. First, while emancipatory feminism has a broader remit to understand oppression, neoliberal politics has also tamed publics, such that crowd-sourced, single-issue politics and social media constructed narratives define politics. Even with huge demonstrations in streets, such a politics is extremely limited and faces power structures increasingly impervious to such pressures. In other words, marketised rationalities have priced this in and governments that privilege the sovereignty of capital perform attentiveness but have no intention of taking this further into transformative agendas. The defeat of the organised working class, in the global North and South, has placed subaltern forces on a defensive footing with an orientation around point of production issues. Economism and narrow, single-issue politics dominate unions. This has to be surpassed and trans-working-class politics has to emerge. Similarly, women's politics has to become trans-feminist and environmental politics has to reach for trans-environmentalism. Intersecting crises make this absolutely essential to build a broader convergence of social forces. Emancipatory feminism can both engender a politics beyond a narrow issue-centred focus and unite these forces. This is a challenge it has yet to overcome in practice.

Second, and as corollary to the previous point, Donald Trump's ascendance into the White House upended even liberal feminism. He mainstreamed a crass capitalist patriarchy, objectifying women as sexual objects and brought an angry white male machismo to the fore. While the worldwide Women's March on 21 January 2017 – a day after his inauguration – attempted to push back the 'Trumpian effect', globalised and emboldened other right-wing politicians committed to capitalist patriarchy. In countries such as Brazil, Hungary, the UK and the Philippines, this has expressed itself sharply as part of new right-wing political projects. Illiberal, socially conservative and authoritarian politicians, such as Trump, came to power through the ballot box; products of decades of neoliberal rule but now showing the full-blown anti-democratic face of the neoliberal class project. These political projects are remaking gender orders and power relations, with grassroots subaltern women on the receiving end. In the USA, its highest court – given its conservative composition – has reversed the right to abortion, pushing back a crucial gain of second-wave feminism. More generally, the authoritarian neoliberal right wing is positioning states and their coercive capacities to advance greater law and order control, build hi-tec surveillance 'border wall regimes' and increase the incarceration of blacks, migrants and refugees. With the worsening climate crisis and the limits to adaptation, millions are going to be on the move on the planet (IPCC 2022). This has already begun, with women and children already facing these challenges in different parts of the global South. In this context, exclusionary nationalisms need to be confronted head on with counter-hegemonic political projects capable of leading society through accelerating and deepening the just transition. This is a crucial challenge for emancipatory feminism.

Third, and building on the previous point, emancipatory feminism has the intellectual resources to advance a deep, as opposed to a shallow, anti-capitalism. In this regard, systemic alternatives to the global crisis of socio-ecological reproduction demand nothing less than a post-carbon capitalist society. Within strands of ecological Marxism, ecological socialist feminism and indigenous feminism, conceptions of the commons, subsistence economies, democratic planning, alternative provisioning, ethical engagements with the techno-sphere, care labour, decolonial knowledge and democratising the state furnish the basis for a democratic eco-socialist project. In this volume several chapters articulate such democratic systemic reforms, based on constitutive forms of power from below, as crucial for the deep just transition. WoMin African Alliance on the continent is reimagining a transformative and eco-feminist approach to a renewed pan-Africanism, as evidenced by Hargreaves chapter in this volume. Important lessons can be learned from Rojava (see Azeez in this volume) about the transformative role of indigenous feminism in advancing an emancipatory project. In South Africa, resistance to carbon capitalism and worsening climate shocks have thrown up numerous fronts of struggle: against coal pollution and against further extraction, including coal, off-shore extraction and fracking for gas and oil; food sovereignty campaigning; reclaiming the water commons in the context of drought; and the Climate Justice Charter process (now supported by over 260 organisations) (Satgar and Cock 2022). These are democratic eco-socialist forces with potential to coalesce around a political project with answers to the intersecting crises of socio-ecological reproduction. The challenge is to advance consciously in this direction, with emancipatory feminism anchoring this political leap.

NOTES

1 In this regard Anderson's *Marx at the Margins: On Nationalism, Ethnicity and Non-Western Societies* (2010), Brown's *Marx on Gender and the Family* (2012), Achar's *Marxism, Orientalism, Cosmopolitanism* (2013) and Mojab's *Marxism and Feminism* (2015) are apposite.
2 See Arruzza (2013), Bhattacharya (2017a), Ferguson (2020) and Fakier et al. (2020). In the South African context, see Fakier and Cock (2009) and Mosoetsa (2011).
3 For the first time since the end of the Second World War, there are now neofascist parties in the German and Swedish parliaments and several right-wing parties rising in other parts of Europe.
4 See Fraser (2015) and (2021).

REFERENCES

Achar, G. 2013. *Marxism, Orientalism, Cosmopolitanism*. Chicago: Haymarket.
Aguilar, D.D. 2015. 'Intersectionality'. In S. Mojab (ed.), *Marxism and Feminism*. London: Zed Books.
Anderson, K.B. 2010. *Marx at the Margins: On Nationalism, Ethnicity and Non-Western Societies*. Chicago: University of Chicago Press.
Anderson, K.B. 2020. *Class, Gender, Race and Colonialism: The 'Intersectionality' of Marx*. Daraja Press and Monthly Review Essays.
Arruzza, C. 2013. *Dangerous Liaisons: The Marriages and Divorces of Marxism and Feminism*. London: Merlin Press.
Bakker, I. 2007. 'Social reproduction and the constitution of a gendered political economy', *New Political Economy* 12 (4): 541–556.
Bhattacharya, T. (ed.). 2017a. *Social Reproduction Theory: Remapping Class, Recentering Oppression*. London: Pluto Books.

Bhattacharya, T. 2017b. 'How not to skip class: Social reproduction of labour and the global working class'. In T. Bhattacharya (ed.), *Social Reproduction Theory: Remapping Class, Recentering Oppression*. London: Pluto Books, e-book, pp. 68–93.

Bohrer, A.J. 2022. 'Marxism and intersectionality: A critical historiography'. In D. Fasenfest (ed.), *Marx Matters*. Leiden and Boston: Brill, pp. 242–268.

Brown, H.A. 2012. *Marx on Gender and the Family: A Critical Study*. Leiden and Boston: Brill.

Fakier, K. and Cock, J. 2009. 'A gendered analysis of the crisis of social reproduction in contemporary South Africa', *International Feminist Journal of Politics* 11 (3): 353–371.

Fakier, K., Mulinari, D. and Räthzel, N. 2020. *Marxist-Feminist Theories and Struggles Today*. London: Zed Books.

Ferguson, S. 2020. *Women and Work: Feminism, Labour and Social Reproduction*. London: Pluto Press.

Fraser, N. 2015. 'Legitimation crisis? On the political contradictions of financialised capitalism', *Critical Historical Studies* 2 (2): 157–189.

Fraser, N. 2017. 'Crisis of care? On the social-reproductive contradictions of contemporary capitalism'. In T. Bhattacharya (ed.), *Social Reproduction Theory: Remapping Class, Recentering Oppression*. London: Pluto Books, e-book, pp. 21–36.

Fraser, N. 2021. 'Climates of capital', *New Left Review* 127 (Jan–Feb): 94–127.

IPCC (Intergovernmental Panel on Climate Change). 2022. 'Climate change 2022: Impacts, adaptation and vulnerability: Working Group II contribution to the Sixth Assessment Report of the IPCC.' Accessed 7 March 2022, https://report.ipcc.ch/ar6wg2/pdf/IPCC_AR6_WGII_FinalDraft_FullReport.pdf.

McNally, D. 2017. 'Intersections and dialectics: Critical reconstructions in social reproduction theory'. In T. Bhattacharya (ed.), *Social Reproduction Theory: Remapping Class, Recentering Oppression*. London: Pluto Books, e-book.

Mies, M. and Shiva, V. 2014. *Ecofeminism* (second edition). London and New York: Zed Books.

Mojab, M. (ed.). 2015. *Marxism and Feminism*. London: Zed Books.

Mosoetsa, S. 2011. *Eating from One Pot: The Dynamics of Survival in Poor South African Households*. Johannesburg: Wits University Press.

O'Connor, J. 1996. 'The second contradiction of capitalism'. In T. Benton (ed.), *The Greening of Marxism*. New York and London: Guilford Press, pp. 197–221.

Salleh, A. 1994. 'Nature, women, labour, capital: Living the deepest contradiction'. In M. O'Connor (ed.), *Is Capitalism Sustainable? Political Economy and the Politics of Ecology*. New York and London: Guilford Press, pp. 106–124.

Satgar, V. 2015. *Capitalism's Crises: Class Struggles in South Africa and the World*. Johannesburg: Wits University Press.

Satgar, V. 2022. 'Marx, the commons and democratic eco-socialism'. In D. Fasenfest (ed.), *Marx Matters*. Leiden and Boston: Brill, pp. 181–197.

Satgar, V. and Cock, J. 2022. 'Ecosocialist activism and movements in South Africa'. In L. Brownhill, S. Engel-Di Mauro, T. Giacomini, A. Isla, M. Lowy and T.E. Turner (eds), *The Routledge Handbook on Ecosocialism*. London and New York: Routledge Taylor and Francis Group, pp. 179–188.

Vogel, L. 2013. *Marxism and the Oppression of Women: Towards a Unitary Theory.* Chicago: Haymarket Books.

Williams, M. and Satgar, V. (eds). 2021. *Destroying Democracy: Neoliberal Capitalism and the Rise of Authoritarian Politics*. Johannesburg: Wits University Press.

CONCLUSION

Ruth Ntlokotse and Vishwas Satgar

A s mentioned at the beginning of this volume, Jacklyn Cock and Meg Luxton, contributors to volume 1 in the Democratic Marxism series in 2013, invited a research focus on socialist feminism as crucial for the renewal of feminism, after the setbacks of second- and third-wave feminism.

We take up their invitation in this volume, and build on it in two ways. First, Cock and Luxton emphasise the life-making role of social reproduction and its centrality within capitalism. The chapters in this volume take this further to argue the conditions for social reproduction today are meeting the total crisis of capitalism. Implicated in this is the hegemonic role of liberal feminism that has been mainstreamed as 'feminism' over the past four decades of global restructuring of capitalism. Today, social reproduction is being gridlocked by the systemic crisis tendencies of patriarchal capitalism such that life-making at a societal scale and in households is in jeopardy. Covid-19 has amplified and revealed more sharply the worsening of the crises, not just of social reproduction, but of socio-ecological reproduction; subaltern women, labour and nature are all interconnected in this crisis of life-making. Liberal feminism has fallen short in this context; its exclusionary class, race and ecological aspirations have proven to be complicit in the oppression of subaltern women. Second, Cock and Luxton invited us to clarify what a politics that takes social reproduction seriously would be all about. What would it look like? Various chapters in this volume explore this in relation to women's resistance before and during Covid-19. Their resistance includes the search for a renewed pan-African feminism at the frontlines of anti-extractivist struggles; women leading the defence of Rojava; women building food sovereignty pathways in communities, villages, towns and cities; women championing climate justice in mining-affected communities; women transforming the androcentric and gender division of labour in mining; women understanding the limits and challenges of the structural class location for African women; women contesting macro-economic policy and women seeking to improve the working conditions of nurses. This is not an exhaustive list, but certainly highlights important examples of a fourth wave of feminism.

This volume contends that emancipatory feminism is finding its expression much more prominently in the fourth wave of feminism. It has the potential to clarify and define this wave. Emancipatory feminism is certainly eclipsing liberal feminism as grassroots women search for a politics at the frontlines of the crises of socio-ecological reproduction. At the same time, emancipatory feminism is building the capacities to confront a new extreme right wing marching across the planet in the name of nativist, patriarchal, socially conservative and exclusionary nationalisms. Such a right wing is either 'post- or anti-feminist'. Both these tendencies suggest either that women's oppression has been addressed or that women's emancipation has gone too far and therefore feminist gains must be rolled back. In many places, religious fundamentalism, articulated with patriarchy and capitalism, is giving warrant to this reactionary politics. Embracing world making and constituting power from below positions emancipatory feminism to build alternatives and advance political projects in resistance to the challenge of right-wing polarisation. Democratic deepening and democratic systemic reforms give this form of emancipatory feminism a powerful democratising role. Convergences between Marxist feminists, socialist feminists, eco-feminists and indigenous feminists are, however, crucial and this volume embraces and fosters this dialogue in order to find genuine universals that will become a basis for the building of domestic and transnational unities. The post-modern notion of difference is now understood: there is no monolithic social category termed 'women'. However, at the same time, accentuating difference in the name of 'black socialist feminism' or 'white eco-feminism' is politically irrational, given the worsening global crisis of socio-ecological reproduction and the descent of societies into authoritarian and, in some instances, neofascist politics. Emancipatory feminism holds out the potential to transcend both academic and political polarisation, as it seeks to deepen transformative anti-capitalist resistance.

At a practical level, political demands for Covid-19 fiscal support (basic income, unpaid labour transfers and other relief measures); ending hunger through food sovereignty; preventing climate harm through accelerating and deepening the just transition; climate jobs and free, quality and accessible public health services have the potential to rally women, even if they are not feminists, together with wider society. These positive solidarities, affirming of emancipatory alternatives, enable women to lead the reimagining and remaking of society in struggle. Nonetheless, the organising challenge of movement building looms large. Emancipatory feminists are aware of this challenge and the importance of feminist education and consciousness raising, as opposed to merely crowd-sourcing street politics to make symbolic noises. Many examples in this volume showcase variegated practices: coalition building, giving feminism ideological and political control in autonomous territories, building grassroots alliances, movement building and encouraging transformative trade unionism. The march of emancipatory feminism is just gaining momentum and already it is demonstrating creative forms of mass organising. This has the potential to generate truly conscious feminist organisation – a necessity if there is going to be an adequate response to the global crisis of socio-ecological reproduction and an advance to a democratic, decolonial, eco-socialist, feminist world.

CONTRIBUTORS

Hawzhin Azeez is a Kurdish academic, activist and poet who spent close to four years in the Rojava region as a participant in the rebuilding and reconstruction of Kobane.

Asanda-Jonas Benya is a senior lecturer in the Department of Sociology at the University of Cape Town. Her work focuses on the intersection of gender, class and race.

Christine Bischoff is a sociologist at the University of the Witwatersrand, Johannesburg. Her main areas of research are trade unions and employment relations.

Jane Cherry is the executive manager at the Cooperative and Policy Alternative Centre in Johannesburg. She is also an activist and organiser in the South African Food Sovereignty Campaign and the Climate Justice Charter Movement.

Jacklyn Cock is a professor emeritus in the Department of Sociology at the University of the Witwatersrand, and a research associate of the university's Society, Work and Politics Institute (SWOP). She has published widely on gender, militarisation and environmental issues.

Samantha Hargreaves is the founder and director of the WoMin African Alliance, which works with partners and allies in 16 countries across Africa to expose the mechanics and gendered impacts of a patriarchal extractivist development model.

Inge Konik is an associate professor in the Department of Philosophy at the Nelson Mandela University in Gqeberha, and an associate editor for the journal *Environmental Humanities*. Her current research focuses on materialist ecological feminism, ecologically promising value systems, and environmental and feminist cinema.

Jane Mbithi-Dikgole is currently a lecturer and research supervisor at the South African College of Applied Psychology.

Courtney Morgan is a campaigner for the African Climate Reality Project, worked on the Climate Justice Charter for South Africa, and is active in the South African Food Sovereignty Campaign.

Ruth Ntlokotse is a committed gender activist and has been involved in trade union politics for 16 years. She is deputy president of the National Union of Metalworkers of South Africa, and in 2022 she was elected president of the South African Federation of Trade Unions.

Sonia Phalatse is a feminist economist researching and writing at the intersection of climate and economic justice.

Vishwas Satgar is a veteran activist, democratic eco-socialist and edits the Democratic Marxism series. He is an associate professor of International Relations and is the principal investigator for the Emancipatory Futures Studies in the Anthropocene project at the University of the Witwatersrand.

Busi Sibeko is an economist and researcher whose work has ranged from macro-economic policy, including feminist economics at the Institute for Economic Justice, to research support for the labour constituency, to co-chairing the Budget Justice Coalition in South Africa.

Dineo Skosana is a senior researcher and project leader for the Nature and Society cluster and at the Society, Work and Politics Institute (SWOP) at the University of the Witwatersrand. She coordinates the coal project, which investigates South Africa's transition from coal to renewable energy.

INDEX

Printed and bound by CPI Group (UK) Ltd, Croydon, CR0 4YY

09/06/2025

14685824-0001